NORWAY TO NASSAU

My Exciting Life of Faith and Service

Blessings
A Morris Russell

A. Morris Russell

Printed in Canada

ISBN: 978-1-4866-1088-4

Word Alive Press
131 Cordite Road, Winnipeg, MB R3W 1S1
www.wordalivepress.ca

WORD ALIVE
—P R E S S—

FSC
www.fsc.org

MIX
Paper from
responsible sources
FSC® C016245

Cataloguing in Publication information may be obtained through Library and Archives Canada

Acknowledgements

I would like to acknowledge the incredible support of my home church in Larbert, Scotland, and of Global Outreach Mission. I have also been blessed with wonderful support from the churches of my pastoral ministry in New Brunswick, Newfoundland, Ontario (Toronto, Burlington, St. Catharines, Binbrook, and Unionville), Nassau, Bahamas, Bonaire, Haiti and Jamaica.

I would also like to thank my wonderful family and friends for their support during this process.

In loving memory of Adaline Betty Jamieson,
my wife of thirty-six years,
and to Sarah (Morag) D. A. Forrester,
my wife of twenty-nine years.

Foreword

Pastor Russell has been a personal friend and counsellor since I met him in the summer of
1967 when he was in his second year as pastor of First Baptist Church, St. John's,
Newfoundland.

Pastor Russell has been working on this book for several years, and I have
discussed the project with him at several intervals. During his entire ministry,
beginning as a young missionary to the Laps above the Artic Circle in Norway,
followed by his rural and large community ministry in Canada and the Bahamas,
he has kept detailed records and taken many pictures to document his lifetime
experiences. Those experiences have been incredibly varied and encompass times
of great joy, sadness, danger, conflict, and blessing. Thanks to his diaries, the
pages of this book contain many details of those experiences and demonstrate
his unwavering trust in the faithfulness and protection of God in every aspect of
his life. His story reaffirms that just as in Bible days, God can still turn ordinary
people into great missionaries.

He has documented his early life and education in Scotland, his conversion,
Bible College training, marriages, and call to mission work. From an early age,
Pastor Russell has been a very disciplined and conscientious individual. Arising
early each morning, he spends a couple of hours reading, meditating, and praying
in preparation for his ministry responsibilities. He always attempts to present a
fresh word from the Lord; even in rural ministry when he served four churches
on Sundays he prepared a different message for each congregation. His sense of
humour was a great asset in his ministry and dealing with people.

Pastor Russell has firm convictions and strong leadership skills. In his
ministry years he was energetic and highly motivated to do his best for his
Lord at all times and in every situation. He has strong doctrinal persuasions,
which he enunciates clearly with scripture references. He has no time for liberal
theology or doctrinal compromise and has spoken strongly against these trends at
conferences where church leaders tried to water down some of the long accepted

tenets of Christianity. He has always been attentive to family life details such as birthdays, anniversaries, marriages, and deaths, making sure proper recognition is made of every person involved.

I commend this book to you because it is a faithful record of a faithful servant who has served his Lord without fail for more than sixty-five years. He has suffered many hardships privately, and I have heard him quote the scriptural passage in Hebrews 12 about how the Lord disciplines those he loves, following which he would add: "I wish the Lord didn't love me so much." This book records some of those difficult times in his life as well as many of the happy times of ministry and family. May the Lord use this record to challenge its readers to a life of enduring faith.

R. Clifton Way, MD, FRCPC.
Former Professor of Pediatrics, Memorial University of Newfoundland
Professor Emeritus, Faculty of Health Sciences, McMaster University

Preface

The publishing of this book coincides with the celebration of the sixty-fifth anniversary of my ordination to the Christian ministry. This took place on June 25, 1950, in Larbert Baptist Church, Stirlingshire, Scotland. It was in this church that I came to personal faith in the Lord Jesus Christ and later, along with eight others, was baptized and received into membership. It was here that I was mentored, grounded in the Word of God, and taught how to share my faith, develop my talents in music, give my testimony in open air meetings, and minister in sister churches in central Scotland. It was in this church that my wife and I were commissioned as the first missionaries to go out from the church. We served with the mission then known as The European Evangelistic Crusade, serving in Lapland and Northern Norway.

This book is published with a desire to bear testimony to God's grace and faithfulness. My prayer is that it may challenge others to commit their lives to the Lord and Saviour, Jesus Christ, and to His service. May it challenge pastors and missionaries to realize that there is no higher calling in this twenty-first century than to preach and teach the Word of God with power and conviction, and to realize that this supersedes the increasing dependence upon and proliferation of programs in this generation. God has promised that His Word shall not return void, but it shall accomplish that whereto He has been pleased to send it.

All that has been accomplished in this book bears testimony to the centrality of preaching of the life changing Gospel of God's redeeming grace and love, and the value of teaching the Word of God. My life and ministry have not always been perfect, but all that I have been privileged to do has been done with a desire to bring glory to God, to see sinners saved, and to see believers strengthened.

Yours in His Glorious Service,
A. Morris Russell

1

From Letham to Lapland

"Can any good thing come out of Letham?"

Letham is a very small village located near the banks of the river Forth, in the Parish of Airth, Stirlingshire, Scotland. It is in the heart of Scottish history that covers James VI, Mary, Queen of Scots, Robert the Bruce, William Wallace, and many others. When I lived in Letham in 1928, the village consisted of "the cottages," which was the housing provided for the miners, and "the terraces," located on the opposite side of the village green, which was the housing provided for management personnel. A small co-operative general store was located at the corner of the village. The nearest primary school was located in Airth, the centre of the Parish. The children from the village had to walk two miles—rain, hail, or shine—to attend school.

The village grew up around the coal mine. The coal bing (slag heap) dominated the village. It was like a mountain, and I remember it very vividly from my boyhood. The mine itself was very deep, and it extended out under the river Forth. Because of this, there was always a problem of water draining into the mine. My father and two older brothers, John and George, worked waist deep in water while mining the coal. Coal was necessary for use in the iron works nearby in Falkirk, Carron, and Larbert. Carron Company owned most of the mines in the area.

My Father, Henry Russell, was a miner and a soldier. He was a non-commissioned officer with the artillery. He fought in the Boer War, served in India, and also fought in the First World War. He was very active in community affairs, having served as a parish councilor, and he was a director of the local co-operative society and very highly respected in the community.

The Change of Life

My Mother, Ann Bell Smillie Russell, was an amazing woman. She was born to George and Agnes Smillie at Black Loch, Slamanan, Scotland. I don't remember my grandfather; however, I have vivid memories of my grandmother. She was a godly woman, often seen with her Bible on her lap. The other book that was a constant companion was *Fifty Years in the Church of Rome* by Pastor Chiniquy. It was the story of his conversion.

My mother was the eldest daughter and second eldest child in a family of fourteen. Because of this, she helped to bring up the rest of the family, which was good training for when she had her own children. Not only was she a good housewife and mother, but she was very active in the community, the Red Cross, and other committees. When the miners were on strike, she was very much involved in the soup kitchens providing food for the families of miners. She was always very much in charge, a strict disciplinarian, a great cook, and had an open door policy of hospitality. She was a surrogate mother to her siblings, a master at home remedies, and a loving mother.

With five boys and two girls of her own, she certainly had her hands full. My father was a soldier as well as a miner and he also had a brief spell working in the gold mines of Australia. One day my mother, while in her mid-forties, announced to my father: "Henry, I think I'm pregnant again."

"Go on, lass," my father responded. "It must be the change of life."

Little did they realize what a change it would be—I was the "change of life!" I had the privilege of being born into a loving, caring, God fearing family. I, Arthur Morris Russell, named after my father's brother, was the seventh child in our family. My mother gave birth to me in the bedroom of our miner's cottage.

There was always something exciting going on in such a large family. I have memories of playing on the large village green and of exploring the coal bing. We could also cook potatoes in the smoldering coal that was always present. One of the dominating sites of that whole area was Airth Castle, located on a promontory halfway between Letham and Airth. It had been built in the late thirteenth century and was burned by James II in 1488. However, it was restored and enlarged over a period of time. Today it's a very grand and popular hotel.

Nearby, in the Dunmore Estate, stood a very unique structure built of stone and in the shape of a pineapple. The Earl of Dunmore built it in1761 as a birthday present for his wife so that she could sit on the balcony and view the beautiful and extensive gardens. One other pineapple structure exists in Holland.

In the 1970s the estate was restored to its former glory and can now be rented as a holiday home.

The Dutch influence was all around us. Between Letham and Airth there was a large carse area (really an extensive bog). Since the Dutch were experts, they were invited to drain the area and build dykes so that the peat could be cut. This also provided excellent and extensive arable land.

The Preparation for Living

I believe that God has had His hand on my life over these eighty-plus years. This will become more and more evident as my story unfolds. From that little village I have travelled half the world. I have lived and worked in the high Arctic, working amongst the Norwegians along the coast high above the Arctic Circle. My travels and ministry have taken me to the Sami people (Laplanders) in the interior. I lived and ministered in Eastern Canada for twenty years. For over twenty years I lived and ministered in Southern Ontario. Then I came to the close of my full-time ministry after almost ten years in The Bahamas. During that time I also had ministry in Haiti, Jamaica, and Bonaire.

My ministry and travels have taken me to almost every country in Europe, including several countries in Eastern Europe. It has been my great joy to have travelled and ministered in most of the lands of the Bible, including Israel, Jordan, Egypt, Greece, and Turkey, along with many of the island nations of the Mediterranean. All of this has served to enrich my ministry as a pastor and given me an insight into the challenges and opportunities of missionary activities around the world.

My ministry has taken me to remote areas as well as cosmopolitan centres. I have pastored small country churches with largely rural communities. I have also ministered in large churches, some of which had largely multi-ethnic congregations. I have taught in Bible schools, worked with missionaries, and have had the joy of seeing young men and women go into fulltime service for the Lord. My television and radio ministry has enabled me to stretch the boundaries of my witness for the Gospel. During my sixty years of ministry, I have counted it a privilege to dine with royalty, political leaders, and many world renowned figures.

Smillie Family Morris' mother is on the left

The family of Henry and Ann (Smillie) Russell, Morris is in the centre

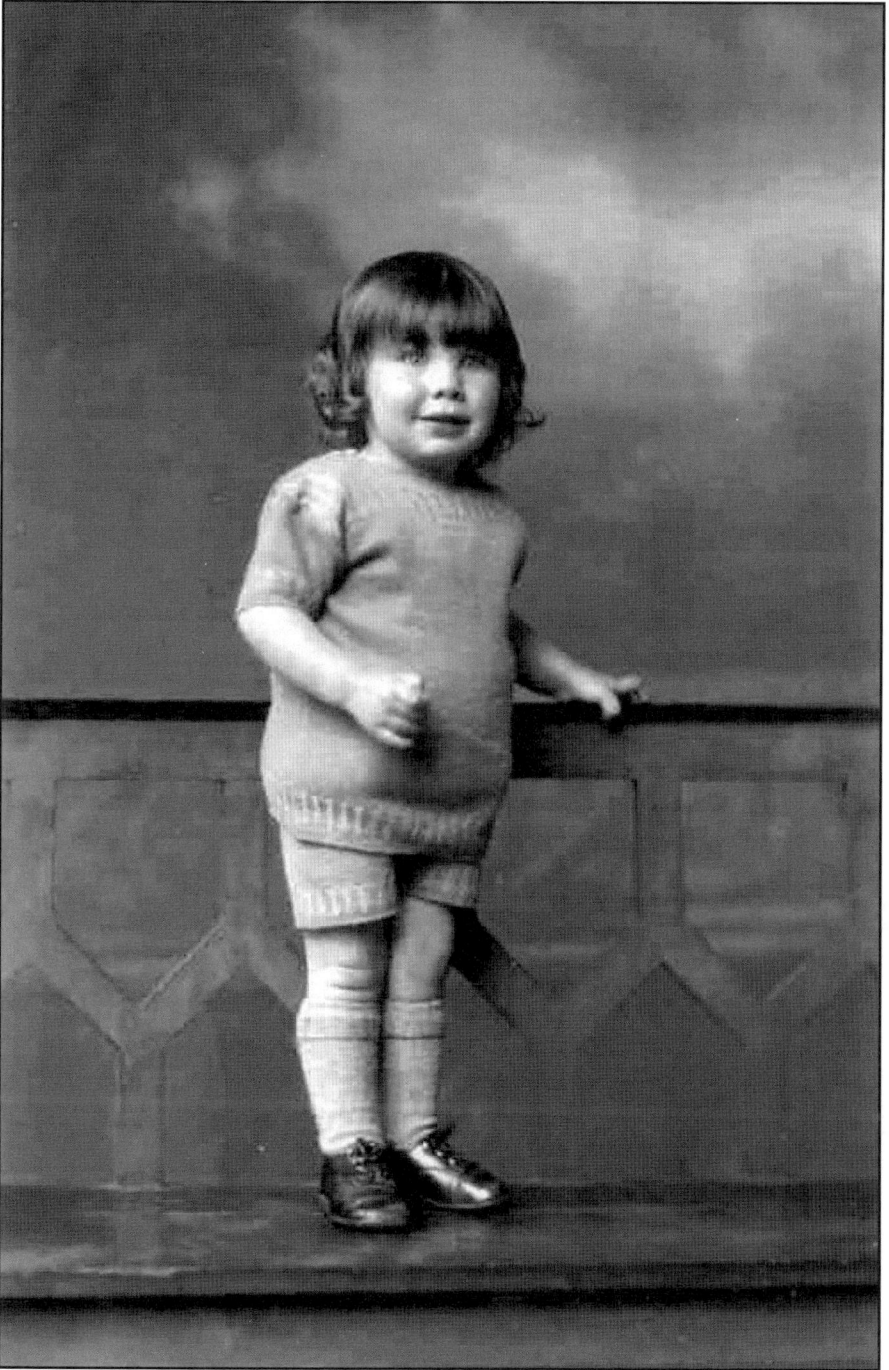

Morris at about 18 months old

2

The Change That Made the Difference

A significant milestone in my life and the life of my family occurred when we finally moved from Letham to Grahamston in Falkirk. My father was no longer able to work in the coal mines because of failing health. This was a result of two situations in his life. During the Boer War, he was shipwrecked twice just off the coast of South Africa. During the First World War he was gassed twice while in Ypres. With the terrible conditions of mud and water in the trenches, his lungs were damaged and he developed a very bad heart condition. Since he could no longer work in the mines, our family had to move out of the miner's cottage. My eldest brother, John, took this opportunity to leave mining for good. My second eldest brother, George, continued working in the mines for several more years. My sister, Agnes, moved to the west side of Scotland where she went into service with one of the affluent families, caring for their children and looking after their home. My brother Henry (Harry) got employment with the Carron Co-operative Society, in the bakery department, and he later went into the meat department.

My brother Watson, eight years my senior, was born in 1920. He was very sick during the first few years of his life and as a result became a deaf /mute. He entered the Donaldson School for the Deaf at Henderson Row in Edinburgh. This was a residential school, so he was only home during school holidays. He and I were very good buddies, having much the same temperament and personality. My mother always said I could use sign language before I could speak. Watson received a very good education, and while there he excelled in sports. He was capped for cricket and received a gold engraved cricket ball. He was honoured for his swimming skills. In his adult life, he became the West of Scotland champion wrestler, Cumberland style.

My sister, Janet, three years older than me, started school in the Northern School just across the street from our home. Three years later I started school there. School was an exciting time for me. I was always learning new things, which is what life is all about. I enjoyed where we lived, mostly because we lived above an ice cream shop. I was very friendly with the store owner. You can be sure that I spent a lot of my spare time there. The store owner was Italian, and he was very kind to me. My reward for helping him was always an ice cream cone or some candy. He would always get a lecture from my mother, because when she would call me for dinner I was never hungry since I had been eating so many candies.

Our home was located right on the main street. One of the fascinating things that captured my attention was the man who went down the street turning on the lights. He was known to everybody as "the lamp lighter." He would leave a trail of light wherever he went. This was absolutely amazing. The other wonderful experience I had while living there helped to lay a significant foundation for my life. We could walk up the street to what was known as the "Miller Hall." It was named after the man who founded it and was a very significant evangelistic centre in our community. It's still there but is now known as the Grahamston Evangelical Church. It was here that I first attended Sunday school.

The lady who taught us was Mrs. Miller, and she had an amazing impact upon my life. I remember that it was very uncomfortable sitting on the hard pews, and my feet couldn't touch the floor, so at times I could be very restless. However, I can still recall the way in which that lady told the wonderful Bible stories. I can also remember how we sang those wonderful choruses, and the excitement of receiving rewards for learning Bible verses.

It was in the services at the Miller Hall that my three older brothers, John, George, and Henry, came to a personal faith in the Lord Jesus Christ. All of them became very active in the Lord's service. Henry eventually trained for the ministry and served in Edinburgh before moving to a church in Chatham, New Brunswick, Canada. Eventually he served at a church in Etobicoke, Ontario, and later in life became the General Director of The Yonge Street Mission in Toronto.

Country Living

After I finished first grade in the Northern School, a major change took place for my family and for me in particular. My parents decided to move from

Grahamston to the country. They bought a house on a good size piece of land in a little village called Torwood, which is located on the main highway that runs between Stirling and Edinburgh. This move was primarily because of my father's health. The village was in the country, in the heart of farming and woodlands, hence the name "Torwood," which means "The Wood on the Hill." Our new home was very quickly given the name "Harann House." This was a combination of my father's and mother's names—Harry and Ann.

The house had a rather romantic history. It was located on the main coach road between Stirling and Edinburgh. At this point on the highway there was a toll house. Our new home had originally served as an inn for the travellers. To this day, rings are on the wall on each side of the front door; it was there that travellers could hitch their horses.

I recall helping my brother, George, do some renovations upstairs. We were installing larger windows. In the attic we found a long coach whip that was used for the horses, and also a coach light. It's recorded that the Rev. Robert Murray McCheyne, when student minister at Larbert Parish Church, would on occasion stay here. Perhaps it was the fact that I grew up in Torwood that I developed a great love for history. Let me come back to that later.

My schooling at Torwood Village School was basic and foundational, while also very comprehensive. Our teacher, Ms. Miller, was an amazing individual. She was strict, loving, concerned, and a wonderful communicator on every subject. She was my heroine and my mentor; we stood in awe of her. The school was a two room schoolhouse with massive oak trees in the front yard and a wonderful playing field at the back ... so different from the school I attended in Grahamston. It was a primary school, and Ms. Miller not only taught "the 3Rs," but she made learning fun. In Science we watched seeds grow; in Music, we learned Scottish dancing. Physical Education included personal cleanliness and good manners. Ms. Miller taught all grades.

Part of our curriculum was the Bible. It was read every morning, followed by prayer. We had to memorize significant portions of the Bible, a task for which we were rewarded. Ms. Miller also took an interest in our families and the entire village. The school was the focal point of life in the village. In addition to all of this, Ms. Miller came back out on Sundays to teach Sunday school. To illustrate her dedication, let me share with you this personal story.

It was probably around the year 1937, and I became ill. I had excruciating pain, so my mother provided nursing care. In those days we didn't have ice available, so heat was the next best thing to be applied. Two days went by and the heat didn't ease the pain, but rather made it worse. Finally I was rushed to the Falkirk Royal Infirmary. Upon examining me, the surgeon concluded that I would need to have surgery. I had appendicitis; my appendix had ruptured, resulting in peritonitis. Since there was no penicillin in those days, I spent three months in hospital. It was a very uncomfortable and slow recovery.

The surgeon indicated that it was a miracle I survived, although he also said that I would have real problems later in life because of the illness. This prediction was fulfilled. Because my stomach muscles were weakened, I have had eighteen hernias repaired as an adult. Again upon reflection, I can see that God had His hand on my life.

Ms. Miller visited me every week in the hospital, and she always brought a treat for me. To make sure I wouldn't miss out on my schooling, she brought in regular schoolwork that I could do while in hospital. This had its benefits, as I was put ahead a grade.

Around this time my father's sister, Margaret, otherwise known to us as Aunt Meg, returned to Scotland from Winnipeg, Manitoba, Canada. Her husband, James Dixon, had died in northern Manitoba. He was a fur trader with the Hudson's Bay Company. It had been a very bad winter and he'd been found frozen to death on the trap lines in the north.

Aunt Meg came to live with us at Torwood. She wanted to pay for her stay with us, but my father refused to accept any remuneration from her. In the course of the discussions, my father said that if she insisted on paying, she could buy a bicycle for his youngest son. I was more than thrilled to hear of this. I got a full-size bicycle with multi-speeds ... but there was a hitch. Since I had just come home from hospital after being there for three months, my doctor put restrictions on my activities. Because of my recent surgery, the doctor said that I could not participate in sports or ride a bicycle for one whole year. So for one more year I admired the bike, I polished it, and I walked it around the back yard—but I could not ride it. You can imagine the count was on until the day that I could ride it with pride ... thanks to my Canadian aunt.

Growing Up in the Country

Living in the country was exciting. We had a forest right across the road from us full of all kinds of wildlife. We could explore the wooded areas, pick the blue bells, relive Robin Hood, and play cowboys and Indians. In my boyhood days we had to create our own entertainment, and that meant we had to be inventive. Our community was a place where we could get together and enjoy each other.

I remember my granddaughter coming home from school one day and asking to interview me about my boyhood days for a project. Among the questions that she asked me was one about entertainment. She looked at me and said, "Papa, what television programs did you watch when you were a boy?"

I looked at her and smiled. "My dear," I said, "television was not invented when I was a boy; we had to create our own entertainment."

Her eyes opened wide.

"But Papa, how did you survive not having television to look at?"

I simply explained to her that we had the joy of creating our own programs and entertainment. No, in my boyhood days we had no television, no video games, and no computers. We made our own entertainment. Upon reflection, we also escaped the negative influences of the mass media. We explored the countryside, played games of our own invention, and enjoyed nature. When winter came, we had indoor activities. During the winter nights we read books and played board games.

In addition to playing and school we also had chores to do. We were responsible for feeding the chickens, taking care of the rabbits, and looking after the dogs and cats. Then there were chores in the house. We had to clean the silver, wash the floors, and make sure that we disposed of the garbage. There was always plenty for us to do. In the summertime we had a large garden with lots of fruit and vegetables. These had to be tended to. We had to rake the ground around the bushes and the vegetables, and we also had to clean out the weeds. We were always kept busy.

Somewhere in those years my buddies and I played "hunting and the hunted." I ran out of the woods down a very steep embankment and could not stop. I ran right in front of the coal truck and was knocked down and knocked out. When the driver of the truck came to me I was unconscious and he was beside himself with fear. He picked me up and carried me into my house. How thrilled my mother and father were when I opened my eyes, wondering what in all the world had happened to me. Again, I would pause to say, I believe that God had other plans for me.

I grew up in an environment with animals and birds always around me. My father, being a coal miner, always had a canary—as was typical in those days. Even the soldiers in those days used them in their tunnels. From this we get the very interesting expression, "living like a canary in a coal mine." It means simply serving as a warning to others. The canary in a coal mine had little control over its fate, but it continued to sing anyway, being willing to face dangers without compromise. The canaries were widely used to determine if any dangerous gases were around.

We always enjoyed our budgies. They developed quite a vocabulary and they were always entertaining us with their constant chatter. We also had lots of hens and a huge red rooster who was the master of the flock. He was a terror to avoid and he ruled the roost. The hens provided us with eggs and the occasional sumptuous dinner, so during the war years there was no lack of variety in our diet. We also had cats and at least two dogs. For fun we had rabbits. I bred the blue and the black Dutch rabbits for show purposes. I had chinchillas, which were also bred to provide fur for the making of gloves that were all the fashion with the ladies in those days.

The most exotic animal we had for a short while was a small monkey that came from South America. This was one my brother had picked up in the dockyard at Grangemouth from one of the ships. This monkey was a real source of entertainment and fun, and it loved to sleep in a little cradle up in our sawmill. It was spoiled by everyone around.

My brother Watson, who was a deaf/ mute, was home from school one day. He was at the back of the house playing with a tennis ball, bouncing it off the gable end of the house and catching it. But one time it dropped on to the sloping roof and rolled into the gutter. To retrieve the ball he swung the iron gate against the wall and figured if he climbed on the rungs of the gate he could reach into the gutter and retrieve it. Unfortunately, on the top of the iron gate were several long, sharp spikes. When he climbed the gate and reached for the ball his foot slipped. As he came down, one of the spikes entered his knee, under the kneecap, and came out above the kneecap. So he hung there, unable to extricate himself. Being a deaf/ mute, his voice could not be heard. Minutes after the accident, my mother came around the corner and found him hanging there, impaled on the spike. She immediately lifted this big sixteen year old boy off the spike and carried him into the house, blood flowing everywhere. Immediately, my mother applied the usual medication she always used in the event of serious injury (I have a few scars that awaken memories of such treatment). Out came the bottle of raw Lysol, which was poured onto the wounds. This was guaranteed to kill any germs. After this treatment, Watson was whisked off to the hospital by my father. Upon examination, the surgeon concluded that the leg should be amputated above the knee. My father strongly objected and refused to give permission for the surgery. The wounds were cleaned and sutured. The leg was saved and Watson lived a very active life until he died in 2008.

3

Changes and Conflicts

The 1930s were significant and formative years for me, and also years of political turmoil in Britain and Europe that would have global impact. The nations were coming out of the terrible economic crash. A political opportunist, Adolph Hitler, was increasingly making himself heard. Nazism was on the rise and spreading its tentacles across the continent of Europe. Around that time, Britain's Prime Minister, Neville Chamberlain, came back from a conference in Europe with a signed Peace Treaty declaring "we have peace in our time." But that, of course, did not hold true. In spite of diplomatic assurances, Britain declared war on Germany on September 3, 1939. It was in this environment that I was growing up, and significant changes were taking place all around me. On February 3, 1939, my father died. This was another blow to my sense of security. He was my hero, and I would miss his counsel.

Around 1937, my brother, George, finally left his work in the coal mines and started his own business, eventually bringing in his other three brothers. My father served as advisor to guide them in their plans. A sawmill was built and started, a truck was bought, ladders were acquired, and a multi-faceted business was established. It was named "Russell Brothers" and offered a variety of services: window cleaning, chimney sweeping, indoor painting and decorating, demolition of old buildings, and a very extensive sawmill supplying firewood and kindling to communities from Stirling to Falkirk. The business thrived. Even my sister, Janet, and I worked there after school and often on weekends.

The War Years

Just when everything seemed to prosper, war was declared and George was called up to the army. My oldest brother, John, was called to the fire service, my third brother, Henry, went to work in the chemical works in Grangemouth, and Watson went to work at the Singer's factory in Clydebank, Glasgow. Our truck was confiscated by the War Department, and our business was effectively closed because of the war effort.

In the meantime, I was transferred from primary school in Torwood to middle school in Larbert. I was advanced one grade. I have never been quite sure if that was because of my ability or if the teacher was glad to be rid of me! I then moved on with my education to Central School.

The war was on, and evacuees from Glasgow, Clydebank, Greenock, and area came to our community to escape the German attacks on that industrialized area. I joined the Argyle and Sutherland Highlanders Cadet Force and eventually became a sergeant instructor in small arms. I also worked in the Post Office for a short time as a telegram boy. I thought I might continue there in the telephone department; however, it became evident that wouldn't be possible since I was colour blind.

In all of this mix, and as a result of the ministry of the Baptist minister, Rev. W.C. Inglis, to our family at the time of my father's death, my mother, sister, brother and his wife and family, and I started to attend the Baptist church. Following the ministry of the pastor one Sunday evening, three of us made a commitment to the Lord Jesus Christ. On February 2, 1942, Gordon Lightbody, Charles Shaw, and I came to know Christ as our Saviour. Later on, nine of us young people, including my present wife, then Morag Forrester, were baptized and became members of the church.

Around this time I was given the opportunity to start my apprenticeship as a plumber and heating engineer with David W. Smith of Stenhousemuir. Miss Katie Thompson, one of our youth leaders, gave my name to Mr. Smith. I had an interview and was hired immediately. Upon reflection, I realize that throughout my life I have never really sought work either in the secular world or in the world of the ministry. The promise of God in Proverbs 3:5–6 has proven true for me: "*Trust in the Lord with all your heart and lean not on your own understanding. In all your ways acknowledge Him and He shall direct your path.*" In my early Christian life I wasn't always clear in my testimony or my lifestyle. But God, in His Grace, kept His hand on me anyway. Eventually I got the proper perspective on life and got my priorities straight.

V.E. Day—Tuesday, May 8, 1945—was a significant day in the Western world. The wonderful news was broadcast that Nazi Germany had surrendered. The terrible six years of brutal war was over in Europe. Seventy-two million people had died as a result of one man's selfish, covetous ambitions. Hitler had brought devastation to so many countries in Europe. Of that colossal death toll, forty-seven million were civilians. Within a few days, churches throughout Britain were packed with war weary people giving God thanks for peace—a peace that had been realized at such high cost. The mopping-up operations would be very important for the future of our world. As a result of the war, one of my cousins died and my brother spent six months in the military hospital recovering from injuries. Following the service of thanksgiving at our church in the little town of Larbert, a big picnic celebration was planned at Anderson's farm in Torwood. What a memorable day. I was able to get photographs of those celebrations, because my uncle in Canada kept me supplied with film, which I couldn't buy in Scotland.

V.J. Day— September 2, 1945—brought the Pacific/ Japanese conflict to a close and put an end to a brutal time meted out to many innocent people. This peace was finally concluded in September of 1945 following the dropping of the atomic bomb on Hiroshima, which killed 140,000 people. Hard on the heels of that was the dropping of another atomic bomb on Nagasaki, on August 9, 1945, killing 72,384. In addition to that, 17, 490 were severely injured. This was another opportunity for a time of thanksgiving for the fact that all the selfish ambition and cruel suppression had been brought to an end. This was followed by services of thanksgiving and then a period of celebration with a traditional picnic at Torwood.

4

The Issue of Priorities

There was a time when I was struggling with priorities in my life. Should I continue as a plumber, or should I seriously consider moving into another area of work? I even considered what God might desire of me in His service.

I'd been rather shallow in my commitment to the Lord and not serious in my Christian life and spiritual growth. It was around this time that the Lord did some serious work in my heart and in my life. I had gone to bed at my usual time and dropped off to sleep rather quickly. However, God had some other plans. Suddenly I was wide awake around 3:00 a.m. The room was flooded with light coming from a full moon against a cloudless sky. I was overcome with an incredible conviction that the Lord Jesus Christ had come, and I was left behind. I'm not prone to dreams, and I've never had a nightmare or been susceptible to great emotional display. What I experienced that night was quite out of character for me.

I lay in my bed for a few moments and not a sound was heard. Everyone in our community had dogs, but none of them were even barking at that time. The main highway was nearby, but there was no sound of traffic. Family members were in the house, but not a sound was heard anywhere. I got up and went to look out of my upstairs window. I had never seen such bright moonlight, and with not a sound anywhere. Nothing was moving … not a breath of wind. I was all the more convinced that my family had been taken and I was left.

I got down on my knees beside my bed and wrestled in prayer with God until the break of day. I got down to business with the Lord. From that moment on, in fact, I presented my body, soul, mind, and spirit *"as a living sacrifice, holy, acceptable unto God, which is* [my] *reasonable service*" (Romans 1:1). The Scriptures say "*… do not be conformed to this world, but be transformed by the renewing of your mind, that you may prove what is that good and acceptable and perfect will of God*" (Romans 1:2) These were the words that came to my mind from the book of Romans. From that moment on it was no longer my will, but God's will, be done in my life. Little did I dream what this would mean in the years ahead.

Since the older members of the family had moved away, I was left with many of the responsibilities. I looked after the chickens, maintained the fruit and vegetable gardens, and for a time I cultivated black currant bushes and had the opportunity to make some money from them as I mailed them out to people in different parts of the country. In the fall of that same year I worked at McEwen's farm during the harvest time.

We were given time off school to help with the war effort. I had the responsibility of driving a team of horses to bring in the grain and harvest the potatoes. Throughout the year I also worked at Anderson's chicken farm, helping to look after the chickens. I packed the eggs for private deliveries and also took care of different chores on the farm. One time Mr. and Mrs. Anderson went away for three months in South Africa. With the help of one of my buddies, I was left to look after the operation, which meant that I could earn extra money. I turned all of my money over to my widowed mother, and she gave me my pocket money and took care of all my needs. So from a very early age I knew what work and responsibility really meant.

One day I was witnessing to my work mate, Jim MacNab. I had my New Testament in one hand and a cigarette in the other.

"If I met you on the street, I would never have known you to be a Christian," Jim said.

I asked him why, and his answer hit home to me: "That cigarette in your hand."

I got up from where I was sitting, went over to the stove, took the pack of cigarettes out of my pocket, and tossed them into the stove. I haven't smoked from that day to this. I didn't want anything to hinder my witness amongst those with whom I came into contact.

5

My Call and Preparation for the Ministry

All but one member of my family was musical. We had an old-fashioned pump organ in our home that I learned to play when I could barely reach the pedals. I eventually bought a piano accordion and took lessons for about three months. I had a very short stint playing Scottish dance music; however, I was very involved with a musical group in our church. We led in the music and used our talents in open-air meetings, churches, and other events. Eventually I found it very useful in my work in Lapland and Norway and in my ministry in churches where I have pastored over the years.

While pursuing my apprenticeship as a plumber, I became increasingly aware of the fact that God had other plans for my life. I was the sole breadwinner at home. Mother had a meagre pension at this particular time, so my earnings were very important. One day I approached my mother about the fact that God was calling me to Christian ministry. Her response was very supportive and very wise. She said this to me: "I'd like you to finish your apprenticeship first and then plan from there." I've always been thankful for that advice.

While continuing with my apprenticeship, I was also very active in our church. I was part of our branch of the NYLC (National Young Life Campaigners) under the leadership of Agnes Nicol and Katie Thompson. Under their leadership our group grew significantly. We had in-depth Bible study, augmented by a study led by one of our deacons, James D. Taylor, who was a well-known and greatly appreciated lay preacher.

Great emphasis was placed on the importance of the practical application of all that we learned. This meant involvement. We had a youth choir, which I had the privilege and joy of leading. Saturday evenings we were often invited to sing in churches and mission halls around the area in which we lived. The choir would sing, but we also had solos, duets, and quartets. Usually two of our group would be designated to give testimony to their faith. Quite often I would be asked to preach.

In the summer months on Saturdays we would travel by bus somewhere in the area. There we would have a picnic, then we would go out and distribute tracts, ending the day with an open air meeting in the town square or park. For several years I conducted a children's meeting in our local park. There I made good use of my accordion, used object lessons to teach the gospel, and also flannelgraph to illustrate Bible stories.

During this time I became increasingly aware of the fact that God was preparing me for ministry, so in 1947 I enrolled in the Evangelical Baptist Fellowship Bible College in Glasgow. The college was founded by the Rev. John Shearer to combat the increasing theological liberalism that was spreading throughout Scotland. While I was finishing my apprenticeship as a plumber, I attended the college several nights each week throughout the winter of 1947 and 1948, travelling some thirty miles to Glasgow each evening, plus doing projects at home. Eventually I left my job as a plumber and enrolled full-time in the college, where I was a resident student for two years.

As students we were rooted and grounded in the Word of God, taught by Godly men, and equipped for the work of the ministry. My ability to be there full-time was made possible by the Lord's wonderful provision. Two factors played in this. My father had been a soldier for a good part of his life, but became an invalid as a result of what he had suffered during the First World War. Since I was the son of a veteran, I qualified for financial assistance for a college education. Along with this, one of our church deacons, Mr. J.D. Taylor, who had an interest in my life and was also a county councilor in the Stirlingshire Council, pled my case. As a result, financial provision was made for me to cover the cost of tuition and board at the college. To God is the glory!

As a student I had a number of ministry assignments, including one in a suburb of Glasgow called Auchenshuggle. There I conducted a children's meeting one night per week. On Sundays we were out preaching in some of our churches. My plan was to prepare for pastoral ministry, but God had other plans. As a result of preaching at an open-air meeting in Edinburgh, I met and became friends with a young lady named Adaline Betty Jamieson. She was very active in her church, the Spurgeon's Memorial Church, and in St. Andrew's Mission Hall.

She had come to a personal relationship with Jesus Christ during evangelistic services conducted by the Rev. John Scroggie, who was a brother of the well-known Dr. W. Graham Scroggie.

We soon realized that God had drawn us together to equip us for a ministry. She had been born in Shetland to Tommyann Sinclair and James Adam Jamieson. Her background of island life and isolation would fit her well for the isolation and island ministries that would be ours together. Also, the Shetland Islands have a strong historical tie to Norway.

Eventually her family moved from Shetland to Edinburgh, where her father became the lighthouse keeper in Leith Harbour. Leith is the port of Edinburgh and was a very busy one in those days. Her mother became renowned for her Shetland knitting. Some of her knitting is displayed in the museum in Edinburgh. She also was a part of the Highlands and Islands Home Industries, doing school programs, and travelling to Chicago and New York for British days in large department stores. As a result of this, she became very well acquainted with the beloved Queen Mother. In Leith, Adaline Betty Jamieson attended the Leith public school, and after that moved to Trinity Academy. She was the middle child of five girls.

Summer Student Ministry

In the summer of 1949, I worked with the Scottish Evangelistic Council in the Scottish Borders at a place called Duns. I was asked to be in charge of the team. We conducted several children's meetings each day; we distributed gospel tracts and had open-air meetings in the surrounding villages. During our time there I had the unique experience of preaching in the Pre-Reformation Church at Polwarth and dining at the Hume Mansion on two occasions. This is an area steeped in political and religious history.

The church itself has an amazing history. In the entrance of the church was a massive rock that was hewn out and used as a baptismal font. At that time, the children were immersed, not sprinkled. To the left of the pulpit there hung what was known as the "Death Knell"—a large bell that, in times past, would be used on the occasion of a burial. The person carrying the bell would walk ahead of the casket as it was being carried into the cemetery, ringing it to ward off the evil spirits. Such was the superstition in those days.

Under this church, beneath the area of the pulpit and the communion table, is a crypt. This is the burial place of the famous Hume family, one of whom in more recent years became the Prime Minister of Great Britain. Looking through a grating, one could see a number of very old caskets. The story is told that the crypt was the hiding place of Patrick Hume, a fugitive in 1683. He hid there for four weeks and was fed with food smuggled from the kitchen of the Hume Mansion by his daughter, Lady Grisell Hume. She endured great hardships, risking her own life, to protect her father and family. He was allegedly implicated in the plot to assassinate Charles II.

Patrick Hume (or Home) took a leading part in the Scottish Reformation. Sir Patrick Hume fled to Holland in 1684, assisted by his daughter. I counted it a special honour to follow in the footsteps of those who were willing to pay a price for their faithfulness to God.

Following my stint in the Borders, I stopped in Edinburgh to visit my girlfriend. Then I went home to have my laundry done and pack and get ready to go to Keswick Convention in England's Lake District. I was to be assisting my brother, working at the S.U.M. camp, and of course attending the convention meetings. Little did I realize how that week would change the course of my life and ministry.

I joined the charter bus that would take me to Keswick. God, I believe, guided me to sit beside someone I had never met before. Upon introducing myself, I discovered that he was a pastor in Glasgow. His name was Rev. Donald Stuart. As we continued on our journey, it was interesting to discover that he was also the Scottish director of the European Evangelistic Crusade, later to become known as Global Outreach Mission.

Mr. Stuart had recently returned from a trip to Norway where he had participated in a series of evangelistic meetings conducted by Dr. James A. Stewart, founder of the above mentioned mission. While in Norway, the Rev. Donald Stuart had had a very interesting conversation with Mr. Enock Wangberg, leader of the Nordland og Lapisk Bibel Misjon in which he was made aware of the need for workers in northern Norway and amongst the Lapps (Sami people) in Lapland. Mr. Stuart shared the need with me as we travelled toward Keswick. I had never given any thought to missionary work; my plans and preparation were always looking toward a pastoral ministry.

On arrival at Keswick in mid afternoon, I immediately went to the S.U.M. camp where I would be assisting my brother in leadership. The first evening, I attended the first meeting of the convention. What a joy it was to share with over three thousand believers from Britain, Europe, and around the world. I was so looking forward to a week of fellowship and ministry with some of God's choicest servants.

The Week that Changed my Ministry

I made my way back to the camp after the evening service. As I walked through the entrance, I suddenly collapsed in a heap with severe pain in my stomach. The ambulance was called and I was rushed to the Mary Hewitson Hospital in Keswick, England, where I spent five days. All kinds of tests and x-rays were performed, but no reason for my pain could be found.

As I lay there on that hospital bed, my conversation with Rev. Donald Stuart kept coming to my mind. I sought refuge in the Word of God. Again and again, God directed to me to Isaiah chapter six. This I read over and over and over. Early in the morning of the fifth day, I read over and over that eighth verse: *"Also I heard the voice of the Lord saying: 'Whom shall I send, and who will go for Us?' Then I said, 'Here am I! Send me.'"* At that point I realized that God was calling me not to the pastoral ministry, but to the work in northern Norway and Lapland. There, still in my pain on that hospital bed, I said, "Lord, if this is what You want me to do, then I am willing to go where ever you say."

Suddenly, the excruciating pain that had gripped me for five days was gone. I had had a busy year in college and a busy summer working in the Borders of Scotland. The only way the Lord got my attention was to get me in a hospital bed. Again, I am reminded of those words, *"For I know the plans I have for you … plans to prosper you and not to harm you, plans to give you hope and a future"* (Jeremiah 29:11, NIV). Fortunately I was able to take in the closing meetings of the Keswick Convention. It was then that I went forward and offered myself for overseas service as the Lord would lead.

Upon returning home, I immediately got in touch with my girlfriend, Adaline Betty Jamieson. I shared with her how God had worked in my life since we had last talked. Prior to this we had discussed the fact that God was preparing me for the pastoral ministry, and she had committed herself to serving the Lord with me; therefore, I felt it wise to inform her that I would now be going overseas. I made it clear that if she didn't feel she could make this change, then I was willing to break off our relationship. I was thrilled to discover that in her early Christian life she had expressed a desire to be a missionary. Wow! The Lord had prepared the way!

During the second half of 1949 we were accepted by the European Evangelistic Crusade for work in northern Norway and Lapland. I returned to college for what would be my final year. It was advisable that my girlfriend, who became my fiancé that fall, should have some Bible school training. She was already a very highly skilled secretary. She had skills in writing, including being a poet, along with an ability to sing and be in leadership; however, Bible school training would be vitally important towards helping her in the ministry.

In order to do this, she would have to resign from her very secure job and apply to a suitable Bible school for a one year course. She would also need the money to make all of this possible. To this end we prayed, and the Lord miraculously provided all that was needed.

In the fall of 1949, she applied and was accepted at the Bible Training Institute, known as the "BTI" in Glasgow. She commenced her one year course, staying in residence and becoming involved in the many activities of the school. It was a wonderful time for her. There were a number of students at the school who were the product of the Hebridean Revival, which took place in the 1940s under the Ministry of the Rev. Duncan Campbell.

We were both studying in the same city but several miles apart. We were allowed to see each other once per week. I would take the street car to where she was, then we would go to a little café down the street from the college, and there we would get a meat pie and cup of tea each. We could talk there in relative comfort. On the occasion of her twentieth birthday, on November 14, 1949, my mother joined us at the home of the Jamieson family, where Betty and I were formally engaged. What a happy occasion. Plans were now underway for the future.

During my time at the college in Glasgow, I was able to exercise my plumbing and carpentry skills. This helped pay for my tuition and board. At that time, Rev. Austin Stirling and Mrs. Stirling looked after the students who were in residence. They had purchased a home in a small village outside of Glasgow with the idea of eventually retiring there, so I was asked if I would be willing to do plumbing and carpentry work for them during my spare time. To this I readily agreed. This provided me with extra money … keeping in mind that I would need to buy an engagement ring. I was able to save for one, and with a little help from my mother I proudly presented a beautiful diamond ring to my fiancé, Adaline Betty Jamieson.

During one of the summer's activities, I worked at a shipping company in Grangemouth. I was very fortunate to have this job. The ships brought in lumber from Finland to be used as pit props in the local coal mines. Since I had a college degree, I was given the responsibility of keeping tabs on the number of props that were offloaded from ships and then shipped to the coal mines. I was paid very good wages. I was also able to preach on the weekends in the different churches around our area. Truly the truth of that Scripture became very real to me: "*And my God shall supply all your need according to His riches in glory by Christ Jesus"* (Philippians 4:19). It is exciting to walk in the way of the Lord.

The remaining months of 1949, and the first half of 1950, were hectic and exciting. I was not doing the degree program at college, but rather the pastoral diploma, so by the end of May, 1950, I would be finished my formal studies. Late in 1949, I was smitten with a bad case of the mumps. This was not the most pleasant disease for a man in his early twenties. I had to stay home from college, but managed to keep up with my studies.

In the early part of 1950, in preparation for my June wedding and then heading to "the field," I decided I should have some dental work done. The dental appointment was made for March. Some extractions had to be done, and then partial dentures fitted. Amongst the extractions were two molars. This work had been done on a Friday. When I got home, I discovered that I was bleeding profusely, and nothing would stop the bleeding. It was the weekend, so the dentist recommended that I go to bed, sit up, and have the minimum of movement. With the extreme loss of blood I had become extremely weak. My mother and my fiancé looked after me. My fiancé sat up all night with me to make sure that I was okay.

By Monday it was critical. The dental surgeon was called in. He arrived with his assistant and went to work immediately. During that time I was in and out of consciousness. A blood vessel had been torn, causing the extreme bleeding. Eventually the dentist was able to put in sutures. In the meantime, his assistant had passed out at the sight of all the blood, so my fiancé bravely served as assistant to the dentist. It was thought that I might have to go to the hospital for a blood transfusion; however, after a short time, although I was weak, I was eventually able to return to class at the college. My future mother-in-law was deeply concerned that my dentures would not be fitted before the wedding, which was scheduled for June 30, 1950. My fiancé— bless her—said, "I will marry him as planned, teeth or no teeth."

It's wonderful to experience God's plans and purposes unfolding each step of the way. It is so reassuring to know that He is in control. June 22 was my last day at E.B.F. College. Mr. Graham, President of the college, spoke to the student body from the text "*I being in the way, the Lord led me*" (Genesis 24:27, KJV). What a challenge to those of us who were stepping out into the ministry.

My ordination service was held at Larbert Baptist Church on June 25, 1950. This was so fitting, since it was here that I came to know Christ as my Saviour and Lord. It was here that I had been discipled; it was here that I had my first opportunities to preach and give leadership in so many areas. The Rev. John Shearer, principal of the college, preached and conducted the ordination service. Rev. Shearer spoke on "The Burning Bush." He reminded all of us that the fire in our hearts should be kept burning by self sacrifice. The ordination hymn was "Lord Speak to me that I May Speak."

One of the amusing parts of this service was the different prayers that were offered. One person prayed for me and my "girlfriend," another prayed for me and my "fiancé," and still another prayed for me and my "wife." I kept hoping that they were praying for the same person! It was such a joy to have so many of my family, friends, and fellow students there on that very special occasion. It was also so special to know that we had so much support in prayer from my home church as we set out in the Lord's service. By the way, I did get my dentures in time for my ordination and my wedding!

Immediately after my ordination to the ministry, we were plunged into the final preparations for our wedding. We were married at 1:00 p.m. at Hope Street Baptist Church in Leith. The service was conducted by my brother, Rev. Henry Russell. Having been a pastor for over sixty years, I've discovered that every wedding has some special things. Our wedding was no exception. While the wedding party was standing at the front of the church, the flower girl, my bride's youngest sister, said, "Betty, I need to go to the bathroom." Another sister, sitting nearby, took care of the emergency.

The reception was held at The Kintore Rooms on Queen Street in Edinburgh. Immediately after the reception, we were off on the first leg of our honeymoon, which was somewhat different than what happens for a honeymoon today. We made our way to the railway station and travelled by train to Gourock, where we stayed at the Ashton Hotel on the first night of our life together. In the room that evening, we knelt together and committed our lives to the Lord, to the ministry to which we had been called, and to each other.

In preparation for settling in for the night, we opened our suitcases. Oh, yes … my sister-in-law, Pearl, had been at her devious work. Confetti was spread between each layer of clothing, and my pajamas were carefully sewn together. Oh well … what are sisters-in-law for? The next morning, July 1, we packed our suitcases and walked to the pier, where we boarded one of the Clyde steamers that would take us to Ardrishaig in Argyleshire. From there we took a taxi to "The Shieling," a beautiful little romantic cottage located between Ardrishaig and Lochgilphead.

After dinner we settled into our very comfortable bedroom. The next morning when we came down for breakfast, we were greeted with congratulations. The owners of The Shieling had seen our wedding photo in the *Scotsman* newspaper. Sunday we made our way to Lochgilphead Baptist Church. That evening I was invited to speak at the open air meeting in the square, and we were invited to the home of the pastor, Rev. and Mrs. Duncan MacNeil. On Wednesday evening I spoke at the mid-week service. We had a wonderful week of excellent weather. We decided to hire bicycles to enable us to explore the area .One day we cycled along the path beside the Crinan Canal. We were out several miles when my bicycle got a flat tire, so I had to walk back several miles. Oh well, I was only twenty-two years old then. Saturday came all too soon and we headed back to Larbert and Edinburgh, where we received a royal welcome.

Morris and Adaline Betty Jamieson Wedding day June 30th 1950

The five Jamieson girls-Betty in the centre

6

The Final Days of Preparation

Soon after getting home we had to shift gears very quickly. On July 12 we had to travel down to our mission headquarters at St Leonards-on-Sea. I will never forget entering the living room and seeing the motto above the fireplace: "Dare you go where the Holy Ghost leads, and leave the consequences with Him." Throughout my life that has been my motivation. While there I did extensive work around the gardens. My wife and I became involved in conducting meetings on the beach in the afternoons and evenings and had many opportunities to talk to people about the Lord.

We were back in Larbert and Edinburgh by August 12, 1950, the day of our departure. We had a number of meetings in the general area. During the day we spent time packing and then shipping our goods to Norway. We had farewell gatherings at Larbert and Edinburgh, and on August 11 we had our final farewell at Eldon Hall in Newcastle. We had some last minute needs to be met before we boarded the ship on August 12, and the folks at Eldon Hall were very kind. We received a gift that enabled me to buy a pair of shoes and other personal items, with money to spare. How the Lord provides! On Saturday afternoon, August 12, our family came down to Newcastle from Scotland to bid us bon voyage. It was a very emotional send-off. As the ship pulled out from the dock, the crowd that were gathered sang that great chorus: "Got any rivers you think are uncrossable; Got any mountains you can't tunnel through; God specializes in things thought impossible; He can do just what no other can do." How often we would prove that in the days and years ahead.

Late Sunday afternoon we docked in Bergen, Norway. It was a typical Bergen welcome… it was raining! On the ship a young man from Bergen had befriended us. Since we had a few hours to spare before we were to board the train that would take us to Oslo, he offered to show us around the city of Bergen and the other key sites. We went up the mountain by cable car and got a panoramic view of the city and the surrounding area. Later in the evening we boarded the train that would take us on an overnight trip to the capital city, so we arrived in the early hours of the forenoon, not knowing who would meet as. We stepped out onto the platform of the railway station looking very British and hoping someone would identify us. Suddenly we heard our name being called; we then made our way to the information desk of the railway station, and soon we were introduced to a six foot six giant of a man whose name was Enock Wangberg. He would become our interpreter, our friend, our introduction to Norway and the Lapp life, and also a fellow worker. We were whisked off to be part of the missions conference in the town of Moss. There we met many of our European workers.

The workers were from Germany, France, Holland, and Italy. What a time of ministry and fellowship we had together. We stayed with the Bye family, who became very supportive of our work in the North. From Moss we travelled to the capital city of Oslo, where we had meetings. It was very interesting that there we should meet Dr. O. J. Smith of the People's Church in Toronto, Canada.

The trip to northern Norway with our friend, Enock Wangberg, would take us nearly one week. It was a trip on "Riks Vei 50," the main highway from the south to the very north of Norway—almost all of it on gravel road. We set out on a journey … an adventure, an experience… that would impact us as a couple committed to serving the Lord for the rest of our lives. Little did we realize to what extent this would be true. Growth, maturity, variety, complexity, fulfillment, rewards, demands, satisfaction, humbling experiences—all of this and very much more would characterize the ministries in which I have been involved over these sixty plus years. They have taken me to so many countries and have caused me to be involved in many cultures. How humbling to think that God in His sovereign purposes would care to use me, having come from such humble background, to be thrust into service in so many different ways.

Our first stop on our journey north was the city of Trondheim. It was in the cathedral there that all the kings of bygone days were crowned. Not far from there is the grave of St. Olav, Patron Saint of Norway, and the one who brought Christianity to that country. While there we also saw the place where Dr. James Stewart was used of God to bring about revival in 1949. It was indirectly through this revival that we were called to Norway and to Lapland. While in Trondheim we stayed at the mission home. From there we continued on our journey north, stopping at different places along the way to make contact with various friends of the mission.

Eventually we arrived in Tromso, where we stayed at Ebenezer in Tromsdalen, where Ms. Hulda Wangberg, Enock's sister, lived. Hulda became our language teacher and our advisor regarding the culture of the North. While there I went to Tromso to check on our luggage being unloaded from the ship that had been sent from Newcastle. We then had to transfer it to a local boat, which would take our luggage to Espenes.

I would like to note here what happened to our barrel of china and linen when it was taken off the ship. I made my way to the pier to supervise the unloading of our luggage, which contained all of our worldly goods, including wedding presents and our wedding china. As I watched them unload our luggage, I was horrified. Our most important stuff was packed in a barrel. They rolled it onto its side and kicked it down the gang plank where it bounced on to the pier. I was sure our china was broken. I said nothing to my wife at that particular time, because I wanted to check out things for myself. When we eventually got to Espenes and unloaded our things there, the first thing I did when we got the barrel home was open it. To my great surprise, not a single thing was damaged or broken—thanks to my sister-in-law's careful packing and God's protection. It was then that I revealed to my wife what had happened at the dock.

From Tromso we went on to Nordreisa for the dedication and official opening of Bethesda, the mission hospital. This took place on September 9, 1950. We eventually arrived at Sobakken, which was to be our home, on September 22, 1950. This would be our headquarters for most of the time we served in the North. On September 24 there was a welcome gathering for us arranged by a group of local believers called "Vart Hap," meaning "Our Hope."

Enock Wangberg stayed for a few days to help us get acquainted, and then he left for the South, leaving us amongst people who knew no English (and we who knew no Norwegian). The only thing we could do was ask for God's help. When we would go out into the community, we were always armed with an English/Norwegian dictionary. And so we navigated through the daily needs, and through God's infinite grace we were able to cope in our new surroundings. From the humble beginnings of Letham and Shetland, here we were three hundred kilometres above the Arctic Circle. Our mission was to be found faithful in serving the Lord, proclaiming the unsearchable riches of Christ, and providing the ministry of reconciliation.

Preparation for our First Winter

Our main task was to get the house into shape before winter and the dark period, "Morke Tiden," when the sun never shines. We had to fix the roof, secure the windows, and paint the kitchen. We had no running water, so we had to bring it by bucket from the brook behind the house. When it froze over, I cut a hole two feet deep in the ice with an axe. To keep it from freezing over again, I covered the hole with burlap and then with branches.

One of our major tasks was to build an outdoor toilet. This meant digging a pit and then building the outhouse over it. I located the building halfway between the house and the building that would be our chapel. This way it would be accessible not only for us, but also for those who attended our services. This sounded like a good idea when there was no snow on the ground; however, when we had snow (which was all winter), it meant having to dig a long path through the snow from the house to the outhouse. This was not easy when one was in a hurry, so planning ahead was an important strategy. It was decided to make it a "two-seater." It was duly stocked with neatly cut squares of newspaper, as no toilet paper was available.

One incident I should recall was very humorous, although also very serious. My wife had made the trip to the two-seater. It being dark, she took her flashlight with her. Going about her business, she laid the flashlight down on the other half of the bench, from where it rolled and dropped through the other hole into the pit. Oh dear! What a problem! Upon returning to the house she announced the mishap. Being the brave, chivalrous character that I was, my response was: "You lost it; you find it."

We struggled through that first winter learning the language as we lived with the people, listening to the Norwegian radio, and reading, as best we could, the newspaper. In this way we were building our vocabulary, developing the ability to make the right inflections, and putting the verbs and definite articles and indefinite articles in the right place. Thankfully the Lord truly gave us the gift of tongues.

As we met with the group of believers, my teaching and preaching consisted of reading in the Norwegian Bible portions of scripture with the main theme, and then reading the appropriate additional verses. This helped me to explain my thoughts for the group. Then we always had prayer sessions where they prayed in Norwegian and my wife and I prayed in English. We also learned the familiar hymns in Norwegian, and most of them I could play on my accordion or my guitar.

Prior to going into the ministry full-time, I had done a lot of children's work. While in college, I became acquainted with the group called "The Bible Club" movement. Knowing I would be going into the children's work in the North, and knowing the value of reaching adults through the children, I acquired a whole set of flannelgraph figures, covering most of the Old and the New Testament stories. With a built-in ability for art work, I learned to draw backgrounds on the flannel cloth, so with the figures and the backgrounds we had visual aids to augment our language limitations and thereby communicate with relative ease with the children. In addition to this, I played the accordion and guitar. I acquired some Norwegian choruses and the tunes. Now all we needed was the children, so we started children's work.

The first winter was certainly not boring, but was rather a very busy time. It was a time of adjusting to climate, culture, customs, and community. The store keeper, the lady in charge of the telephone central, the man who was a government employee in charge of road maintenance, snowplowing, and trucking, the postmaster, the family of Ingolf and Esther Strand, the small group of believers, and others all contributed to our effective adjustments, increased language skills, and day to day coping abilities. Coupled with that was the fact that we were newlyweds, novices in housekeeping, and getting to know each other. We were the only English speaking people in the community, so we had to learn to get along with each other since there was no one else with whom we could speak. Of course we could not "run home to mother," either. In addition to all of this, God had blessed both of us with a great sense of humour. We could laugh together at life in general and our language bloopers in particular.

On one occasion we had been invited to the home of a Norwegian lady, Elisabeth Solvol, to have a Norwegian meal. She was one of our local believers. One of the customs in Norway is to thank the hostess for the meal, and when especially thankful, to mention by name the food that was served. Being desirous of expressing thanks, my wife wanted to say "thank you for the hen" (Takk sa meget for honen); instead, because of the wrong inflection and pronunciation, she said "Takk sa meget for hunden," which actually meant "thank you so much for the dog." Our hostess saw the funny side of it and said, "Look, the dog is still running around in the yard." Oh the joys of learning another language!

Long nights, no daylight, no telephone, no electricity, very cold weather, lots of snow, no insulation, no storm windows … all contributed to making life interesting, at times exciting, as well as stressful. In November of that first year, my wife celebrated her twenty-first birthday. Our hope was that she could at least talk with her parents on that special occasion. Not having a telephone, we had to go to the telephone central in Espenes. The switchboard was manned by Miss Andreasen. We sat there for several hours while the operator tried to make a connection with Edinburgh, Scotland. It was all in vain. We had to leave when the switchboard shut down for the day. Oh well … it was a different birthday!

We trudged back to the house where we sat across the table from each other, in kerosene oil lamplight, and celebrated her twenty-first birthday several thousand miles from home and family. This experience convinced us that we should take care of the "no telephone" situation. I went to enquire about having a telephone installed and was promptly told that I would be supplied with a phone and wire, but would have to install it myself. Perhaps my connection with the British Post Office and Telephone was not in vain after all. I promptly strung the wire from the road to the house and connected the telephone. Voila! We had a telephone. We had a connection, albeit limited, with the outside world. We were also introduced to the exciting experience of "the party line," which consisted of multi customers on one line, each with a distinctive ring.

In later years when I started travelling in my ministry, I would call home regularly to my wife. This produced a lot of excitement. When I would call, our phone would ring, and this ring would be heard on the neighbours' phones. I would then hear one click after the other as they picked up their phones so that they could listen in for the latest news. Once my wife and I launched into our conversation in English, which no one else could understand, and we could hear the other phones being replaced with expressions of disgust.

As we made our way through the first winter, we decided that we should have a stand-up bath. We had a large barrel that served as a bathtub in which we could stand and have a bath. Excitement was in the air. We got everything ready. With two pails and a large double handed pot, we went down to the brook at the back of the house, cut through the ice, and filled the containers with ice cold water. Each of us carried a pail along with the double handled container between us. We headed back up the snow-covered slope to the house. Halfway up the slope I slipped and fell flat on my face. The containers of ice cold water emptied on top of me, soaking me to the skin. This was not the bath I had envisioned. It was so cold that I froze to the ground.

I said to my wife, "You go on to the house and stoke up the fire while I peel myself off this ice. Get some fresh clothes from upstairs and I'll dry off in front of the fire and put on fresh, dry clothes."

Standing by the fire I waited for my wife to come down the stairs with my clothes. Some time went by before she came. When she finally came I asked her what took so long. She said, "I was laughing so hard at the sight of you lying sprawled on the snow I had to compose myself before coming down, thinking you might get upset with my unsympathetic laughter."

That first winter held its challenges. I decided that the kitchen needed painting, so I went to work on it. We bought the paint and a paint brush, and I set about painting the kitchen. I did it by the light of a small kerosene lamp, since it was dark all day. I completed the job and was very proud of my work; however, with the return of the sun in February, my pride was soon deflated. The strong daylight revealed that there were many missed spots. Oh well! It needed a second coat anyway.

Our support through the European Evangelistic Crusade was certainly not generous. As with all of the workers throughout Europe, we were a "faith mission." This meant that if the support did not come in, we got nothing. Our support was set at approximately $56 per month; however, often we were informed that only half that amount would be available. Sometimes this would be augmented by a "C.A.R.E." parcel from friends in America. Usually the standard box would contain canned goods and some dry foods. Once we received a whole chicken in a can. It was amazing how much we could get from that one chicken—several meals from the meat plus soup from the bones. The parcel also contained a can of bacon … again, so tasty. We used the bacon fat on our potatoes (when we could get them). There was also Spam and tins of salmon. What excitement when one of these parcels arrived!

To augment our diet, I would on occasion borrow a rowboat and row out to the Arctic Ocean to fish. The fish were very plentiful. Given the fact that the Lord provided us with the deep freeze as big as all outdoors (in the wintertime), we could just leave the fish outdoors for a few hours. Once they were frozen, we could store them in our little earth cellar under the house.

Our living room floor was covered with old-fashioned linoleum. We could brag about it providing us with an indoor skating rink. The floor was so cold that first winter. My wife would mop the floor, and before it was completely dry it would freeze. We had an open fireplace in the corner of the living room, but it was useless in providing any semblance of warmth. With a straight chimney the heat all went outside, so my next job involved tearing out the old fireplace and replacing it with a stove.

It was quite common practice to cover the linoleum with boat varnish, so clearing out what little furniture was there, I went to work and varnished the linoleum. After two to three days it was dry enough to touch, so I replaced the furniture over the newly varnished floor. It looked great, but come Sunday we encountered a problem. Our group of believers gathered together in different homes each week for fellowship, Bible study, and prayer, and it was our turn to host. We were looking forward to this, now that the kitchen was painted and the floor had a fresh coat of varnish. When it came time for prayer, as was the custom, we all got on our knees to pray. Once the prayer session was over, the problem manifested itself. The women wore heavy woolen stockings, and the men wore heavy woolen pants. When everyone tried to get up from their knees, they were stuck fast to the newly varnished linoleum. We then discovered the reason—the woolen material and the body warmth softened the varnish. It hadn't really dried, but was actually frozen. There was lots of laughter, and I suggested that maybe this was not such a bad idea. It was one way to keep the saints on their knees.

Our first Christmas in the North was a memorable one for us as a couple, for the community as a whole, and in our work amongst the children. Christmas Eve was special. This was when they gathered in our chapel, which was not anywhere near ready for full use. However, we made it usable. My wife did a great job of baking cookies and cake, enough for all the children and the adults who came. We acquired an evergreen tree, decorated with tinsel, and lit it with … yes … real candles. The tree was set in the middle of the floor, and everyone gathered around to sing Christmas carols, one of the favourites being, "I am so glad each Christmas Eve, t'was then that Jesus was born."

I led the singing with my accordion. This was followed by the Christmas story told with the visual aid of flannelgraph, which augmented my limited Norwegian vocabulary. After the service, people would go home to celebrate "Julen" (Christmas)—not with Santa Claus, but with "Jule Nissen" (an elf-like character). All of this happened during the "Morke tiden," or dark time, which started in November and didn't end until we saw sun again in February. This was a difficult time for the people, and many would suffer from a type of melancholia known as "Arctic Sickness," now called SAD (Seasonal Affective Disorder).

The years we were in the North were those immediately following the Second World War, when Norway had been occupied by the Germans. When it became evident that the Nazi regime was showing signs of crumbling and were being overpowered by the Allied forces, the Nazi forces began retreating from across the Northland. The retreating forces demonstrated their cruelty. They practiced what was known as "the scorched earth policy." As they retreated, they burned the houses and other buildings behind them, leaving the North in flames. This was captured in the book entitled *Finmark i Flammer*, or *Finnmark in Flames*. The Northerners were herded to the coast, where they took refuge in whatever kind of boat was available, and fled south. Many died of exposure. Children were born, but many became sick; it was a terrible tragedy.

The Germans valued their stronghold in the North because from there they could intercept the convoys that were making their way to Murmansk. The Norwegian government was in exile, and the Norwegian forces took refuge in the United Kingdom, but they continued their fight against the occupation forces in Norway. They did sabotage work, which frustrated the enemy and also boosted the morale of the Norwegians. One of the great stories of this time was *The Shetland Bus*. The main character in that story was Shetland's Larsen.

Norway was finally rid of the enemy, and peace was declared, but the road ahead was tough. As a result of the forced migration south, the Nordland and Lappish Bible Mission established a ministry to take care of the sick and the elderly. Thus the home at Malvik was established. The Norwegian government undertook the major tasks of rebuilding the settlements of the North. The town of Hammerfest and many inland communities were the focus of their attention.

When we arrived in the North, there were still many evidences of the occupation. There were the ruins of the German barracks, some military vehicles, and ships that had been sunk with parts of the hulls still sticking out of the water. One famous ship was the *Tirpitz*, which was part of a major victory for the Allied forces. Rationing was still in force; fruit and vegetables and clothing were in short supply. The milk that we bought from a neighbour was blue in colour and had a strong taste due to the fact that the cows were fed turnips. We took raw cod liver oil and we ate cod liver.

In spite of this, general productivity was still very low in the winter months. There were not very many other types of vitamins available. Many people were still nursing emotional and physical scars from those terrible years of occupation. Some of their family members had died in concentration camps. Others were imprisoned and mistreated for their refusal to cooperate. Still others had fraternized with the Germans and were subsequently ostracize by their neighbours.

It was in this environment that we were called to minister; it brought to us its particular challenges and wonderful opportunities. Winter was challenging with the snow, subzero temperatures, and challenges in the travelling we had to do. I learned to ski—not for pleasure, but to facilitate travel from one place to the next. We also bought a "spark." This was essentially a chair on long runners. One could sit on it and the other person with one foot on the runner could then kick with the other foot to propel it along, or the seat could be used to carry groceries and other parcels. In other words, it could be used more or less like a scooter.

February was an important month. We could anticipate the close of the dark period and return of the sun. I would get up each morning, stand at the kitchen window from where I could look up the valley, and each day hope to catch the first glint of sunlight that would mark the end of the dark period. How we rejoiced to see the light and feel the benefit of the sunrays!

Through all of this we were very much aware of God's enabling grace, His daily provision, and our increasing fluency in the language. One time we made a trip by local boat to Tromso to meet up with Enock Wangberg's sister, Miss Hulda Wangberg, who lived at Ebenezer in Tromsdal, which was just across the sound from Tromso. Here we stayed for three weeks. Two things occupied our time here. First, we had intensive language study with the aid of a very capable teacher. We dealt with grammar, sentence structure, and the refining of our pronunciation. Secondly, we conducted Bible training sessions for local leaders working as lay workers in a number of surrounding small villages. This involved theology, Bible exposition, hermeneutics, and dealing with practical application.

While we were there we conducted the evening meetings, Sunday services, and children's meetings. My wife and I sang; I played the accordion and guitar, and we both shared in the ministry of the Word. We made contact with the Baptist church in Tromso, where we became fast friends of the pastor, Gulston Ohrn, and his wife, Lily, and family. This also gave us opportunity to minister there, and eventually I was given a letter of commendation from the Baptist district secretary of the North, Pastor Gustav Flatebo. This enabled us to move freely amongst the Baptist congregations and minister to them. This was an added blessing. We would get some extra remuneration from time to time, and thus augment our meagre financial resources. The Lord will provide! One of the reasons this letter was valuable was because of any suspicion that may have surrounded my name, "Russell." The only other ones with this name were known to the general public as "The Russellites," commonly called "Jehovah's Witnesses." They took this name from their founder, Charles Russell. Oh well … what's in a name? So this letter cleared us of any suspicion.

There was a very definite side benefit arising from the harshness of occupation and the deprivation that the people experienced, and that was an incredible openness to, and interest in, the message of hope provided in the Gospel. This was first evidenced in the evangelistic crusades held by Dr. James Stewart in Norway in 1948 and 1949. A spirit of revival broke out in Trondheim, the crowning capital of Norway. It was in this city cathedral that Norwegian kings were crowned. The citywide crusades started in one of the larger churches, but very soon the crowds were so great they moved to a larger auditorium, and attendances continued to increase.

Dr. Stewart was able to minister through an interpreter, one of whom was Pastor Knut Anderson, who was a youth secretary for the Baptist denomination in Norway. They had to move to the largest available place in the city of Trondheim—Trondheim Cathedral. The spiritual life of the city increased, souls were saved, and people's lives were transformed.

There were many who believed that Dr. Stewart made a mistake in not continuing the meetings; however, just four years after the end of World War Two and the liberation of Norway, there was a very obvious hunger and thirst for righteousness. So while we struggled with the climate, the meagre support, the limited resources, and the difficulty in travel, we discovered that whenever we went to small villages on the islands and the mainland, we always had outstanding overflowing attendances of children and adults at the meetings we conducted. As soon as we arrived in any place, word spread and the people came. Here again was one of the advantages of the telephone party line. Children and adults came face to face with Jesus Christ.

The first baptism we ever had was in the stream behind the house. The stream was fast flowing. It was fed by water from the ice and snow of Boringfjel, the highest mountain in our area, and the water was extremely cold and greenish in colour. We dammed up the stream so that it would be deep enough. We had to baptize the candidates against a fast current so that they wouldn't be carried away by the force of the water. At one of the baptisms there was a bit of concern expressed. The top of the lady's head had not been completely immersed. A very quick answer was given: "Oh, we just did the bit that the priest forgot." Being baptized by immersion was not an easy decision because of the opposition encountered by the state church priest and sometimes family members. One lady whom I baptized met very strong opposition from her husband. He said, "If you get baptized by those dissenters, I'll shoot myself." She was baptized, but he reneged on his threat to shoot himself.

A. Morris Russell in Kautokeino Costume-Lapland

Our oldest daughter-Adaline- in Kautokeino Dress

Kautokeino family

7

Respite from the Rigours of the North

In May of 1951, we were to have a break from the rigours of the North. God provided the finances to enable us to attend the field conference of the mission to be held in Grindevold, Switzerland. We travelled by boat from Espenes to Narvik. From there we travelled by train to Stockholm in Sweden.

Narvik was an important port in Northern Norway. Before the war, Sweden shipped its iron ore by rail to Narvik. There it was loaded onto the ships and transported around the world. The Germans invaded the port, arriving in what appeared to be the freighters. Once in the harbour, they unloaded their "cargo" of soldiers who immediately took over Narvik. They wanted to use this port and its connection with Sweden (who incidentally had declared neutrality) so that the Germans would be able to ship Swedish iron ore to their own ports to meet their needs for their war machine. Now that the war was over, we could use this railway to travel south through Sweden.

The problem with the Norwegian railway was that it only came as far north as Bodo. At this time the Norwegian relationship with Sweden was still very strained. In spite of Sweden's neutrality, they were still very much pro-German, and the Norwegians were not happy about this.

The Norwegian kroner, which was their currency, was not strong, so we couldn't exchange it for Swedish kroner, which was very strong. This created problems. In those days we had no credit cards, as they weren't available to the general public at that time. We boarded the train in Narvik that would take us through Sweden south to Stockholm.

As we left Narvik, we got a view of the fjord. There we could see the remains of the German ships that had been sunk by the British. The mountains were high and covered with snow. We could see the ski tracks that crisscrossed the frozen lake. There lived the Swedish Sami folk (the Lapps), and their tents could be seen up on the mountains.

We were soon travelling through barren land with many kilometres between each house. We were fortunate to have a berth on board the train, so we were able to have a good rest. As we travelled south, we saw less and less snow and more and more houses and larger stretches of fertile land. Twenty-three hours later we arrived in Stockholm. We were able to spend the night in a small hotel called the "Esplanade," which was a very small tourist hotel not far from the dock and the railway station.

The next morning we didn't have enough money to deposit our luggage in the storage room at the station, so one of us sat watch over the luggage while the other took the opportunity to walk around the city of Stockholm. There were no wheels on the luggage in those days, so it wasn't easy to carry them around with us. To throw some complications into the mix, my wife was five months pregnant with our first child. One could always see the funny side of this—this was the product of long cold nights in December and January, and of course the pill hadn't been invented yet! We did have enough money to buy a package of cookies, though, which served as our lunch and dinner.

That day passed without any major incident. In the evening we were able to board the train that would take us on the ferry to Denmark, on through to Germany, and to our destination, Switzerland. Now we could exchange our Norwegian money for Danish kroner and get some food. Hallelujah! Norway and Denmark were on friendly terms, having both suffered at the hands of the German occupation forces. I still recall scenes of German people picking through the rubble of places that had been destroyed by the final offensive of the Allied bombers.

We arrived in Switzerland and were met by Mr. Douglas Stuart, the American director of the mission, and also Mr. Armin Hoppler, our field director from the office in Winterthur, Switzerland. We were promptly driven to a mansion located on the shores of Lake Bodensee that had once belonged to Napoleon and was now a home operated by the deaconesses of the Evangelical Lutheran church. This was a place where we could relax and recuperate courtesy of Rev. and Mrs. Stewart and several of our American friends.

It was a bit of Heaven on Earth. We were pampered in a loving, caring environment. Every morning we were awakened by the beautiful harmonious voices of four of the deaconesses singing some of the wonderful hymns, one of them being "Gott ist die Liebe," as they walked along the corridors of each floor of the mansion. We enjoyed the good food, the fellowship, and the fun. We participated in the devotions each day, and my wife and I would sing in Norwegian and English while I accompanied on the piano. The deaconesses noted that my wife was pregnant and took special care of her.

The day before we had to depart for the missions conference they had a special time for us. They presented my wife with a beautiful set of hand knitted baby clothes for our anticipated first child. God is so good. At this point in time deep emotions well up within me as I reflect upon the goodness of the Lord in the land of the living. We were able to spend time with our leaders, explaining our work in the North. They did not realize the difficulties we encountered.

Our Missions Conference

We were checked into the conference a day ahead of most of the other European missionaries. I was enlisted to help with the last minute preparations and also pick up those who came by train. The Sunday opened with a communion service. What a precious time of fellowship with a deep sense of oneness in Christ! I talked with one of our workers from Spain as we stood on the veranda, dwarfed by the majestic mountains around us. He shared his heart cry for Spain in the 1950s. Life in Spain for the Evangelical Christians was not good. Opposition and oppression were rampant. He had even spent time in jail. With tears in his eyes he said, "I stand here talking with you in the midst of this majestic beauty, and I feel like a bird let out of the cage."

Can I ever forget this week? The fellowship, prayer, fun (oh yes, missionaries can have fun), and the generosity of our fellow workers to us was overwhelming. One missionary gave me her second camera, which was much better than my old black-and-white camera. With this gift we could promote the work of the North in a much better way. Another missionary promised me a bicycle, which he shipped to me sometime later. This enabled me to travel from place to place and not have to walk so far. We realized we weren't alone. This support was most encouraging.

At party time skits were the order of the day. I acquired a tartan travel rug, pinned it around me to represent a kilt, danced the Highland fling, and sang some Scottish songs—much to the amusement of all present. The fellowship that week encouraged and strengthened us after a long hard winter in the far north. The deep spirituality that was evident from the head to the newest missionary on the field shone through in every aspect of the work. Truly it was worthy of the name of Christ, and of the great work founded by our beloved leader, Dr. James A. Stewart and his dear wife, Ruth.

Having Rev. Douglas Stewart, brother of Dr. Stewart, and his wife, Mary Sue, with us was a great inspiration to all. The mornings were spent in prayer and the ministry of the Word of God. In the afternoons we enjoyed exploring the world around us. We took the chair lift up one of the mountains where we enjoyed the very delicate edelweiss poking through the melting snow, along with many other Alpine flowers. We visited the glaciers and the fascinating ice caves. Taking in the majestic handiwork and beauty of God's creation was an overwhelming inspiration.

In the evenings we heard from the workers in the difficult and different countries. Many were dealing with the aftermath of the war, the refugees, and the rebuilding of Europe. There was much evidence of a disillusioned people with a great spiritual void seeking answers to life. This gave our missionaries an overwhelming number of opportunities to provide physical and emotional care, along with the message of the Gospel.

Originally it had seemed impossible that we could attend the conference, but God marvelously provided. We had needed the fellowship and support of the missionary family. This would stand us in good stead upon our return to the North with its isolation, harsh winter, and difficult travel conditions. The Sunday mornings were wonderful, as were the devotional times each morning. It all brought us so close to the Lord.

At the end of the conference we packed and started to head back to our various fields of service, but we had one more place of ministry to go to first. On our way home from Grindevald, we stopped to take part in a service in the city of Berne, Switzerland. Many of us took part with testimonies and the quoting of John 3:16 in all of the languages represented in the group. Then we had a mass choir, which I had the privilege of conducting. This was a climax to an incredible week as we bade tearful farewells to our fellow workers.

Summer 1951 with its Challenges and Excitement

The summer of 1951 saw us engaged in children's day camps at Solbakken. Upon reflection, this was similar to what eventually became known as D.V.B.S., or Daily Vacation Bible School. We had games, Bible verse memorization, and Bible stories each day. Snacks and treats were provided for the children.

During that summer, electricity was brought into our house. This was an incredible contribution to a more comfortable and civilized lifestyle. One of the modern conveniences was having running water in our house. I dug a trench from the stream at the back of the house to the basement of the house and laid a pipe in our earth cellar. Then I hooked up a pump. In this way, I was able to install a sink in our kitchen, which was a luxury "par excellence."

Excitement mounted as we looked forward that summer to the visit of my mother and my wife's sister, Pearl. Neither of them had travelled outside of the U.K. before. This was to be a new experience for both of them. My mother and Pearl had travelled from Newcastle, England, to Bergen, Norway. There they picked up the *Hurtigruten*, which would take them to Tromso. We met them there, and then we travelled by the local boat to Espenes.

What a joy to have family with us! There was a lot of talk for the next few days, and they got a fair taste of life in the North. We climbed mountains, visited the Sami folk, got to see the reindeer, attended meetings, and got a taste of Norwegian fare and reindeer meat.

Pearl went back to Scotland after three weeks. She flew out of Tromso on a flying boat that took her to Bergen, and then from there she took the boat to Newcastle and then the train to Edinburgh. She arrived back to work on the Monday, where she faced a problem. Her work companions inquired where she had been. When she told them of her experiences, they concluded that this explained the sores on her legs and elsewhere on her body. She obviously had picked up some disease in Lapland, so she was immediately sent home from work. The doctor had no idea what this so-called disease was. Pearl contacted us in Norway and explained the situation. We very soon realized what the so-called disease was. She was the victim of a very bad reaction to mosquito bites.

Yes, mosquitoes can be a problem in the North. The eggs are protected by the snow, and when the snow melts, the eggs hatch. They are vicious insects. They attack both humans and the reindeer, which is why the reindeer seek a patch of snow to lie down on to have protection from the mosquitoes.

My mother planned to stay on for several months in the North. She would then be able to help my wife when the baby was born and also provide company for my wife when I had to be away on some of my ministries. As the time of the anticipated arrival of our first child drew near, we had to make plans accordingly. The decision was made to move to Nordreisa and check in at Bethesda, our mission hospital there. Two rooms were made available to us to provide accommodation for ourselves and my mother. This also meant that my wife would be close to the doctor, nurses, and the midwife.

While in Nordreisa at the hospital, I was able to exercise my plumbing, carpentry, and painting skills. I also visited the patients and ministered to their spiritual needs. We had the opportunity to make good contacts with the patients who came in from surrounding communities. This made it easier for us to go to those communities to do some follow-up, as well as have some evangelistic meetings. We also had some of the Sami people from the Kautokeino tribe come to the hospital to have their babies and have their medical needs attended to. This gave us the opportunity to make very interesting contacts that would serve us well in our future ministry amongst the nomadic people.

We also had held regular services at the hall that was attached to the house where the hospital manager lived. This was the time of year when some of the berries were ripe, so my mother and my wife went out picking multebaer, which are called bake apple or cloud berry in English. They are delicious, so when my wife made them into jam they were a great addition to any meal. They are a beautiful golden yellow when ripe and very high in vitamin C.

On Thursday, August 30, we received word that my wife's grandmother had died in Shetland. At times like this we were very conscious of the fact that we were so far removed from family and home. One day my mother was sitting by the window in the hospital common room. Her facial profile was emphasized by the light coming from the window. One of our Christian friends went in to visit my mother and to have an opportunity to use what little English he knew. Immediately upon greeting my mother he asked her, "Are you one of Abraham's children?"

When my mother inquired as to why he would ask that question, he said that he was just looking at her nose.

"Oh," she said, "the reason that I have a nose like that is I fell down the stairs and broke it." Another reminder not to judge by appearances!

Storslett was the business centre in that area. In the centre of that community was the Lutheran State Church. On one occasion, on May 17, which is the Norwegian National Day when they celebrate their independence from Sweden, we all decided to attend the state church. We were classified as the dissenters; however, the state church priest, who was not kindly disposed to dissenters, took advantage of our presence in the service to instruct everyone in the congregation that those who did not "baptize children" or "christen" them should have a millstone hung around their neck and be cast into the depths of the sea. Rather a far-fetched interpretation of that scripture, which makes no reference to baptism at all.

Just about this time we celebrated the first anniversary of our arrival in northern Norway. It was hard to believe that so much had happened and so much had been accomplished. We gave God all the glory as we reflected upon the ministry we had been able to exercise, and for the fact that we had developed such fluency in the language. Not everything has been easy, though. We'd faced opposition from the people in many and varied forms, but we gave God thanks for the opportunity to share the glorious Gospel with so many.

Our family grew by one on September 19, 1951, when Adaline Anne Russell saw the first light of day. The given names were the combination of her mother's name, Adaline, and her Grandmother Russell's name, Anne. She was delivered by a midwife named Fru Volstad at the mission hospital. She had to be registered by the local state church priest, the only one authorized to register births in the community.

We stayed on at Nordreisa for several weeks. This gave my wife opportunity to regain her strength, as well as allowing the baby to be better able to travel to our home in Espenes, a distance of some five to six hours travel. The most natural thing was for the baby to be breast-fed; however, her mother developed breast abscesses that were very painful and difficult to treat. The midwife told my wife that she would likely have breast cancer when she reached her late forties or early fifties. This actually happened. My wife had a radical mastectomy and died when she was fifty-six years of age.

Homeward Bound

The time came for us to make our way back to Espenes with our new daughter. We packed all our stuff into the hospital vehicle, affectionately called "The Surrebus." It was an old German ambulance, a relic from war years. Birger Rudd, the hospital manager, was the driver. My wife and Adaline Anne rode up front for warmth and a measure of comfort. My mother and I rode in the back. It was a gravel road all the way, so we bumped and bounced along hour after hour, and for the first time in my life I saw my mother experience travel sickness. She wasn't used to this, but then who could survive the kind of roads we travelled on? These are some of the joys of our travel in the North.

We were concerned about my wife's health with the painful recurring of breast abscesses, her need to look after the baby, and the fact that I would have to be out travelling again. We had a very good doctor who was responsible for our area. He attended to my wife faithfully. On his visits he always liked to use what limited English he knew. Once he was checking out my wife's lungs with his stethoscope. Searching in his mind for the right English words to tell her to breathe in and to breathe out, he suddenly said, "Yes, now I know, inspire and expire." So much for our wonderful English language!

He not only was our doctor, but he also became a close friend. We discovered he had been married to a lady in Trondheim who had become a born-again believer. He didn't like this change in her life or her new lifestyle, so he left his medical practice in Trondheim and came north to be the community doctor in our area. When he discovered that we were Christians, he began to ask questions. He told us that he was living with a woman in the North and had two children by her. He eventually came to faith in Christ as a result of our discussions with him. His dilemma now was how to handle the two women in his life. We encouraged him to go back to his wife in Trondheim, who was willing to receive him. This he did. We also pointed out that he had a responsibility to the children in the North. This he also did. So we were used to bring healing to him, as he also was used to bring healing to us.

We were able to get one of the teenage girls from Over-Espenes to come and live with us to do the washing and to help look after the baby and stay with my wife when I had to go out to meetings in the area. She was an excellent help and also relieved me of much worry.

Our ministry expanded and developed as I worked with Enock Wangberg and Ernest Jensen. I now had my bicycle, which I could load on to the local boat and travel to different ports on the island of Senja, Norway's second-largest island, and also on the mainland. I would load my stuff onto the bicycle and travel from community to community. With our sleeping bags with us, we could bunk down in the community hall or stay with some friends along the way. This enabled us to have children's meetings and evangelistic outreach events.

Up to this point I worked mostly in Tromsfylke (the county of Troms), and we had only the occasional encounter with the Sami, the Laplanders. This would come later and would necessitate much more extensive travel, along with Enock Wangberg and the support of Norland og Lapisk Bibel Misjon. Before leaving this area of our ministry, let me share yet another incident of God's amazing provision for our daily needs. The mission had informed us that since funds were low, we would be getting only half of our allotted money. This would be the equivalent of approximately $25 for the month. This meant that we were not able to buy very much in the way of food. We had just had our breakfast one day, and as we prayed we mentioned our needs to the Lord. We had fish, which I had caught, but we had nothing to go with it, so in my prayer I made mention of the fact that we really would appreciate it if the Lord would provide us with some potatoes. Having finished our devotions, I put on my jacket and made to go out.

"Where are you going?" my wife asked.

"I really don't know," I replied. As I put my hand on the door knob, someone put their hand on the outside door knob. The door opened and there stood Elizabeth Solvol, one of our dear friends who lived about three to four kilometres from us. I invited her into the kitchen, and we sat and talked for a little while. During our conversation, she told us the following story:

"I was on my way to the post office when I felt the Lord telling me to take something to the Russells. I went back into the house and the only thing I had were these."

She handed me a brown paper bag. When I opened it, I found two to three kilograms of potatoes. The Lord promised, "… *before they call, I will answer*" (Isaiah 65:24) and "[I] *will supply all your need*" (Philippians 4:19). Who said being a servant of the Lord wasn't exciting?

At this point we were well into our second year of ministry. Our language skills had vastly improved, and we were well acquainted with the culture and customs. It felt like we were at home and accepted by the people. The motto in our mission headquarters went something like this: "Dare you go where the Holy Ghost leads and leave the consequences with Him." If followed, He promised He would provide a most exciting and rewarding life with eternal values the priority. What more could one wish for? This was to set the pattern for my ministry of well over sixty years in thirty-five countries. It brings to mind the lyrics: "How can I say thanks for the things He has done for me—things so undeserved that He gave to prove his love for me. The voices of a million angels could not express my gratitude; all that I am and ever hope to be, I owe it all to thee. To God be the glory, for the things He has done."

One day, Enock Wangberg and I were travelling to a community in the Lyngen area. He told me an amazing story about a group of people and the amazing sixth and seventh books of Moses. These are attributed to Moses and have their roots in Egyptian magic. This part of Lyngen was a stronghold of those who held to the powers of the sixth and seventh books of Moses. They claimed that they are an addendum to the Talmud, although there is no mention of them there. They are also an addition to the Pentateuch, the first five books of the Bible. One day a man was brought to the mission hospital in Nordreisa. He had cut his foot with an axe. Someone had read from these magic books; however, this had not stopped the bleeding. By the time he got to the hospital, infection had set in and he had to be flown to Tromso, where they had to amputate part of his leg. This illustrates the widespread superstition found amongst the people of the

North. Enock Wangberg wrote his Master's thesis on this particular subject for the University in Oslo. False doctrine, the power of the state church, superstition, and the hangover of Animism amongst the older generation did not always make it easy to share the good news of the Gospel of the Lord Jesus Christ.

There was a real mix of emotions in a period of around two weeks. We had the news of Grandmother Sinclair's death in Shetland. This was difficult for my wife, because she had grown up there. Then there was the great joy of welcoming our new baby girl into the world and into the family. Then came the glorious good news that Pop, my wife's father, had committed his life to the Lord Jesus Christ!

We had made a commitment when we married that we would pray for Pop every day of our married life until we heard that he had come to know the Lord Jesus Christ as his own personal Saviour. We received his letter—the only one he ever wrote to us—and what a thrill to receive that good news. Pop was a very special person. He was a lighthouse keeper in the lighthouse at the pier in Leith, which is the port for Edinburgh, Scotland. He was interviewed on one occasion by a reporter from the *Scotsman* newspaper. The reporter described him as, "a big, strong, silent, Shetlander."

Pop had been to an evening evangelistic service where he heard a message—a message he had heard many times, but that night he was under deep conviction. The next day at the lighthouse he got down on his knees, repented of his sin, and received Jesus Christ as Saviour and Lord. Knowing that we had committed to pray for him every day until he yielded to the claims of Christ, he put pen to paper and wrote that letter. The angels in Heaven rejoiced as did we, three hundred miles above the Arctic Circle.

All during that period of time, our call to ministry, sharing the good news of the Gospel, ministering in the hospital, conducting children's meetings, holding gospel meetings along the coast up the long fjords of the North amongst the fisher folks and the nomadic people of the reindeer, exercising my plumbing and carpentry skills in the hospital, equipping the doctor's office, getting ready to welcome him, was done to the glory of God. He chose us to be a part of this exciting ministry

In October of 1951, I was back up to Tromsdalen, where I taught some classes for lay leadership from some of the smaller, out-of-the-way places and communities. This was a very worthwhile ministry, as it helped to multiply the outreach ministry through those who lived in those different areas. During this time, when I had time at home in Espenes, I also worked on the chapel, finishing the inside of the building. By this time we were in our second winter.

Now that we had the baby, we had a few more concerns. We had to make sure that she was warm and provided for. I was joined by evangelist Roald Nilsen from southern Norway, who helped with the work on the hall and helped in the ministry amongst children and the adults. It was good to have the support and fellowship. In spite of the fact that my wife struggled with health issues and had the responsibility of the baby, she was still very much involved in the work. She was very active in the children's and young people's work. From time to time she would go on a baking spree, whenever we had a care package from our American friends. Then we would put on a feast for the children. She was also involved in singing and sharing in the devotions.

To make life a little easier, in November we got an electric stove. This was made possible by some friends. In spite of this, my wife had another spell in bed. She wasn't getting a chance to build up her strength. The big question was whether she would be able to make it through the winter up in the North. Our doctor was really very good. He was deeply concerned about the recurring abscesses, so he gave my wife regular doses of penicillin.

In the meantime, we were seeing very good responses from the children, young people, and the adults, with new people attending regularly. This was a source of encouragement in the midst of my wife's ongoing physical problems.

That winter was tough going. Blizzards, high winds, deep snow, and extreme temperatures were the order of the day. We had to cut down and chop our own wood. We got a supply of coal that came from Svalbard, an archipelago located halfway between the most northerly part of mainland Norway and the North Pole. Svalbard was committed to Norway around 1920, with other signatory nations given access to it. Norway and Russia mined the coal in that region. Longyearbyen is the main community. The coal, when it was mined, came in the usual lumps; however, once it was exposed to the outside elements, it disintegrated into small granules. We would mix it with water and add it to the stove. It would then cake together and give off excellent heat.

By December it was extremely cold with lots of snow. Adaline Ann was growing very healthy and was excited about life, but my wife had been struggling with her health. Now that she had been getting penicillin regularly, however, she was gradually improving.

I had been extremely busy with so many physical things calling for my attention. This was so time-consuming that little time was being given to study and preparation for the different meetings I had in the area. It was difficult to feed others when I was not feeding myself.

Periodically I had to make a trip to Tromso to take care of different matters. Sometimes I would travel by bus, which was a six-hour trip. Sometimes I would travel by boat, which would be an overnight trip. While in Tromso I would often minister in the Baptist church there on the Sunday. Anytime I was away I had to make sure that my wife had enough food and enough fuel to keep her warm and comfortable until I got back home again.

Christmas was a wonderful season. Thanks to friends in Scotland and in America, we had all the Christmas trimmings. We had canned turkey, canned plum pudding, and lots of small gifts to be given to the children. My wife was able to do all the baking for the feast. This was our second Christmas, and we had over eighty children and adults in attendance. The year 1951 was brought to a close with a watch night service. The chapel was filled. The service went from 10:00 p.m. until just past midnight. What a climax to the year! Through it all, thanksgiving was made for God's enabling grace and faithful provision and knowing that His strength is made perfect in our weakness.

The year 1952 started out as a very busy time. Near the beginning of February, we rejoiced with the return of the sun after a long dark period. My mother was still with us. Sometimes she chose to stay home rather than face the winter weather. One evening in the mountain area not far from us, one and a half metres of snow fell in one night.

Ernest Jensen and I planned a trip that would take us around the second largest island in Norway, the island of Senja. With bicycles loaded with our gear, accordion, guitar, flannelgraph equipment, and our rucksacks on our back, we set out on our evangelistic trip. Our plan was to have children's meetings in the afternoon and gospel services each evening. We cycled for about twelve kilometres on gravel roads that had been plowed by the snow plow. We had a contact where we stayed for three days. That evening, no meetings were being held, so Jensen and I spent time translating some children's choruses from English into Norwegian.

We sent word around the community that children's meetings would be held in the afternoon and gospel services in the evening, either in the community hall or in any available school. My diary reminds me that we sang one of our newly translated children's songs in English, "Sunshine Corner," and then in Norwegian. This was very fitting, since we saw the sun that day for the first time after the long, dark winter. It lifted one's spirit as we escaped the doldrums of the winter.

The winds were so strong, the snow so deep, and the frost so hard that the reindeer were dying from hunger. Because of their weakened condition, they were falling victim to the wolves. We too were battling the strong winds and low temperatures while walking waist deep in snow, but we plowed on from place to place, holding meetings for children and for adults, giving out tracts, and sharing the good news of the Gospel. We were always welcome and were grateful for the hospitality extended to us. We were so glad to be on the King's business. While on this tour, we heard on the radio that King George VI, of the United Kingdom, had died from coronary thrombosis and complications from lung cancer. His daughter, Elizabeth, would now become Queen.

Although the winter was hard in the North, it had its compensations. The men folk were home, and they could be reached with the Gospel. Yet the amount of snow and the deep frost made it difficult to travel with bicycles, or even to walk. Sometimes we would travel twenty-five kilometres in a day. Sometimes we were able to travel by regular ferry; otherwise, we would have to have an open boat.

While travelling I always tried to keep in touch by phone or letter with my wife and my mother, but this wasn't always easy. On one leg of the tour we had to walk five kilometres up the mountain with rucksacks on our backs and all of our equipment on our bicycles. It was so cold that when we would breathe in, our nostrils would freeze together.

As we worked with the schoolchildren, we discovered that some of the teachers were Christians. Some had come from the South and felt that it was their calling to minister in this way in the North. Because of isolation and difficulty in travel, we encountered many unusual things.

While in this community on the island, a young father came to visit us. We discovered that he was a backslider, and we had the joy of seeing him come back to the Lord. He told us about his two-year-old daughter who was quite ill, so we went home with him and prayed for the little girl. Before we left that community, we discovered that she had considerably improved.

In one community we had a meeting in a room that actually was a part of the barn. We ministered to the accompaniment of the noise of the animals. On this trip, my friend, Jensen, got some bad frost bite on his face. We had to rub his face with snow to get the circulation going again. During this same trip I called my wife to see how things were going. She was doing much better, but my daughter, Adaline, was down with the measles.

We got back home after three weeks on the island. We had walked and cycled many kilometres, had meetings in most of the communities, and saw some respond to the Gospel call. We were tired, but nevertheless rejoicing in the Lord.

8

The Rollercoaster of Emotions

We were not long home when we got word that the Strands' little girl, Liv Marie, had died on February 20. This demonstrates the emotional swings in the ministry. We had been rejoicing in a wonderful ministry on the island, and now we were being called to minister to a family in their sorrow. In addition to this, it was the first funeral I'd ever conducted. I'd have to work on my appropriate Norwegian language so that I could communicate well in this time of sorrow. Here we were rejoicing in our five month old daughter, and now we were seeking to comfort the family whose six-year old daughter had just died.

Liv Marie had never walked. She was blind and deaf and could not talk. Her intake of food was mostly in liquid form. She was severely physically and mentally challenged, yet her mother gave her such love over those six years of her life. We went along to visit with the mother. We read from the Word of God, prayed together, and wept with her in her sorrow. The father was a carpenter and was working in Hammerfest—a long ways from home. It would take him two or three days to get home.

Two days after her death, we had the coffining service for little Liv Marie. We shared words of comfort with the family. The lid of the coffin was fastened down, and then we carefully carried it out to the barn where the body would be preserved by the cold frosty weather. The burial service was delayed for one week, to allow time for the father to get home. It also would take this time to open the grave, since the ground was frozen to a depth of perhaps five or six feet.

The day of the funeral went from 11:00 a.m. to 5:00 p.m. It was very demanding and draining emotionally and physically. We began with the service at the home, attended by family and friends. While this was happening, there was a very heavy snowfall. Following hymns and scripture reading and a brief message, the little coffin was transferred to a truck to be taken to the cemetery about three kilometres away. Everybody walked there. Making our way to the grave site, we carried the coffin through the deep snow. Hymns were sung, Scripture was read, and the little coffin was lowered into that frosty grave. We then shovelled the earth and snow back on top of the coffin. Everyone returned to the house for a meal, followed by a closing service.

By the time my first funeral over, I was completely drained. When we had a visit with the mother and father a few days later, the mother said something that I've never forgotten over sixty years of ministry: "We want to thank you not just for the wonderful service, but for visiting me following Liv Marie's death. You not only read Scripture and prayed with us, but most of all, you wept with us."

My prayer throughout my ministry has been, "Lord, grant that I may never lose that sense of compassion as I minister to the people given to my care." Liv Marie's older sister, Grethe, was a regular attendee at our children's meetings and Sunday school.

We could always count on her to memorize scripture verses and be faithful in attendance. As an adult, she became very successful in her professional life. For most of her career she worked with the Norwegian government, and at the time of this book's writing, she was in the Vice Consul at the Royal Norwegian Consulate General in New York City.

Her brother, Edward Johann Strand, was born in 1952. Later in life he was diagnosed with "Usher's Syndrome Type I." He was born deaf and had very weak eyesight. Gradually his sight deteriorated, and he is now legally blind. At nine years of age he was sent to the school for the deaf in Trondheim and was there for ten years. Around forty years of age his sight deteriorated drastically. At that point he started to learn the Braille language. He's a tall, handsome man who has worked in the library for over thirty years at the University of Tromso. He's able to function effectively through the various electronic media available to him, and at home he enjoys "reading" on the Internet. It's really amazing to note how successful these folks have been, coming from such a small community.

A few days after the funeral of Liv Marie Strand, we visited Margit Espenes, who had just given birth to a girl. One experiences the many lows and highs of ministry life. This girl, Kristin Espenes, granddaughter of our senior leader in Espenes, now lives in South Africa. She is now Mrs. Kirsten Tuv. She got in touch with me in 2009, fifty-seven years after I first saw her. She is now a journalist … another success story.

9

A Never to be Forgotten Missionary Trip

Enock Wangberg and I set out on what would be a momentous, unforgettable trip. It was late March and we were to travel by car to Nordreisa; however, on the way to the mission hospital we hit snow-covered roads. As we rounded a bend on the road, behold a huge, powerful snow plow was heading toward us on our side of the road, and there was no place to go. On our side was a high rock face; on the other side was a sheer drop to the fjord below. We met head-on. Obviously there was no damage to the snow plow, but the front of our car was split in two. Miracle of miracles … even with no seat belts in those days … neither of us was injured. We thanked God for His protection.

We had to stay at the ferry station overnight so that we could give a statement to the police in the morning. We then got the ferry across the fjord, minus the car. On the other side we were met by the hospital manager who took us to Nordreisa. The next day was Sunday. In the morning we had the children's meeting, and in the afternoon we had a hymn sing in the hospital corridors for the patients. In the evening we had a meeting for the adults in the meeting house. For the next few days I did some plumbing maintenance work at the hospital. On Friday we started packing our rucksacks with clothes, Bibles, books, and tracts. Wangberg and I set out on a trip that would be forever etched in my memory. Even sometimes today when I happen to be out in the snow, with high winds and bitterly cold temperatures, I have unpleasant flashbacks to that time in the North. But more about that later as the trip unfolds.

The hospital manager, Birger Rudd, and some of the staff came to wish us God's speed. Some were wishing they could travel with us. The local boat took us to Sjaervoy. There we would join the larger boat, the *Hurtigruten*, which would take us to Hammerfest. Instead of arriving at midnight, however, it didn't arrive until 3:30 a.m. In the North we often said that we went by the calendar rather than the clock.

Once on board we bedded down for the balance of the night. We slept until about 7:30 a.m., and then got up and washed and had breakfast. While having breakfast, I asked Wangberg if there were any stops between here and Hammerfest.

"No," he said. "It's a long way between the raisins." This is a saying that came from the war years. During the Nazi occupation of Norway, food was strictly rationed. The Norwegians enjoyed their raisin bread, but because of the stringent rationing, they seldom got enough raisins for making the bread, so only a few raisins were used. Hence the saying to describe few and far between: "It's a long way between raisins."

We finally got into Hammerfest at 9:00 a.m. the following morning, having travelled about three hundred kilometres. Hammerfest is the most northerly city in the world. In the middle of the town stands a prominent meridian marker that marks the northern end of Struve's Arc, or curve. This is an imaginary curve on the earth's surface from the North Pole south to the Black Sea. Not far from here is the Nordcap, or North Cape. This is the most northerly point of land in Norway, and only the Svalbard Islands separate you from the North Pole. This represents a very interesting area of the continent of Europe. It became a very important territory for the Germans after their occupation of Norway. This area became heavily fortified, and Hammerfest was a major base for the Germans. It became more strategic after the Germans invaded the Soviet Union in 1941. For the Germans, Hammerfest became the main U-boat base and also an important supply base so that the German ships could attack the Allied supply convoys that were making their way to Murmansk on the Kola Peninsula and Russia.

When it was evident that the tide was turning against the Germans in the fall of 1944, they began what was called "the scorched earth policy," as described previously. Their attitude was, "If we can't have that, no one else is going to get it." So the German troops not only burned and plundered some of the surrounding communities, but completely destroyed the town of Hammerfest. They looted and burned and forcefully evacuated the population. By February of 1945, the only building left standing was a small funeral chapel. Keep in mind that all of this happened in the worst of the winter. Some people—men, woman, and children of all ages—made it south in whatever water transportation they could find. Many died of exposure.

We visited Hammerfest in the aftermath of this wanton destruction, when slowly the city was being rebuilt and the survivors were returning; however, evidence of the cruel results of the work of the army that was bent on conquering the world was everywhere to be seen. Now the reconstruction was evident everywhere, and the infrastructure was being carefully established.

We held meetings in homes, since community halls had not yet been built. Everywhere there was a hunger for God and for the Good News. We had the opportunity to make some gospels, tracts, New Testaments, and Bibles available to the people. We travelled from place to place along the fjords, mostly by boat and occasionally by horse and sleigh.

One of the places we visited was a seniors' residence in Bokelv, where we were welcomed by Miss Dorothea Lem. She was one of the very radiant Christians in that area. The home existed since before the war, but like everything else, was burned to the ground by the Germans. At the end of the war Dorothea came back, and with generous donations was able to rebuild the home. Here she welcomed seniors from communities along the Porsanger Fjord, which is Norway's fourth longest fjord. Most of the people there are of Sami extraction. At the home they could spend the evening of their lives in relative comfort and Christian love. We spent two days there ministering to the seniors, and we had meetings where we invited folks from the neighborhood to come and join us.

We moved from here by boat to Indre Billefjord. We expected the boat to come at 1:30 a.m. It finally arrived at 6:00 a.m. The joys of travel in the North! We'd waited almost six hours. We eventually got over to the other side of the fjord where we got the bus that would take us to Karasjok, a trip of almost nine hours. The snow was deep … higher than the bus. Karasjok was where Andreas Wangberg, father to Enock Wangberg, started his work amongst the nomadic people of the North. One day Andreas Wangberg bought a copy of a Norwegian Bible from a Bible Society colporteur (peddler of books). When he got home, he began to read the Bible and through that came to a personal faith in Jesus Christ. At that time he was twenty-three years of age.

The Story of the Lappish Bible

The following story about his father and his father's ministry was told to me by Enock Wangberg in 1952. This I have confirmed through some writings in Norway.

Andreas Wangberg became convinced that he should leave fishing and become a "fisher of men." He was a living testimony of Romans 10:17: *"So then faith comes by hearing, and hearing by the word of God.*" He also wanted to share this Word with others. Shortly after making this decision, he made his way to Scotland, where he came in contact with Robert and James Haldane. These two men were comfortably wealthy and had been used in evangelism throughout Scotland. Through their ministry, churches were established, and they became part of the Baptist witness there.

Through his time with these servants of God, Andreas realized that he should be baptized by immersion. Following his visit to Scotland, he became overwhelmingly convinced that he should commit his life to preaching the gospel. The following year he went to southern Norway to study and better equip himself for the ministry he was about to do. He made trips to Britain and to America, where he carried out his evangelistic ministry. He later married a young lady from Mjondalen in southern Norway.

At first they thought of going to China, but it soon became clear that they should minister in Norway instead. One child was born to them, but when he was only three months old he died. They later had another son who died when he was twenty. Two other children were born, Hulda and Enock. Both of them I had the privilege of knowing and working with in northern Norway and Lapland.

In the spring of 1903, Andreas Wangberg and an English friend made their way to Lapland. They soon realized that while Norway was sending missionaries to other lands, no one was really ministering to the deep physical and spiritual needs of these nomadic people of the North. Andreas Wangberg came back from that trip thanking God for closing the door to China and with an overwhelming burden to minister to the people of the North. Out of this was established a ministry that would be called "Nordland og Lappisk Bibel Mission." Eventually the mission published a magazine entitled *Ekko fra det hvitte land.*

In order to do an effective work, it would be important to have the Scriptures in the language of the people. Andreas Wangberg checked in Norway, in Sweden, and in the Bible Society headquarters in London, but there was no Bible to be found anywhere in the language of the Sami people of the North. He then decided that he would spend time living amongst the Lapps, learning the language, and then eventually producing the Bible in Lappish.

In the spring of the year he set off. Arriving in Tromso, he was in for a big surprise. Here in this small town he found Bibles in the Lappish language! How could this be? The story is absolutely intriguing, and worth repeating here to show how God can turn tragic circumstances into situations that will bring glory to Him.

The following story was told to me by Enock Wangberg, son of Andreas Wangberg. Later I was able to confirm this by some of Andreas Wangberg's own life story in the Jubilee issue of *Ekko* magazine in 1953, and also in other sources that were available to me. The circumstances under which the Bible was translated into the Lappish language are truly 'stranger than fiction.'

Blessings out of Tragedy

What became known as "The Kautokeino Uprising" took place in Kautokeino in 1852. In Sweden there was a state church priest—in other words, Lutheran—by the name of Lars Levi Laestadius. He was of Sami ancestry and later married a Sami woman. He was born in Lapland in Sweden on January 10, 1800. As a state church priest he served in several different parishes; however, by his own testimony, he carried out the services of a priest but had no personal faith.

Eventually he came in contact with Moravians. Through the witness of one of these ladies who spoke of her personal faith in Christ, he came to a personal relationship with Jesus Christ. At this time, Laestadius lived in Karesuando. In 1828, a simple log cabin meeting house was built for him. It's still standing today, and some years ago my wife and I visited here while on a Scandinavian tour. It was from here that his renowned religious revival began to spread.

He had a great burden for the Sami people, a great concern for the widespread use of alcohol, and a desire to see them have a more meaningful spiritual life and lifestyle. That influence is very much a living force amongst the Sami of Sweden, Finland, and Norway. Interestingly enough, the Kautokeino rebellion grew out of this spiritual revival led by Laestadius. This can happen sometimes when religious fanaticism takes control of spiritual problems—taking initiatives with a human effort rather than letting God work through our lifestyle and our witness. Spiritual warfare requires spiritual weapons, such as the Word of God, prayer, and submission to the leading of the Spirit of God.

Sometimes we take matters into our own hands and the results can be devastating. This is what happened in Kautokeino in 1852. A group of Sami took matters into their own hands. They were convinced that the local merchant had a great influence on the people for his own monetary ends. They also felt that the state church was close to the government and the liquor industry. Alcoholism was very common and was seen to be very much a part of the culture, so these followers of Laestadius were taking matters into their own hands and were determined to put an end to this. They became very aggressive, and they attacked those who personified those ills. The end result was that the local sheriff and merchant were murdered. These rebels beat up their servants and went on to beat up the local priest, leaving them near to death. Then they burned down the merchant's house. Other Sami stepped in to break up the rebel group and put an end to the mayhem. Two of the Sami rebels were killed, and the others were arrested and convicted. They were sentenced to life imprisonment. Two of the rebel leaders, Mons Somby and Aslak Haetta, were beheaded for their crime. All of the other men who were arrested were sent to Akershus in Oslo. The women who were involved were imprisoned in Trondheim.

Among the males who were imprisoned in Akershus was an eighteen year old lad named Lars Haetta. He was too young to be executed, so he was sentenced to life imprisonment. While in prison he became a born-again believer. He became deeply concerned for the spiritual well being of his own Sami people in the North. He recognized the need for the Bible to be translated into the Sami language, and he realized how important it would be to use his time wisely while in prison. The prison authorities cooperated with Lars to enable him to work on this important work of translation.

The young man was so well behaved that the king was approached and asked if he could be set free because of his good behavior and time served. So after serving fifteen years, he was released. It took him twenty-eight years to complete the translation of the Bible into the language of the North Sami people. This incredible work was later revised by an official translator and was printed in 1895.

This was the work of a compassionate, repentant, former murderer. These were the Bibles that Andreas Wangberg discovered in Tromso. Right there and then, with all the money he had, he bought five hundred Bibles and six hundred and fifty New Testaments. From then on he travelled the length and breadth of Lapland, sharing the Gospel and distributing the Word of God. He claimed the promise found in Isaiah 55:11:

> So shall My word be that goes forth from My mouth; It shall not return to Me void, but it shall accomplish what I please, and it shall prosper in the thing for which I sent it.

Out of these humble beginnings in 1903, the ministry in the North was established. This was continued by his son, Enock Wangberg, and his daughter,

Hulda Wangberg, with whom my wife and I had the privilege of working in the 1950s. It was also a joy to be able to be involved in distributing Bibles, New Testaments, and Gospels as I travelled amongst these dear people. It was a special joy to be able to follow in the footsteps of such a spiritual giant.

10

The Modern Missionary Journey

Let me return to my travels of 1952. On April 3, we finally arrived in Karasjok. There we met up with Wangberg's long time friend, Rolf Gustavson, who owned and operated the largest store in the community. We were welcomed with open arms. We spent some time visiting with many of Wangberg's friends. We also saw the house where Wangberg and his wife had lived for the first three years of their marriage. This house had been burned by the Germans, just like so many others in Kautokeinos. We visited the two schools that provided the Sami children with their education. We hoped that here we could have some children's meetings later on.

The following day we packed Bibles, New Testaments, Gospels, and tracts and headed across the border into Finland. We made our way along the frozen Tana River to reach the place where we had hoped to meet some people. In the guest house we left Scriptures for future guests. We made visits to a number of families with whom we shared the Word of God. Some folks here had formerly been deported to Siberia, but had now returned home. We visited a number of families and shared the tract "The Simple Way of Salvation." We certainly prayed that individuals would come to know Christ as Saviour and Lord.

One of our visits was with a Laplander. He made the typical Lapp knife, so I bought one, as it's always handy to have. We sold a number of Bibles and New Testaments to replace some that had been lost when the Germans had burned down their homes.

It was on this first trip to Finish Lapland that I encountered a sauna in its primitive form. It was a small building out in the yard. In the centre of the building was a fire and stones. There was a designated time for men and a designated time for women. The fire was lit under the stones. When the stones were hot, snow would be brought into the building and thrown onto the stones to generate steam. After an appropriate time in the steam, the individuals would go out and roll in the snow. Using small branches, they would whisk each other, thus stimulating circulation. It is a very satisfying form of punishment!

During this visit we gave three girls a Gospel of John and told them that if they memorized ten verses from John chapter1, they would receive a prize. On our return the next day, they each recited the ten verses and they each received a New Testament in Lappish. It was so rewarding to minister to these dear people. They told their stories of the terrible things they had suffered at the hands of the Nazis—of the loss of valuables, special memorabilia—all destroyed by the scorched earth policy of the occupying forces. It was an opportunity to bring words of comfort with the reminder that we are not to lay up treasures on Earth, where moth and rust corrupts and where thieves break in and steal. But rather we are to lay up treasures in Heaven.

Back in Karasjok on Sunday afternoon, we had a large meeting for children in the school. Their eyes were glued to the flannelgraph as I shared the message of the Gospel with them. We gave out Scripture portions as they responded to the questions that were asked. The next day I was able to sell a number of New Testaments at a local café frequented by the Sami people. When I was out walking, I was able to talk to some people in the community. I encountered a man who had lost his Bible and his hymn book as a result of the burning in Finnmark. He was so glad to get a copy of the Bible from me and was willing to pay several times the price to have it. Oh, what a need!

We were very much aware of the cultural conflicts between the Norwegians and the Sami folk. On the one hand there was a desire to assimilate, but on the other, a desire to preserve. Wherever and whenever we had the opportunity, we had meetings in which we sang and ministered the Word of God. We sowed the seed and God gave us the increase.

We had to move on from Karasjok to Kautokeino. This would be a new experience for us, and our mode of transportation would be quite different. It would be a multi-passenger snowmobile built by Bombardier of Québec, Canada. They had tracks on them, a Chrysler engine, and a wooden body. Very usable in the far north and able to carry twelve passengers at a time!

We left Karasjok around 10:15 a.m. Today this would be about a two hour trip, but back then it took us about eleven hours. When we left Karasjok, the snow was over one metre deep. About one hour out the vehicle veered off the track and the snow was almost covering the snowmobile. We were actually travelling along the path of a frozen river. We all piled out and used shovels and long poles to get back on track. Many times it was twenty kilometres between even the faintest signs of life. One could only see snow as far as the eye could see.

We finally reached the state mountain cabin. Here one could find shelter and some food, and a Lapp family acting as managers. We waited here for another snowmobile to take us on to Kautokeino. After almost a five hour delay, we left at 7:30 p.m. However, our time was not wasted. We made contact with other people, and we distributed some of our literature. In this area, the Sami people were getting ready to move to the coast with their reindeer, which they did every spring.

We eventually arrived in Kautokeino around 10:00 p.m. We certainly had experienced some of the difficulties and also the Lord's protection and provision through those hazardous days. On Saturday, April 12, 1952, we went to visit the state church priest. We had a very good visit with him, and he asked us both to preach in the church the next day at the regular service. This we agreed to do; it was Easter Sunday, April 13—a wonderful opportunity to proclaim the Easter message.

The service was conducted in the Norwegian and Lappish languages using an interpreter. Between three hundred and four hundred people (with dogs and children) and a few tourists gathered for that memorable Easter Sunday. I preached in the early part of the service, and Wangberg preached in the latter part. What an opportunity to share the glorious good news of the resurrection of the Lord Jesus Christ.

The Never to be Forgotten Trip

Wangberg and I had bargained with a Lapp to provide us with reindeer and sleighs to take us from Kautokeino across the Vida (basically a stretch of white wilderness) to Nordreisa. It took us most of a day to come to an agreement. We finally settled on four reindeer and four sleighs for a price of three hundred kroner. We loaded our rucksacks, our skis, and all our gear on to the sleighs, and at 10:30 p.m. we set out across the white wilderness for Nordreisa.

The moon was bright, the air was crisp, and there was a canopy of stars and, of course, the Northern Lights. The Aurora Borealis gave a magnificent Technicolor light show across the Arctic sky that seemed to dance on the crest of the snow.

After about thirty kilometres we stopped. Our guide wanted to make sure the luggage was secure and also took the opportunity to smoke his pipe. Soon we were off again. Shortly after midnight we came to two very small houses … really glorified shacks. After the usual greeting of "Bora Beivi," our guide indicated to the occupants that he would like to borrow a small pan so that we could boil up some reindeer meat later on. We continued on our journey, giving them the assurance that he would return the pan on his way back.

So we travelled on, not a sound save the swish of the sleigh runners, the rhythmic padding of the reindeer hooves, and the silent testimony of God's creative hand. All was going well until, suddenly, the flat terrain changed and we started to descend a steep slope. All chaos broke out! The sleighs kept running into the back legs of the reindeer, which would trip them up. Then next thing we knew, Wangberg's sleigh, his reindeer, and he himself turned a complete somersault, right into the deep snow. The result was a broken shaft on the sleigh and some very nervous reindeer. We repaired the broken shaft and resumed our journey, which was now across a frozen lake. In the distance we saw a government hut. These were made available by the government and found scattered all over the wilderness area of the North. They were made available primarily for government agents and other travellers. Usually there would be wood available, a small stove, and bunks built into the wall, but no bedding. You just slept in what you were wearing at the time.

We finally arrived at the hut around 6:00 a.m. and immediately made some coffee. Shortly afterward, our guide took the reindeer up the side of the mountain to where they could dig through the snow and get some of their staple food, lichen. This is a very healthy source of nutrition for the reindeer. Their front hooves are like shovels, and they can dig through the snow to get their food.

We slept until noon hour. When we got up, we boiled some reindeer meat and made some coffee. No forks or knives or plates were available, so we fished out the meat with our hands and ate. It's amazing what hunger will do.

In the afternoon I went out to search for some small branches. Using my large Lapp knife, I cut down some of the branches and then cut them into suitable lengths for firewood. This would replace what we had used and would be available for the next traveller who came along. Then I tried on my skis to make sure that they fit well, in case I needed them later on. Towards evening we wanted our guide to collect the reindeer so that we could get on our way; however, it wouldn't be that easy. His response was, "Now we will make some more coffee," and "now I will have a smoke," and "now I will collect the reindeer." At that point he lit his pipe, and the next minute he was fast asleep.

About half an hour later, he woke up saying, "Now we will drink some coffee."

At that point I stepped in and said, "No more coffee until you get the reindeer hitched up and ready to go; then you can have coffee, but not before." He eventually agreed.

We set out again at 12:30 a.m. It was a problem to get the reindeer to go, perhaps because of the recent incident in the middle of the frozen lake. We became a tangled mess. The reindeer that was pulling the sleigh carrying our baggage got its horns stuck in the sleigh that our guide was driving, so the Lapp just took out his large knife and cut off that piece of antler. Then he had to cut off a piece on the other side to balance it. To provide a bit of encouragement to us, our guide told us of another Lapp who had crossed this lake earlier in the season. He broke through the ice and lost two of his reindeer!

Shortly after this, everything began to deteriorate. We came to an area with small bushes called dwarf birch. They were in soft, deep snow; slowly but surely, we were becoming entangled in these small bushes. We and our reindeer were floundering. I ended up waist deep in snow, my reindeer facing one way and my sleigh the other. The reindeer became very skittish. Whenever I tried to move, the reindeer became very startled and the situation got worse. It was some time before we got things back in order and started to climb from the lake to higher ground. No sooner had we got there than a terrific storm broke loose. I'd been through storms before, but never one like this one. We had to draw ourselves into our shell of fur that we were wearing with only a sufficient slit to allow us to see.

Before long our guide said, "I'm sorry. The weather is breaking up so fast I wouldn't dare go further with my reindeer."

Wow! What now? This was about 7:00 a.m. It felt somewhat like the Chinook winds were carrying mild temperatures and the surface of the snow was melting, so we had no choice. We took time and organized things into our rucksacks. They weighed probably about twenty kilograms. We strapped on our skis. Up to this point in the North I hadn't travelled very far on skis, so this was going to be an experience. We paid our guide, bade farewell, and set out on the balance of our trip that would eventually take us to Nordreisa.

We committed our travel to the Lord, seeking His guidance. Miracle of miracles, we found the head of a valley. Feeling fairly confident that this would lead us to where we were going, we set off down the slope. It was wet snow, almost like sleet. Our feet were wet, and we were miserably cold. We were now down to the bottom of the valley; this was just over an hour after we had parted company with our guide. Right there was a massive rock. We sat down on the lee side of the rock to get some shelter. We got a pair of dry socks from a rucksack, took off our wet socks, and put the new pair on. Oh, it felt so good!

While finding shelter, the words of a hymn came to mind: "The Lord's our rock; in Him we hide, a shelter in the time of storm." After we felt somewhat rested, we continued on. Eventually we found a wood cutter's hut, within which we also found some potatoes and a can. We got some bark from the trees and lit a fire inside the hut. We filled the can with snow and melted it over the fire, and we put the potatoes in the can and boiled them and ate them right there.

The weather conditions were deteriorating, so we didn't waste any time. We decided to leave our rucksacks there in the hopes that we could get them at a later date. We were so cold, so wet, and so tired. We took this opportunity to dry our skis and wax them. Then we continued on our journey, as it was getting dark. We started out again around 5:00 p.m. Around 11:00 p.m., we saw quite a riverbank overhang; it looked like a suitable place to find some shelter. We trampled down the snow and stretched out on top of our skis so that we could get some rest, which was really the wrong thing to do, as we could subject ourselves to the possibility of hypothermia.

All this time it was snowing very heavily. A short time later we woke up; we were frozen and shivering violently. Fortunately, we had matches inside of our furs. I tried to get them out, which I did eventually, but with great difficulty since my hands were shaking so badly. We started a little fire by the riverbank so that we could get some heat. By 2:00 a.m. we set off again down the valley. It was very hard going because of the biting wind and the driving snow. Around 3:30 a.m. we came across another wood cutter's hut. We were burning a lot of energy because of the terrible weather and the hard skiing. Here we settled down for a brief nap.

We woke up at 5:00 a.m. It was still snowing very heavily. Over a foot of snow had fallen in the time we'd been sleeping. By this time we were convinced that we were in the right valley, the Reisa Valley, and for this we gave thanks to the Lord. We set out again, plowing through the deep snow. A little over an hour later we came upon Hansen's place; now we knew for sure that we were in the right valley. Praise the Lord! We received a real northern welcome and hospitality—and a real breakfast. The first regular meal we'd had in four days. The daughter of the house laid out for us a spread of bread, margarine, and boiled fish. I can taste it now even as I record this experience. We wanted to pay them, but they wouldn't accept anything.

After we had eaten, one of the sons drove us down to the Jensen's place in the valley of Bilto. It was a distance of four kilometres. When we arrived there, Mr. Jensen was busy packing his rucksack and was about to set out to find us. The Hansen fellow said that he would go right up the valley and collect our rucksacks and bring them down to us.

The folks at the mission hospital had been very concerned. They'd contacted some of the people in Kautokeino and learned from them that we had left there on Sunday, but now it was Thursday. The doctor in the hospital worried that we may not survive the storm. The Jensen's contacted the hospital, who in turn contacted my wife, as soon as we arrived. There was great jubilation knowing that we were safe. Birger Rudd, the hospital manager, came up to Bilto and collected us. How glad we were to be back in civilization! We truly praised the Lord for His watch and care over us and for bringing us through the valley of the shadow. In my Norwegian New Testament, I read from John 12: 26: *"If anyone serves Me, let him follow Me; and where I am, there My servant will be also."* What a precious promise!

We were conscious of the aftermath of those stormy and stressful days. On Friday morning I called my wife; it was so good to hear her voice again. She informed me that Mr. Hoppler, the field director, had called. He had suggested that we should make a trip back to Scotland for a restful break. So after we had contacted him again, we made plans to do just that.

On Saturday, April 19, we left Nordreisa by boat to Skjaervoy, where we picked up the boat that would take us south. I got off at Finsness, and Wangberg continued south to Trondheim. Someone came from Espenes with a small boat that would take me home. I arrived home at midnight. What a joy to see my wife, our daughter, and my mother. I was exhausted, but HOME!

Over the next few days I wasn't well. No doubt the strain of being lost, battling the weather, as well as burning so much energy, was taking its toll. Still, to this day, if I have to be out in the wintertime and there is a strong wind, blowing snow, and low temperatures, I have flashbacks and head for the indoors as quickly as I can.

Now that we were going to Scotland, we had about one week to get everything in order. We were glad it was happening, because it meant my mother could travel with us back home. We would take the local boat to Tromso, where we would take care of a number of matters, and then we'd take the larger ship south all the way to Bergen. From there we would take the ship to Newcastle, and then we would travel by train to Edinburgh. Since Adaline Ann was registered as a

Norwegian citizen, we had to register her at the British Consul in Tromso. Here she got a British birth certificate and was added to our passport.

We Came Apart for a Rest

On Tuesday, April 29, 1953, we set out on our trip back to Scotland for some R&R. We enjoyed visiting the various ports on the way south. On the Wednesday evening we had a service on board with the assistance of one of the crewmembers who was a Christian. We met in the dining room later in the evening. We crossed the Arctic Circle, and later on we were joined on board by Pastor Gustav Flatebo, who was the secretary for the Baptist work in Norway.

We arrived in Bergen on Saturday after five days travelling south. Late Saturday evening, on May 3, we set sail on the last leg of our journey home. On Monday morning we disembarked around 7:30 a.m. in Newcastle. After clearing customs, we called my wife's mother in Edinburgh to announce our arrival. We took a taxi to the central station for our trip north to Edinburgh.

After seven days of travel, we were finally home.

What a welcome at the station in Edinburgh! Mum, Pearl, Muriel, Ina, Harry, and Mae were all there to meet us. Now that we were back in Scotland, there was so much to do. Immediately we had to go to the food office in Edinburgh to get our ration cards. Everything was still rationed in Britain, as it was in Norway. On our first Sunday home, I preached both morning and evening in Edinburgh. Then we had to travel down to London to our mission headquarters where we could give a report of our work that we had been doing in the North. While there we met our director, Mr. Reed, our executive secretary, Ms. Ethel Kay, and her assistant, Jenny Weeks.

While in London, we were booked for a series of missionary meetings where we had the opportunity to show our slides and minister the Word. We also had the opportunity to minister alongside of the Rev. Geoffrey King of East London Tabernacle. Then it was back up to Scotland where we had a busy schedule of meetings in Edinburgh, Larbert, and Glasgow, as well as two of the Bible colleges. My wife and my mother shared the platform at Larbert Baptist Church women's meeting. This was the very first time my mother had ever spoken in a public meeting. She did an excellent job of sharing her experiences during her ten months with us in the North. She never did learn to speak Norwegian, except for a few words. We often had a laugh at her expense. She always thought that if she spoke a little louder, the Norwegians would better understand her Scottish/English accent.

11

Physical Rest and Spiritual Renewal

Courtesy of some friends, we were able to take a week of vacation at the Ancaster Hotel in Creiff, Scotland. It was the second anniversary of our wedding. Here we enjoyed rest and relaxation; the weather was fabulous, and the countryside was so welcoming. It was a great time to renew our energies and be refreshed spiritually.

In July we had the joy of attending the Keswick Convention in England. It was here that I had responded to the call of God to go to Lapland. It was like returning to my "Bethel," as I recalled the struggle on a hospital bed in July, 1949. After a demanding year of giving out, preaching, children's meetings, and teaching the leaders at the Bible school, this would be a week of being fed spiritually. We were able to sit at the feet of some of the spiritual giants of that day: Rev. A.T. Haughton, Dr. W. Graham Scroggie, Dr. Alan Redpath, Dr. Stephen Olford, Mr. Fred Mitchell, and Dr. G.B.Duncan. All of these men of God took us deeper into the Word and closer to the Lord as they fed us spiritually from the Word of God.

I had the privilege of speaking at the Methodist Church on Tithebarn Road in Keswick on Sunday evening, as well as at a number of the prayer meetings and devotional times. How blessed we were to have these opportunities. For some time we were exercised about the need for a vehicle for our work in the North— the type of vehicle that would provide us with not only transportation, but also accommodation. While at Keswick we heard that such a vehicle was available by one of the missions, so we went one day to check it out. It was exactly what would meet our needs. It could sleep four, had gas cooking facilities onboard along with a built in generator for power, a public address system, and a pullout platform at the back with the pulpit. This was exactly what we needed, and the price was only about $500.

In our house prayer meeting that evening, we claimed this vehicle for the work of the Lord in northern Norway. At breakfast the following morning, we were informed that the money had been provided. Praise the Lord! It was Friday, July 18, 1952. That evening at the closing communion service, the Rev. Duncan Campbell spoke of how the Lord had worked at the Hebridean revival in Scotland. God's Spirit was at work amongst us.

We arrived back in Edinburgh on Saturday, July 19. It was so good to see our daughter again. We were booked to return to Norway on September 6, and we had a busy time getting everything ready. We had a full schedule of meetings for the remaining forty-four days. In addition, we had to take care of arrangements for shipping the vehicle to Norway. Our friend, Bert Rob of Edinburgh, owned and operated a service station and garage. He checked out our vehicle thoroughly and serviced it at no cost to us. We then took the vehicle over to Larbert to be near my mother's place. There a group of young people from our church thoroughly cleaned the vehicle inside and out. Some of the girls made drapes for the windows and equipped it with some pots and pans and dishes.

In the middle of all of this, I had to go to Humbie in the south of England to minister at a boys' camp. Then on Friday, September 5, we drove the van to Newcastle and had a final meeting at Elden Mission in Newcastle. The next morning we got the vehicle on board the ship and checked in for our trip to Oslo, Norway. When we arrived in the Oslo, it took us four and a half hours to get everything cleared through customs. While in Oslo we took part in the tent meetings that were going on in the city.

The Return Journey North

On Friday, September 12, we set out for the North. It was a distance of around twelve hundred kilometres from Oslo to Espenes, and in those days it was mostly gravel roads. This would take us some three hundred miles above the Arctic Circle. We finally arrived in Espenes, our home, on Wednesday, September 17, after six days of driving. We were tired but very glad to be home.

It was rather hectic getting back into all the activities. I had to take the Caravan to Tromso to be certified. The customs people had to come up with a figure that would determine how much we would pay for duty on this vehicle, and then it would have to be licensed. I had to sit my driver's test so that I could acquire a Norwegian driver's license. This actually took two weeks altogether.

Then my wife and I and two other missionaries were involved in teaching Bible school for two weeks for local lay leaders. We had sessions in the morning, afternoon, and evening. I taught Doctrines of the Bible.

12

Sharing the Light of the Gospel in the Arctic Night

By October it was getting into the dark period, and we had to have lights on all day. As well, the snow was getting very deep, and all of this takes its toll on energies and emotions. Thanks to the Christmas C.A.R.E. parcels from America that year, we had all the extra things we needed for a big gathering in the chapel for children and adults. There were one hundred and six children and about forty adults there. We sang Christmas carols, and I shared a film strip on the birth of Christ. We had treats for everyone and food for all. This gathering made an incredible impact on the whole community. One young man could sometimes be a problem if he wasn't in the children's meeting, but outside causing trouble. His favourite activity was to switch off the electricity from the outside. We talked to him and worked with him, and it's amazing how God can change a young life. Today that young lad is grown up and is one of the spiritual leaders in that community.

Having the Caravan was a great asset to our ministry; however, we had no service stations anywhere near us. I became quite the mechanic, keeping the vehicle in operating condition. That first winter with the vehicle presented its own peculiar challenges. The vehicle had been built and used in Britain. It was a 1939 Morris commercial engine and chassis. Since we were three hundred miles above the Arctic Circle, and temperatures could get well below zero throughout the winter months, we were aware of the fact that a built-in heater would be a blessing, so we made a formal request that such a heater would be a decided help. We received a very curt reply from the British director, who informed us that the installation of a heater would be out of the question. This would be a luxury! Oh well, keep wearing a fur jacket, fur hat, fur boots, and fur gloves while driving—and do not forget the ice scraper.

New Location, New Challenges, New Opportunities

The year 1953 would mark a new era for us in the North. On January 13, we moved to Nordreisa, where we would be near the hospital. I always did a lot of maintenance work there. I would also be able to conduct regular services at the hospital, and then we would be able to minister in many of the smaller communities in a radius of some thirty to forty kilometres. In this way we could maintain contact with people who had been patients at the mission hospital. A great plus was the fact that we'd also be in close contact with the Sami from Kautokeino. They came down to this part of the country with their reindeer during the spring and summer. We felt that this would give us a greater field of service.

A new house had just recently been built across the road from the hospital. The hospital manager had been talking with the young couple who owned it, and they were interested in renting out part of the house. That year we moved into the main floor of the house. It was just absolutely amazing. There was a kitchen with a sink, hot and cold water, and cooking facilities. It also had a living room, two bedrooms, and a bathroom with a shower, wash basin, and toilet. The Lord will provide! Already the van was very useful, as we were able to transport some things to Sorjosen, including a coffin being shipped to a family.

It was the dark period. I found it hard to study and concentrate. This area was not without its problems. When the Lord wants to do a work, Satan can really be busy stirring up the opposition. Our opposition came from the sect who followed Laestadius. They were egged on by the state church priest. In spite of this, we had wonderful meetings in the surrounding communities, even when we had open opposition from the group called "Haugianer." This was an elite sect that functioned within the state church but was in opposition to the established church.

Hans Nielsen Hauge travelled the length and breadth of Norway as an itinerant lay- preacher. He was in prison for nine years. From the nineteenth century on it was illegal to have religious gatherings outside of the state church. He spoke out against the church establishment, yet he upheld the doctrines of the Lutheran Church. Their opposition to those of us from the Baptist persuasion grew from the fact that we didn't practice the baptism of children. Sometimes their exuberance exceeded their knowledge, and it would disrupt our meetings. Their pietism appeared to some, as what one writer called, as a "holier than thou attitude." In spite of this, we had at least eighteen different communities where we could have meetings for adults and children—sometimes in homes, sometimes in halls.

January of 1953 was a terrible winter with lots of wind and very heavy snow. Sometimes it would be four feet deep. We had an eclipse of the moon, which was a rather awesome experience. While in Nordreisa I had my twenty-fifth birthday. We had many different and unusual experiences. One day a man's dead body was picked up at the side of the road. He had fallen off his wagon, so his wife and family had to be informed. When doing this, we were able to share the good news with the bad news.

It was amazing that some adults and children would walk for over five kilometres to attend our meetings and think nothing of it. When preparing for ministry, quite a number of things were not included in the curriculum. There was no training for performing the services of gravedigger or funeral director. Neither was there training to cope with being a motor mechanic. No lectures were given on how to deal with the medical needs of accident victims, or serving as an ambulance driver. All of these things I have done, and through them been able to minister to so many people.

The most unusual thing of all happened on Sunday evening, February 15, 1953. I had no training for it, except growing up in the country and working on a farm. I'd had a very busy day and was not feeling well … mostly it was a lack of energy from trying to cope with the fact that it was the dark period. I had gone to bed early, but at 11:00 p.m. there was a pounding on our door. Our landlord lived in the lower level of the house with his wife and family. They had some animals in a barn on the property. He called me with a great sense of urgency. I quickly put on some warm clothes, and he then told me that his cow was about to deliver and had run into complications. He had called the vet who lived five kilometres away, and he was on his way.

When he arrived, I noticed immediately that he only had one arm! That complicated matters. We started to try helping the cow, but to no avail. An attempt was made to turn the calf, because it was breech; however, the calf was too big for this. Two legs were protruding, so we tried to pull it out, but without success. By this time there was lots of blood around. At the sight of the blood, the man who owned the cow fainted and was lying in the straw on the muck of the barn floor. He was out for the count. By now the vet concluded that the calf was dead; nevertheless, we would have to get the calf out one way or another. He got a special wire saw with very sharp teeth. Since he had only one arm, he couldn't feed it into the womb of the cow, so it was left to me. Following his instructions, I had to be careful not to damage the womb, because then we would lose the cow also. Piece by piece I was able to dismember the calf, operating the saw in a see-saw motion. Then we were able to take out the body of the calf. By this time the owner of the calf woke up, having missed all the gory details. By now it was after 3:00 Monday morning. I was able to chalk up another first—I had assisted the vet, and quite a lesson was learned.

In spite of the winter, strong winds, slippery roads, and snow banks three to four metres high, we were able to keep busy. We had children's meetings, regular services in different communities, and devotional messages for the patients at the hospital at least five days each week. I also did a lot of maintenance work and repairs at the hospital. It was dark, oppressive weather, and the conditions took a heavy toll on our health. However, it was never boring. Not only was I doing a lot of the work in the areas where The Northland and Lappish Bible Mission had contacts, but I also worked with the Baptist work in several small communities and towns.

Some of the staff at the hospital, along with Birger and Hulda Rudd, wanted to go to Kautokeino by travelling up the Reisa Valley by reindeer and sleigh. Plans were made to accomplish this; however, instead of fourteen reindeer and sleighs, our Sami friend brought only seven. We set off on the journey anyway.

The reindeer I had was a bit skittish, which resulted in the reindeer, sleigh, and me tumbling down the side of the mountain. There was no serious damage, and we got everything back to rights again. That first night out we rested in a government hut. There were ten of us altogether in the group hoping to get to Kautokeino. One of the nurses got soaked through to the skin when her reindeer and sleigh broke through the ice. Once we got the fire going, she tried, as best she could, to get dried out.

Part way through the second day, our guide announced: "We have problems. There is no way this whole group can go, because travel conditions are not good. Some of you will have to go back. I don't want to have accidents, and I don't want to lose any of you." Indicating me he said, "Russell here (they always use your surname out of respect) is okay; it doesn't matter with him. He's going to Heaven anyway, but I am not sure about some of you."

At that point in time it was rather small comfort. The hospital manager, his wife, and three of the nurses went on. I took the rest of them back to the hospital. A couple of days later we got word that the group had made it to Kautokeino; however, later on we heard that they couldn't get back out of Kautokeino because of the bad weather.

13

Open Doors, Interesting Opportunities, and Unexpected Challenges

Periodically I had the interesting experience of teaching in a number of the schools. During the Second World War, when the Germans invaded Norway, the Norwegian government, the King, and many Norwegians sought refuge in Britain. Many of the Norwegians lived and trained in Scotland. They travelled back and forth from Scotland to Norway doing sabotage work there, thus upsetting the German occupation forces. So the interest in Scotland was very high. I was asked to teach Scottish history and geography, along with cultural similarities and differences. This, of course, gave me excellent opportunities to make contact with the children and the various communities.

Another skill acquired while in the North was that of "patient transfer service." We had a call from the mission hospital one day. A maternity patient was experiencing complications and would have to be moved to Tromso for care. The air ambulance was called. It was a float plane that landed in the harbour at Sorkjosen. We loaded the lady into our van and drove her to Sorkjosen. We then loaded the stretcher onto a rowboat and transferred her from the boat to the plane. One of the nurses accompanied her. Those deeds of mercy and necessity were always interesting and sometimes challenging. One never knew what exciting happenings a day might bring, so one had always to be ready for the unexpected.

Dr. and Mrs. Larsen were visiting with us for dinner one evening. We had just finished the meal and settled down to a quiet, relaxing evening when one of the nurses rushed over with some bad news. There had been a very bad accident about twenty-five kilometres away involving a group of teenagers. There were two vanloads of teenagers—about fifteen kids in all. Dr. Larsen took off in his car, and I followed in my van after picking up two nurses and two stretchers.

It was not a pleasant sight that met us when we arrived at the accident scene. One load of teenagers was okay. The other was a disaster. These were teenagers from Tromso who were making their way to Nordreisa to participate in a sporting event. A bus had been ahead of them; it had turned a sharp corner on the highway and stopped to let off some passengers. The lead van, containing the teenagers, plowed right into the back of the bus. Seven teenagers were injured, four of them very seriously and the other three less seriously. Now was the time to check out one's emergency skills. Broken bones, concussions, and trauma were evident in all of them. Those were the days of no seat belts and no airbags. Right away we set to work hooking up I.V.s, applying bandages, and immobilizing limbs. It was a frantic time. I transported the three less serious cases to our hospital. Another took the more seriously injured to the hospital in Tromso. We were all emotionally and physically exhausted. Two days later the accident was reported in the county newspaper. In spite of the fact I had never been to medical school, I was elevated in the local newspaper report to the status of "Dr.Larsen's assistant." Chalk that up as another accomplishment. So much for a quiet social evening.

Visitors and Visits

It was always good to have visitors from afar. We welcomed Miss Ethel Kay, executive secretary of our European Evangelistic Crusade Mission in London, England. She was anxious to visit the hospital and our places of ministry, and was always ready to speak at our meetings. Whatever she went to and wherever she spoke, I acted as her interpreter. She was thrilled to visit with the Laplanders and to see the reindeer. I took her out in the van to one of the most scenic parts of the highway in the North, high up on the side of the mountain and overlooking the fjord. When we got down to the bottom of the hill, I turned to her and asked, "Well, Ethel, what did you think of that scenery?"

"I didn't see a thing," she replied. "I was so scared I had my eyes closed all the time."

While Ms. Kay was with us, we took a week and had rallies at Mallangen, Skutvik, Maestervik, Takelvdal, and Espenes, our first home. Everywhere we went we had large gatherings; it was a great blessing as we shared the Word of God with young and old. Around this time two of our nurses followed the Lord in believer's baptism by immersion. This was a great testimony to the community. We also had a visit from Mr. Dunbar from England. He was the man who had made it possible for us to have the van for the work in the North. We had the opportunity to let him see how valuable the vehicle was for us in our work. He shared in the open air meetings, tent meetings, children's meetings, youth rallies, and the work in the hospital. It was a special joy to take him to Kvenangsfjell, where he met many of our Lapp friends.

One of our highlights was a trip we made to Finland and Sweden accompanied by Pastor Gullston Ohrn and his wife, Lilly. We were looking forward to participating in a conference for Baptist pastors from Northern Norway, Sweden, and Finland.

Finnish Lapland and Norwegian Lapland had much in common. They had suffered deeply at the hands of the Germans during the war, their communities had been burned, and their people had been displaced. They were desperately in need of encouragement as they expended their energies, trying to bring some semblance of order into their disrupted lives. Our first stop on our way was Kilpisjaervi. This is the place where the borders of Norway, Sweden, and Finland converge. We visited Karasuvanto and Karasuvando, border towns between Finland and Sweden. It was in Karesuando that Lars Levi Laestadius had his base for his religious revival work.

Rovaniemi, Finland is a very interesting town that straddles the Arctic Circle and is spoken of as the capital of the Finnish Lapland. Today it is a very popular winter destination and advertised as the home of the "Ice Hotel" and Santa Claus. In spite of all my travels by reindeer and sleigh, I never did meet Santa Claus along the way.

It was very interesting to travel from Finland to Sweden. In Finland, one drives on the right side of the highway, while in Sweden, one drives on the left side of the highway. At the border we had to drive through an interesting figure eight so that we would move from the right side driving to left side driving. We drove down into the area of the Gulf of Bothnia, which is part of the Baltic Sea. From the Swedish side of the Gulf, iron ore is shipped to many countries around the world. From the Finnish side, wooden pit props are shipped for use in the coal mines.

This was very interesting to me. In 1948, I worked for the summer months at the Grangemouth docks in Scotland with a gang of men who offloaded those pit props that had come from Finland. It was my responsibility to count the bundles of pit props, which would then be used in the coal mines around the area.

Our destination was the conference at Luleo in Sweden. This was the first Inter-Scandinavian Baptist Pastors' conference ever held, and it lasted for five days.

On the Sunday, I preached in two Baptist churches outside of town. Norwegian and Swedish are very similar languages, so it was no problem to communicate. It was a great time of fellowship and encouragement to all who attended.

Evangelistic Tours

In the fall of 1953, we set out on an extended tour throughout Troms and Nordland Counties. We had meetings in larger centres like Narvik and Harstad, as well as many smaller communities in between. While in Harstad I became very ill with a sinus infection. It was one of the most painful experiences I'd had to that point. We were in the midst of special meetings in Harstad Baptist Church. My wife was very capable, and she took care of some of the meetings we'd planned. Two days went by and my condition was getting worse. Eventually, we called the doctor. He was shocked at my condition. He indicated that he would leave me for one more day, but if the infection didn't break he'd have to operate. Wow! Not a pleasant thought. He told me to sit by the stove, keep the kettle boiling, cover my head with a towel, and inhale the steam. Also, I should get a large basin, fill it with hot water—as hot as I could bear—and soak my feet. Within four hours the infection broke. It was as if a sluice gate had been opened; the pus just poured out. What a relief. The downside, however, was that I had no idea I had so much empty space in my head! I was able to continue preaching for the balance of the week.

Near to Harstad is a small community called Trondenes, which is home to a very old medieval church built of stone. It dates from the late fourteenth or early fifteenth century. The pulpit and the altar are very beautifully decorated. One of the unique things about it is an hour glass located on the pulpit, which served to keep the preacher in check.

From here we moved on to Narvik, where we had a wonderful week of meetings with a very good response. While in town, I visited a dear friend from Espenes who was terminally ill in hospital. I had the opportunity to make sure of his relationship with the Lord. His parting shot as I left the room was, "I'll see you in Heaven." Praise the Lord!

From there we made our way south, having meetings in Oppdal, Trondheim, Lillehammer, and lots of smaller communities in between. By November we were in Raufoss, in Oppland County. In my day there, the main source of industry and employment was the ammunition factory. We had meetings in the Baptist church and also in the surrounding area. While in Raufoss we had permission to have a meeting at the ammunition factory during the lunch time in the canteen.

The greater percentage of those who attended was men. What an opportunity to share the gospel with them!

The balance of our time on this tour was spent in the major population centres in the Baptist churches, the Free Friends, and the Indre Misjon. We had a very rich and rewarding time with the folks in these different churches. There were those who came to faith in Christ. Others came to a closer walk with the Lord. It was good to see some of the lasting fruit from previous meetings in some of these areas. We had good fellowship with Pastor Knut Andersen, Enock Wangberg, and many others. In just over two months of travel, we had fifty-two meetings with adults and twenty-three children's meetings. These were very demanding days, but also very rewarding.

14

Home for Christmas

On December 12, 1953, we boarded the *M.V. Blenheim,* which took us to Newcastle, England. We were heading back to Scotland to spend Christmas with family. We then would spend time promoting the mission throughout Britain, speaking at conferences and ministering in churches. Within a few days we were plunged into meetings. Word soon got around that we were home, and the invitations kept coming. Edinburgh, Glasgow, Larbert, and many places in between, sought our services. Two of the newspapers and one of the magazines had heard about us. They were fascinated by the fact that we had been in Santa Claus Land and travelled by reindeer. Of course our daughter, Adaline Ann, was the main attraction. It was very special to share with family during this festive season.

As we looked into a new year with all its uncertainty, opportunity, and potential activity, the Lord gave us a promise for 1954: *"See, I have set before you an open door, and no one can shut it "* (Revelation 3:8). This was God's promise to the faithful church in Philadelphia. It's His promise to those who are faithful today. We go forward into a new year knowing not what the future holds, but we do know who holds the future.

Very quickly 1954 was shaping up to being a busy time. Our first trip was to the Shetland Islands, where my wife was born, and where we would have some meetings. It was a wonderful time of catching up with some relatives, as well as being able to share about our work in Northern Norway. This was especially significant because the islands were originally a part of Norway and the world of the Vikings. This is very evident in the place names, the dialect, and, of course, the archaeology.

One of the great festivals of the year is "Up Helly Aa." This goes back over one thousand years. It's called "Europe's largest fire festival" and is held on the last Tuesday in January every year. The participants are dressed as Vikings with an appointed Jarl as their leader. It involves a torch lit parade in which a replica of a Viking ship is carried to a hill. At a given signal, the torch is tossed into the galley and is consumed by fire. There is also much singing and dancing to celebrate this occasion.

After returning to the mainland, we were kept busy with church services and missionary meetings all over the central part of Scotland. During those times we had great blessing. We saw some people come to know Christ, while others were challenged regarding Christian service. We also witnessed a renewed interest in missions.

We travelled to the mission headquarters in London, where on April 14 we were able to share our ongoing concern and burden for the work in the North. It was at this meeting that Vivian and Betty James were accepted for the work in Northern Norway. They would join with us in the North to help take some of the load. We were thrilled as we looked forward to their partnering with us.

While in London we were able to attend the Billy Graham crusade in Haringay Arena. We were invited onto the platform and sat with Mrs. Ruth Graham. That evening over five hundred came forward in commitment to Jesus Christ. What a thrill it was to see such a moving of the Spirit of God. Back in Scotland we had an incredible missions conference at the Dunoon Baptist Church. We had booked in at the hotel where we had many visitors. We were also joined by Berger Ruud, our mission hospital manager in Nordreisa. I interpreted for him, and I also did most of the preaching over the weekend. These were times of refreshing from the presence of the Lord.

Following this conference, my wife and daughter stayed on in Scotland while I went on a tour with some of our missionaries from Europe. We were joined by Dr. John Moore. As we moved through England, Wales, Southern Ireland, and Northern Ireland, we had wonderful meetings wherever we went. The crown of them all was in Northern Ireland, where we had meetings in Presbyterian and Baptist churches, as well as in YMCA halls. Every meeting we had was packed to capacity. It was a particular joy to sing with Dr. John Moore that wonderful song, which he wrote, "Burdens Are Lifted at Calvary." I've never forgotten that experience.

I returned to London, where my wife and daughter met me. Along with Birger Ruud and other EEC missionaries, we took the ferry across the English

Channel to Calais in France. From there we took the train for an overnight trip to Bern in Switzerland. From there we travelled by train to Interlakken, and then on to Grindevold, where we would take part in our missions field conference.

One of the highlights of the conference was that two of our missionaries were to be married in the beautiful little country church in Grindevald. The whole missionary family was able to rejoice with them on that special occasion. Besides all of the reports and challenges, the fellowship and prayer times were so uplifting. Here we also met a young Swiss nurse who was coming to join the staff at the mission hospital in the North. Her name was Ruth Oks.

From the conference we headed back through Switzerland and Germany by train. We stopped for a few days at Rendsburg, Germany, where we had fellowship with one of our missionary families. After a few days there we travelled on to Oslo and then to Drammen in Norway. We were in the area for almost two weeks. We had a series of meetings with Pastor Mosige of the Baptist church in Drammen. In addition to that, we had meetings in a number of places in the surrounding areas. These were very profitable, and we were able to generate interest in the work of the North. We saw young people commit their lives in dedication to the Lord's service, as well as a number coming to know Christ as Saviour and Lord.

Along the way we took part in tent meetings in Oslo. We also had some open-air meetings. These were made possible by "The Glad Tidings" van, which was equipped with a retractable platform and pulpit, along with a powerful sound system. At one of our open-air meetings we were so pleased to see that we had a group of police cadets from a training camp nearby.

Travelling up country, we had a major stop at Oppdal. It was always a joy to minister here. There was always a hunger for the Word of God. We had meetings for adults and children, along with some open air meetings. We were always the recipients of the warm hospitality extended to us by the Strand family. It was haymaking time when we were there, and we had a wonderful time bringing in the hay. This awakened happy boyhood memories from when I used to work on the farm. The sawmill was also in operation, so we took part in sawing lumber for the new Baptist meeting house that was to be built.

Two highlights are worthy of note here. On Sunday afternoon, July 11, 1954, we decided to have an open-air meeting in the middle of town. Oppdal is located on the main highway that runs from Oslo all the way to Hammerfest. In my day it was mostly gravel highway. Now, of course, it's paved. Located south of Trondheim, it was always a popular place for the travellers and pilgrims who were on their way to the burial site of St. Olaf, the patron saint of Norway who is credited with bringing Christianity to the country. Here in the centre of town we had the largest open-air meeting we've ever had, with a crowd of around five hundred people—locals, tourists, and people who opened their doors and windows to listen. We sang, I preached, and one could sense the Spirit of God at work. That evening at the local Baptist church we had a significant number of visitors,

The other highlight was the joy of welcoming Betty and Vivian James. They were a Welsh couple who had come to join us in our ministry in the North. How we rejoiced to welcome such reinforcements! Mrs. James had some Norwegian blood in her veins. Her father was Norwegian, and as a result she had a working knowledge of the language. We picked them up at the railway station and took them right to the evening meeting. Mr. Vivian James brought greetings and I interpreted for him. The next day we headed north. On the way we had trouble with the van going up the mountains. We discovered we had blown a gasket and cracked the head. We couldn't get any parts in the Mo-i-Rana area, so with thick brown paper soaked in oil we made a gasket, and with "Radweld" compound we sealed the crack. Necessity is the mother of invention. That held and was still holding when I left the North one year later.

When we arrived back in Espenes in July, at the height of the midnight sun, there was a great welcome gathering for us and the James'. It was so good to be home. Now that we were back and I had some male help, we got down to making some significant plans to improve and expand the accommodations at Solbakken. In the meantime, with the help of Ivar Andreasen and his truck, we drove to Nordreisa to bring our furniture and other belongings down to the Espenes. All went well and we got back safely.

The Nielsens, who had given leadership to the work in Espenes while we were away, were now going back south, so we had a farewell gathering for them.

In between all the meetings we had at Espenes, and our visits out to the small communities, Vivian and I started on some serious projects. One project was that of some major work on the house. Winter would be coming soon, and we needed to do some work insulating the walls and sealing the cracks around the windows to keep out the winter winds and snow. This was a major undertaking, but eventually it was accomplished.

The next major task was doing some major renovations on the chapel. We got help from our good friend, Ingolf Strand. Our goal was to create an apartment as part of the chapel building to provide a living and dining area, two bedrooms, and a kitchen. It was a lot of work but well worth it. We had a trap door in the living room that opened into the area under the chapel. This was inadvertently left open one day, and I fell through that trap door onto a pile of rocks below. Since there were no steps, I had to be lifted out. I obviously survived with only some cuts and bruises.

The next job was to get water from the house to the chapel and the apartment. Armed with picks and shovels, Vivian and I dug a trench from the house to the chapel, probably about fifty metres long and two metres deep to make sure the water pipe was below the frost level. This was to prevent the pipes from freezing during the wintertime. We hooked up a water line from the pump at the house to the kitchen in the new apartment. We were really getting to be modern: telephone, electricity, and now running water. However the outhouse was still in regular service—no modernization there!

Following some of these projects, we went on a trip to the island of Senja, where we had some rallies and a conference, and then to the island of Andoy for more of the same. These were times of refreshing as I ministered the Word and also acted as interpreter.

Later we had a trip to Nordreisa so that we could introduce Betty and Vivian James to the folks there, as well as make contact with our Lapp friends. It was the time for herding the reindeer, when they would mark the calves that were born that spring, and also slaughter some reindeer to provide meat and hides for making clothing. I helped Nils Logje with some of the slaughtering, and we were happy to receive some meat to take home. While there we ate together with them and sang hymns. Berit Logje interpreted my message into Lappish. Later on we went to work and picked "Multebaer," also known as "Cloudberry" in English, or "Bakeapple" in Newfoundland. Any way you say it, they are very good and very high in vitamin C. I recall that day that our daughter liked them so much that she ate too many and was sick that evening. We had another berry we called "Tyttebaer," also known as "Partridge Berry." In Norway, tyttebaer jam would be served with meatballs. It also had medicinal uses.

Since we now had another couple working with us, we were able to diversify our ministry. One of the things we did was to develop our music ministry. We became a quartet and sang in four-part harmony. This went over very well in our evangelistic outreach.

On one occasion we had been out on an extended tour and returned home late Saturday night. We had no time to make plans for services for the next day; however, I heard that the Lutheran minister was going to be at the little mission hall, so I thought it would be good to go and hear him and make contact with him. I was made very welcome. Knowing of my music skills, the local leader asked if I would play the pump organ for the service. I readily agreed. It was very worthwhile to build that bridge and share in that worship service.

In September of 1954, we planned an extensive tour in the area of Vesteralen. This was a major outreach and a very successful one. We were away for thirty-two days. During that time, we had twenty-five meetings in which we sang and preached. At the same time, we had the same number of children's meetings, which were held in the afternoons. For the children we used flannelgraph and filmstrip to tell the Bible stories. We usually had a packed out attendance. It was incredible to see the response of the people. Individuals came to faith in Christ. In one meeting, eleven came to know Christ as Saviour and Lord.

It was also good to share with those who desired a closer walk with the Lord. In one meeting held in the community hall, people were packed in. People stood around the periphery of the hall, and children sat on the floor. The place was lit with kerosene oil lamps. As the service progressed (it should be noted that it lasted for over two hours), the lamps began to flicker and go out one by one. We realized that there were so many people in the hall, and with doors and windows closed because it was wintertime, we were running out of oxygen. So we had to open the windows and doors, which took care of the problem. However, it generated another problem, which was too much cold air. Oh the joys of ministry! When the Lord is blessing, the devil is not too happy.

We had three nights of meetings on a small island in the area. The first night we could sense God's Spirit at work. The second night was a different story. Right from the beginning we were aware of the negative spirit. When I got up to preach, it felt as if there was a stone wall between me and the people. Two young men in the gathering seemed to be the source of opposition. Barely ten minutes into my message, I realized that I couldn't continue. I closed the meeting in prayer and asked the people to go home and pray that Satan be bound and that God would have the victory. The next night we came back together and the Lord poured out His blessing upon us. The day after we returned home from this tour, I had a call from a young man who wanted to come and talk with me. There, in our living room, he poured out his heart and then I had the joy of leading him to a personal relationship with the Lord Jesus Christ. To God be the glory!

After a few days we were off to Tromso to take part in a conference at the Baptist church. This conference was to be led by Pastor Gustav Flatebo, the district superintendent of the Baptist churches. I had the opportunity to lead a number of the Bible studies, and my wife spoke at the women's rally. We took the van with us because it had the PA system, and we had an interesting time with open-air meetings in the town. We parked the van right next to the statue of Roald Amundsen, the Norwegian explorer. As a result of this outreach, several unsaved people came out to the evening rally at the church. We continued with the open-air meetings throughout the week. They made a great impact on the community. One of the other interesting things that happened during that conference was that Mr. and Mrs. Vivian James were baptized by immersion and gave a great testimony. I had the privilege of giving the closing message of the conference. This was a great week of encouragement to the Christian workers, blessing to the church, salvation to the sinners, and glory to the Lord. We soon returned to Espenes to take care of the work there.

By now my wife was pregnant with our second child. Household responsibilities were becoming more difficult, so, through the generosity of some friends, I was able to buy her a washing machine. This made life quite a bit easier for her.

Christmas was upon us, and it was a very busy time. We had great services as we celebrated the birth of our Lord and Saviour Jesus Christ. Christmas Eve and Christmas day were very special. The real highlight was the feast for the children, as well as many adults who attended. Our friends in Britain and America were very generous, so the ladies were able to bake lots of goodies. We all wrapped gifts for the children. The men saw to it that we had the decorations in place, including a large Christmas tree that occupied the centre place in the hall. This was a memorable and much talked about evening, with one hundred and thirty children and lots of adults. It was an evening of carols, food, and fun. So ended 1954—a year of blessing and a year of opportunity.

We looked forward to 1955 to be a year of blessing in the ministry of the Gospel. I quote the following poem:

I said to the man who stood at the gate of the year,
"Give me a light that I may tread safely into the unknown."
And he replied, "Go into the darkness
and put your hand into the hand of God,
That shall be to you better than light
and safer than a known way."
(Minnie Louise Harkins)

As I write this segment, I'm in the position of having read the last chapter. I know the end from the beginning. I've been there and done that; I'm fully aware of the truth of the words of that poem. I learned a long time ago that there is no safer place than being in the centre of God's will.

Perhaps the ministry that was the focus of my attention and involvement in the early part of 1955 was preparing me for what would become my main emphasis. I essentially became pastor of "Tabernaklet," the Baptist church in Tromso. The regular pastor, Gulston Ohrn, had become incapacitated. He'd fallen on the ice and had a bad fracture of the femur bone. He was confined to bed to bring about healing, since they didn't have the surgical expertise that would enable him to be mobile in a shorter space of time. I was asked to be Interim Pastor. In this ministry it was a joy to minister the Word of God to the church proper—to see individuals come to personal faith in Christ, to conduct the Bible study and prayer times during the week, to oversee the Sunday school and the children's work, to be involved in the women's ministry, and to visit with the sick and the shut-ins. This was demanding, but also very rewarding.

Tromso was a very interesting town. It was growing and maturing and overcoming the ravages of the war years. It was also the centre for government administration and international representation. One of the great Norwegians, Roald Amundsen, is highly honoured in Tromso. He was a renowned explorer of the Polar Regions, and was the first to reach both the North and the South Poles in his lifetime. His statue dominates Storgaten, which is the main street in the centre of town. During my time there, I encountered his first mate on the *Gjoa*, Hilmar Hansen, who lived in Tromso. Hilmar Hansen travelled with Amundsen in his explorations from 1903 to 1906 on this ship when he successfully navigated the Northwest Passage, opening up a trade route from the old world to the Orient. The *Gjoa* was outfitted for this passage at the Tollefsen shipyard in Tromso. The son of Tollefsen was a deacon in the Baptist church where I pastored. Amundsen died in 1928 while on a rescue mission in the Arctic. He was only fifty-six years old.

While pastoring in Tromso, I always enjoyed visiting one of the older ladies of the church. She was so kind and had such as sweet disposition. Pastor Ohrn shared with me the story of her life. Life for her had not been easy. She had two sons who, because of their activities against the Nazi occupying forces, were arrested and shipped off to a concentration camp. One son died in the concentration camp, but the second son was released from the camp when peace was declared. He was returned to Oslo, Norway, where within a few short weeks he later died. Yet this lady had such a gracious Christian spirit, with no sense of bitterness in her heart.

One single lady who owned and operated a shop in Tromso had a real ministry of hospitality. To the children she was known as Tante (Auntie) Canny. She was so good to our daughter, Adaline Anne, who loved to visit her. Adaline Anne cherished a doll and cradle that she received from Tante Canny. We were frequent guests in her home.

While I was Interim Pastor in Tromso, we made our home at the Jensens', who were very kind to us. We stayed there the whole time I was at the Baptist church.

In time my wife and daughter came up by boat from Espenes to be close to the maternity hospital. Since we were expecting our second child, it was important that the hospital be near at hand. One Sunday morning at 5:30 a.m., I took my wife to the maternity hospital, since she was already in labour In between the services and Sunday school at the Baptist church, I kept calling, but they always said there was no change. A real blizzard was blowing, with lots of snow. Finally when I called at 10:00 p.m. I was told that we had a healthy son, whom we named Harry Stuart Russell. I didn't get to see my wife and new son until the next day, but we praised God that all was well. There was no Internet in those days, but telegrams and telephone carried the news to family, friends, and fellow missionaries around the world. After six days my wife and our new son came home. After two weeks in Tromso staying with our friends, we went home to Espenes by boat. The trip took us eleven and one half hours.

The Call of the North

While at home, Vivian James and I had to put plans together for an extended trip to the far north for some meetings in Hammerfest and then on into the interior for some work amongst the Sami folk. Part of our preparation was to get Vivian used to some skiing on the flat ground as well as in the mountains. He really had no experience skiing, so he had to get in quite a bit of practice in the event that there might be an emergency when we were away. We left from home with our rucksacks containing some clothes—mostly equipment, old-fashioned hard records made available by Gospel Recordings with music and message in the Lappish language, Bibles, Gospels, and tracts. Of course, we had to make sure we had our skis with us.

It was a very stormy two day trip by boat to Hammerfest. We spent six days in Hammerfest where we had gospel services and children's meetings. It was a very busy and profitable time in our ministry there. From there we took the boat out the fjord, where we got transportation into the interior. Our means of transportation was a Bombardier multi-passenger snowmobile, which would take us from Bosekop to Kautokeino. The trip took us about seven hours.

While in Kautokeino, we stayed with the Nils Logje family. They were very dear friends who also made their summer home at Noreisa near the mission hospital. Logje had the nickname "Stora Nils," which means Big Nils, because he stood out as the tallest Lapp around that area. They had two daughters, Berit, the older one, and Karen Anne, the younger one. The Logje family was held in very high regard. Berit acted as my interpreter on many occasions. She would translate from Norwegian to the Lappish. Stora Nils Logje told me a very interesting story that involved his father and provided some insight into the influences that were brought to bear on the Sami people.

Before the influence of Christianity, these nomadic people were largely Animists. They worshiped nature, rocks, waterfalls, and other parts of the created world. Many gods for them were found in trees and plants. So for the older generations, the influences of their background would surface from time to time. One day Logje's father, with his herders, was herding their reindeer along the slope of a mountain. Suddenly, an avalanche took a significant number of the reindeer into the bottom of the valley. Only a few survived; the majority of them were injured with broken bones. The herders wanted to go down and slaughter the injured animals, which would allow them to salvage the meat and the hides. Nils Logje's father said, "No, what the gods have taken, the gods shall have." What a price to pay!

To give some idea of the caliber of Stora Nils, let me share with you the following story. Two men were up from southern Norway to do some survey work and take photographs around the area of Kautokeino and district, but they encountered some problems. They hiked some fifty kilometres into the centre of Kautokeino and came into contact with Stora Nils Logje. They were invited into his home. Sitting around the kitchen table, Stora Nils shared some of the significant history of Kautokeino and its people. He spoke of the Sami who in 1852 were sentenced to death for their part in the uprising known as "The Kautokeino Uprising." He mentioned Lars Jacobsen Haetta, who was too young to be executed, but was sentenced to life imprisonment in Akershus (I shared this story earlier). When Nil's was telling how this young man translated the Bible into Samisk in the Kautokeino dialect, he became very emotional—so much so that he sobbed and wept, and the kitchen table was wet with his tears before he finished the story. Nils was so thankful to have the Word of God. I look back with gratitude to be able to count Stora Nils Logje as one of my dear friends.

While in Kautokeino, Vivian James and I had numerous meetings and distributed tracts and Gospels in the Sami language. We had our gramophone player with us, so we played records, which were provided in the Sami language and made available to us through the Gospel Recordings Mission. It was Easter time, so there were lots of Sami people in Kautokeino. One of our meetings there lasted for four hours. I played the organ, both Vivian James and I sang, and we both preached.

On Easter Sunday we both attended the state church in the morning. In the evening we had a gospel meeting where we had a large crowd and we both preach the Word of God. The highlight of Easter week was a wedding of a young Sami couple whose families I knew. It was a most colourful sight with everyone dressed in their very best colourful costumes of the Kautokeino tribe. The young couple sat during the whole service, which was conducted in their native language. We were invited to the wedding feast, which lasted for three days. There was Lapp Skaus, which is a type of stew made of reindeer meat. The bride's mother asked me to preach at the feast. I suggested that this might not be appropriate; however, she insisted, saying, that I would never get another opportunity like this to share the Gospel with so many people. So with the help of the man who was the interpreter for the state church priest, I spoke in Norwegian, and he interpreted into the Sami language. I preached for an hour. The mother of the bride told me afterwards that it was like the wedding feast at Cana. That was a very rewarding trip as we saw a number of people come to faith in Christ. We headed back to Espenes after what had been a very profitable trip and ministry that lasted for about four weeks.

15

A Major Intersection: Which Way Shall We Take?

Toward the end of May, 1955, we were at a major intersection in our life. We were struggling with some major health issues and the long winter. The dark days, with no sun day after day, week after week, was playing havoc with my energies. Also, my wife had some major health issues following the birth of our son. Our financial support was very uncertain. Fruit and vegetables were in short supply, and what was available we couldn't afford to buy. We were having serious difficulties in communications with the executive level of the British division of the mission. There was a serious lack of understanding of our travel conditions, the extremes of the climate, and the scattered nature of our population centres. It was totally different from the ministry that was being exercised in the Central European countries. As a result, there was a failure to comprehend that many of our needs in the North were necessities and not luxuries. Furthermore, it was hard for us to accept what was being spent in the administration costs in the United Kingdom. We questioned why it was necessary to have expenditures on the basis of structure changes of the headquarters building in London, just to satisfy personal convenience. Such expenses seemed superfluous in the light of the fact that we would receive letters to inform us that that there was not enough money and we would only receive half of our support.

During our last winter in the North, I hardly slept for about ten weeks. Our mission hospital doctor said that I couldn't survive like that. Essentially, I was suffering from what has now become known as the "SAD Syndrome," or Seasonal Affective Disorder. In short, we were struggling to determine what course of action we should take, and most importantly, what God would have us do.

Our initial commitment was to go and serve wherever we would fulfill God's will for us. Without a doubt, initially, we were called to serve in the far north. Could it be that God was moving us elsewhere, and that our ministry and experience in the North would better equip us for whatever the future would hold? We fully recognized that we didn't know what the future held, but we were confident in knowing that God held the future.

At this time a letter arrived to inform us that we should come to Britain to meet with the executive and some of the board members in London. We now had to prepare for that trip, which was a bit more difficult now that we also had two children. However, packing was done, plans were made, and toward the end of May we left Espenes, bidding an emotional farewell … not knowing when, or if, we'd be back. We stopped at Narvik for a few days and ministered at the Baptist church over the weekend and enjoyed the fellowship of the pastor and many of our very dear friends. Being able to share our conflicting emotions and also being able to pray together was great therapy for us.

We travelled south to Oslo where we were met by Steve and Helen Torbico. They were Americans who had worked in Italy for a number of years. Because of health issues, they moved to Norway and were working in the south. The next day we boarded the ship that would take us to Newcastle, England. The weather was beautiful, the seas were calm, and the service was tops. While on board we met some wonderful Christian people. They had been deeply involved in the Billy Graham London Crusade and were frequent listeners to the *Old Fashioned Revival Hour* and Dr. Charles E. Fuller.

Uppermost in my mind during that trip was the meeting we would be having with the director and some of the board members. While in my cabin, God directed me to Ephesians 4:14, where His Word reminded me that as a mature believer I should be speaking the truth in love. This gave me a deep sense of peace and confidence. When we docked at Newcastle, we discovered that there was a rail strike. In spite of that, we made it to Edinburgh by mid-afternoon. The following evening we were at St. Andrews Mission Hall in Edinburgh. I had the privilege of leading two young fellows to the Lord after the service. We felt that this was confirmation that we were where the Lord wanted us to be at that time.

Farewell to Lapland

We finally got word from headquarters that we should be in London for a meeting with the director and board of the mission. We were welcomed in London on July 6 by our dear friends, Alfred and Jenny Weeks. That evening we had our long-awaited meeting to discuss the issues at hand. Aside from the mission's director, there were only four board members. We were very disappointed. However, we did sense that all was not well at the administration level. We were aware that there was a serious rift and difference of opinion. Without rehashing the details, suffice it to say, we made it clear to those present that to make it easier for all concerned, we would tender our resignation right there and then. This was not an easy decision, but it seemed to be the only reasonable one. We will be forever grateful for the friendship and support of our field director, Mr. Armin Hoppler, our North American director, Rev. Douglas G. Stewart, and a number of the members of the British board. They stood with us in prayer as we sought the Lord's will and guidance for the future.

There was still the issue of returning to Lapland to pack and wind up everything there. However, the director said that I should return alone to do this. At that the board members strongly objected, and indicated that both my wife and I needed to return north to bring fitting closure to our ministry and take care of our personal matters. A note in my diary at that time makes mention of the fact that we weren't sure what the Lord had in store for us; however, we were confident that He had a plan for our future. On August 1, we no longer were counted to be a part of the European Evangelistic Crusade. However, our work was not finished in the North or anywhere the Lord would open doors for service. We were the recipients of greetings and letters assuring us of concern, love, support, and prayer for the future.

One of the things we were able to do was dedicate both of the children at Larbert Baptist Church on July 17, 1955. We felt it wise that we make plans to leave our son, Stuart, in Scotland while returning to the North. My sister, who already had four boys of her own, offered to keep Harry Stuart. It wasn't easy to do this, but we knew he would be taken care off. Adaline Anne would travel with us. She spoke Norwegian, and she also had many friends she wanted to see again.

For the balance of the month and throughout August, we had a wonderful ministry in a number of churches in the central part of Scotland. In the meantime, there were several opportunities brought to our attention where we might serve the Lord; however, we had to return to Norway and the North first. We had ministries for which we were responsible. We felt that we must take time to greet our many friends and, of course, there was packing that had to be done.

We returned to Norway on August 22, 1955. We were met by Steve Torbico, and we travelled north with him by car. This was so helpful and would also mean that Steve would get to see some of the work we were doing in the North. From

September to November—about twelve weeks—we had an exceptionally busy time with a roller coaster of emotions. We had meetings at a number of the places around us. It was most encouraging to see fruit remaining from our previous visits. Also, the Lord was pleased to honour the preaching of the Word again in our final meetings. At Espenes on October 23, 1955, we had an incredible service. The chapel was packed. My wife and I sang and I preached. Many of the folks who were there shared their testimony; this was followed by a feast. It was close to midnight when we finally finished. We travelled to Tromso, where we participated in a conference at the Baptist church. This was a blessed week of fellowship and ministry. The James' and my wife and I ministered with our quartet ministry, and we also took part in teaching and preaching.

On Tuesday, November 1, a crowd of the Tromso folks gathered at the bus station to bid us bon voyage. We were leaving behind many happy memories. It was a very emotional time. We arrived at Narvik to a very warm welcome and looked forward to a week of good fellowship and ministry at the church there. On Tuesday, November 8, 1955, we left Narvik by train for Oslo. It was very dark. The winter was upon us. The sun had gone. It was the dark period. We were leaving the North with heavy hearts and leaving a people we had learned to love. After two weeks of meetings in several places in the South, and having fellowship with coworkers Roald Nilson, Enock Wangberg, and Stephen and Hellen Torbico, we sailed back to Britain. We were physically, emotionally, and spiritually exhausted. My health was impaired, but a change of pace would help to restore my energies, along with support from family and friends. Isaiah 40:31 reminds us that "…*they that wait upon the Lord shall renew their strength*" (KJV).

My second oldest brother, George, had just bought a new vehicle for his business. As part of my restorative therapy, I took on the task of fitting out the interior of the van. Soon I felt refreshed and was able to settle down and give thought to what the future might hold for us. We were back together as a family and looking to the Lord for guidance. In December I was kept busy. I was able to minister in a number of churches pastored by fellow students from college. It was a real joy to renew fellowship with them.

The Unknown Future with an All Knowing God

As we came to the close of a major chapter in our life and ministry, we were excited to see what God would have in store for us. We were presented with three interesting possibilities, so it was a matter of determining what God would have us do and where He would have us go. We had the offer of considering a move to the United States. This would keep us involved with the European Evangelistic Crusade. The thought was that we could use our experience to effectively promote the work of the mission from the American office in Philadelphia. Giving it thought and much prayer, we were convinced that God was moving us to more of a pastoral ministry. Through the local church I could still use my God given gifts of preaching, teaching, and evangelism. In addition to that, I could always encourage the sending of missionaries and the support of missions.

Just about this time two other opportunities presented themselves to us. We had a call from a church in the Shetland Islands in the far north of Scotland. A number of the folks in the church there had heard me preach on previous visits to Shetland and were prepared to extend a call to us. They knew that I had married a Shetlander, and she would have no problem returning to the Islands. In addition to this, the Shetland Islands, from the ninth century to the fifteenth century, were under Norwegian control. Then in 1472, King James III of Scotland annexed Shetland to the Scottish crown. To this day there are many evidences of the Norwegian influence. The very distinctive dialect has borrowed many words and expressions from the Old Norse. The customs and archeology also reflect much of the Viking influence. Putting all this together, with our having lived in Norway and being fluent in the Norwegian language, this call had a strong appeal to us. However, we could neither say yes or no, since another ministry possibility had been presented to us.

My third eldest brother, the Rev. Henry Russell, his wife, and family had moved to Canada in 1954. While communicating with me from time to time, he suggested that we might consider coming to Canada. This immediately awakened an interest that should be explored. As this chapter closes, recalling my life from Letham to Lapland, we can but raise our Ebenezer: "*Hitherto, hath the Lord helped us,*" (1 Samuel 7:12). Could it be possible that God would call me from a little, obscure mining village and choose to use me in ways and places beyond human imagination? Without a doubt, the words of John Newton capture the very essence of my life: "Through many dangers toils and snares, I have already come. 'Tis grace that brought me safe thus far and grace will lead me home." Now, on the threshold of uncharted seas and untravelled roads, we said, "Lord, whither bound." At twenty-eight years of age, I was very much aware of the fact that, by the grace of God, there was a lifetime of ministry ahead—new challenges, new opportunities. As one of my teachers in college used to say: "Gentlemen, hats off to the past; coats off to the future. The best is yet to be."

Having just celebrated the sixtieth anniversary of my ordination and still preaching the Word of God as a humble servant of my Master, my prayer is that I be found faithful in my ongoing service for the Lord. What has happened in the ensuing years will be the subject of another saga.

16

Go West Young Man—
From Norway, to New Brunswick, to Newfoundland,
1956-1976

The first major chapter of my life and ministry closed when we as a family bade farewell to Lapland and Norway. Little did I realize how those years of ministry in the far north would mold and fashion my attitude and commitment to the ministry in the ensuing years. The variety of ministries in which I was involved, the cultures with which I worked, the isolation and remoteness of the territories covered, the complexities of my applications, the measure of responsibilities that called for my wisdom, the limitation of financial and physical resources, and the vital demands on my flexibility all served to equip me for the ministries to which God would call me in the next twenty years and beyond.

After a period of physical, emotional, and spiritual renewal, we as a family were able to concentrate on seeking the mind and the will of God for the future. From December, 1955 into January, 1956, several areas of possible opportunities to minister came before us. Seeking the will of God and listening to the advice of trusted friends and family enabled us to narrow down the options. However, underneath all of this, we were deeply aware of fact that the future was as bright as the promises of God. As we crossed the threshold into the New Year, 1956, we claimed the promise of God in Psalm 31:14–15: "*I trust in You, O Lord. I say, 'You are my God. My times are in your hand...'*"

While waiting, I had the joy of ministering at Clarkson Baptist Church, Glasgow, through the month of January. Upon reflection, I now realize that the Lord was preparing me for what He had in store. Into this mix came a letter from Burra Isle Baptist Church, extending me a call to be their pastor. Since I had other matters under consideration, I wrote them back, requesting that they consider waiting for a definite answer. At that time we were pursuing another path, and we were waiting for some definite information. This would help us determine the mind and will of God for our future life and ministry.

My brother had been encouraging me to consider coming to Canada to minister. At this particular time, a very interesting incident took place in his life that eventually would influence our future. While my brother was ministering in New Brunswick, he had occasion to attend a conference in the province of Quebec. He was travelling back home by train in the company of other ministers and was sitting with a Baptist pastor from New Brunswick. In the course of their conversation, my brother mentioned to him that I might be interested in coming to Canada to minister in a Baptist church. The Baptist pastor indicated that one of the leaders of the Baptist denomination was also travelling on board the train in another compartment, so my brother was introduced to Dr. J. Murray Armstrong, the then General Secretary of the Atlantic Baptist Convention. A chance meeting? A mere coincidence? No! This was no doubt orchestrated by the Lord.

Within a few days I received an airmail letter from Dr. Armstrong. He was so excited to tell me of the need for Baptist pastors in the Atlantic provinces. He requested information about my conversion, training for the ministry, and experience in the ministry. All of this I forwarded to him, post haste. Within a few short weeks, on February 18, 1956, we received a letter extending to us a call to the pastoral ministry of Grand Bay, Brown's Flat, Greenwich Hill, and Oak Point Baptist churches, all of them located along the banks of the St. John River in the province of New Brunswick, Canada. Within a few days we responded and accepted the call to this group of country churches. We didn't realize until later that we were part of a significant migration of Baptist pastors, primarily from Scotland and Northern Ireland.

Let me back track just a little bit to demonstrate how even in the details of immigration and travel arrangements, everything was falling into place. We had to have several interviews at the Canadian immigration office, located in Glasgow. It was necessary for us to have vaccinations, x-rays, a medical certificate from our family doctor, and a thorough medical by the immigration doctor. The immigration officer also informed us that the Canadian government had just passed legislation to make available financial assistance to qualified immigrants to cover travel costs. Hallelujah! Once we were settled in Canada, this money would be paid back to the government, interest free. As Scripture says: *"And my God shall supply all your need according to His riches in glory by Christ Jesus"* (Philippians 4:19).

As returned missionaries, we had very little money, but God knew our need. In the meantime, now that we had proof of employment, our medical certificate was clear, we qualified as immigrants, and our passage money was in place, we needed to book a passage with a travel agent. We'd been making this very much a matter of prayer. Five of us would be travelling—my wife and me, our two children, and my mother. Our son, Stuart, was still not one year old. His first birthday would be on March 6, 1956. If we could make arrangements to arrive in Canada before that date, he would travel for free. This would certainly reduce our travel costs, so we made a visit to Cook's Travel, then located on Graham's Road, Falkirk.

The agent was very apprehensive about being able to make travel plans on such short notice, given the fact that so many people were immigrating to Canada at that time. The agent informed us that there would be a ship sailing from Liverpool, England, in sixteen days time, on February 24. It would be scheduled to arrive in Halifax, Nova Scotia, Canada, on March 3, three days before Stuart's second birthday. However, the agent suggested that there might not be space available for five people at this late date. Besides, it would take a few days to get in touch with the shipping company, and then a few days to get a reply. I suggested to the agent that he make a telephone call to the shipping company so that we could get an answer immediately. He informed us that this would increase our costs, and we agreed to pay the extra. Within minutes we had the answer—there were five spaces left. Would you believe that was the number we needed? Within two days we paid the fares and were ready to go. Now it was a rush to get everything ready. There was our last trip to the immigration office in Glasgow to pick up our medical cards and final papers. We bore testimony to the goodness of the Lord in the land of the living.

On Sunday, February 19, I preached at the farewell service in Larbert Baptist Church, my home church. How wonderful to have the assurance that the prayers of our home church would go with us as we set out on this new chapter of our life and ministry.

On the following Thursday, our luggage all loaded into my brother's van, we headed for Glasgow to board the overnight train to Liverpool, England. The attendant on the train was so helpful, and we settled in to a much needed sleep.

When we arrived in Liverpool, the porters took care of our luggage to be taken to the ship. We had some breakfast at the station, and then killed some time with a walk around the shopping area. Later in the day we took a bus to the docks. Immediately upon entering the customs shed, we were met by a trained nurse who took care of the children while we cleared customs. The baggage master checked our baggage. All our worldly goods amounted to one hundred and twenty one cubic feet, forty cubic feet in excess of allowance. This meant twenty-two pounds sterling extra cost! However, with a bit of rearranging, he was able to bring it down to ten pounds sterling. How the Lord undertakes! Because of the late booking, we were assigned to separate cabins. However, through the kindness of the chief steward and some other passengers, we were finally settled in the same cabin. Thank you, Lord!

Having had such a hectic few days, it didn't take us long to settle down for the night. In fact, when I woke in the morning, I couldn't remember putting my head on the pillow. One could hardly feel the ship moving. Of course, we were in the channel between England and Southern Ireland, so we were in sheltered waters. We were heading towards Cork, where we would be taking on more passengers. Around 10:00 a.m., the flag, signaling that a pilot was needed, was hoisted. Soon we could see the pilot vessel speeding toward us. Very soon the pilot was onboard. Shortly afterwards, the tender, carrying an additional one hundred passengers, came alongside, and very soon the passengers were on board. Now we had a total of seven hundred passengers, all bound for Canada.

It was a glorious day and the sea was calm. Our ship was the Cunard White Star ship, *S.S. Scythia*, a 22,000 ton ship, an older vessel. We were informed that it was making its last trip as a passenger ship. By Sunday morning we were really at sea, with water as far as the eye could see. After breakfast I took part in the morning service in the lounge of the ship. However, that was my last meal and the last activity in which I took part. By mid-day the seas were raging. This 22,000 ton vessel was being tossed about like a cork. As the waves broke over the bow of the ship, I found refuge in my cabin for the balance of the trip. My wife, my children, and my mother never missed a meal. The cabin attendants were very kind to me. They tried every trick they knew to try to get my stomach to settle, but it didn't happen. One day the chief steward arrived at my cabin with a tall green bottle. He said that it might settle my stomach. Looking at the bottle I said to him, "Oh, I never drink wine or alcoholic beverages."

"No! No!" he said. "This is neither; it's a very good quality ginger ale." Even that didn't work. I tell the story of the Scotsman who was travelling across the Atlantic and became violently seasick. He went up on deck to get some fresh air and some relief from his nausea. His buddy came up and got alongside of him. Trying to get his mind off his seasickness, he put his arm around Jock.

"Look, Jock," said his buddy. "See the moon coming up?"

"Oh no," said Jock. "Has that got to come up too?"

So the journey continued. While being tossed about so violently, one could not help but think of God's dealing with Jonah.

On the evening of the eighth day, the dining room was decorated with balloons and streamers. It was the gala dinner night, and a very special meal would be served. My wife talked me into getting dressed and joining them for this wonderful dinner. For the sake of all concerned, I acquiesced. Everyone was happy and celebrating. I finally took my place at our assigned table and was able to take some photos. Then the food arrived. There was turkey with all the trimmings. One look at this sumptuous spread and my face turned green. I hastily made my way to the cabin and left the others to indulge. Oh my! There I stayed until Saturday morning, March 3, 1956.

We were seeing more and more "terra firma," and the more "firma" the less "terror" for me. In a matter of a few hours we would finally arrive. All the coast line was shrouded in snow. As we entered the Halifax harbour, we began to identify people. How thrilled we were to identify my brother Harry and his wife, Mae. The ship finally docked at Pier 21 at 5:30 p.m., March 3, 1956. Immediately, Mr. MacLeod, official of Canadian customs, came on board the ship. He informed me that he'd arranged to have us disembark with the first group of passengers. Very soon we were called ashore, and within a short time we were through with all the passport and customs formalities. We were then introduced to the Baptist ministers and wives who had come to welcome us to Canada. Amongst them were Pastor and Mrs. George Simpson, Pastor Abner Langley, and Pastor Stuart Murray, all from the Halifax area.

In those years many immigrants were coming to Canada and arriving at Halifax, so the various denominations had workers at the port to welcome them. The Maritime Baptist Convention had Miss Doris Wagner as their port worker. She gave us a very warm welcome. There were gifts for the children and packages for us. She also provided great help in guiding us through the various stages. Our large baggage was cleared, and we arranged to have it shipped by rail to Saint John, New Brunswick. This would be the nearest point to Grand Bay, where we would be living. We then made contact with my brother and his wife, who would take us by car to Chatham, New Brunswick—a distance of about two hundred and fifty miles. It was cold and there was freezing rain, so we had to be very careful and drive very slowly.

Around 6:30 a.m. Sunday morning we arrived at my brother's home in Chatham. We were utterly exhausted, but happy to be on terra firma. I got up early with my brother and we were off to a service at 10:00 a.m. at the Presbyterian church in Kouchibouquac (a Mic-Mac Indian word meaning "river of long tides") where I was scheduled to preach. What a welcome and what an experience! I stood up behind the pulpit and couldn't believe what was happening. The floor rose and fell; the pulpit kept moving; I had to hold on for dear life. The problem? My mind and my body were still acting like I was on board the ship in the mid-Atlantic! I still hadn't adjusted to the fact that I was now on solid ground. It was several days before I finally got my balance. However, we continued on with the regularly scheduled services that day. We had one at Black River Bridge, then on to Sunny Corner. Everywhere we went we received a very warm welcome, in spite of the freezing winter weather outdoors. The climax of the day was the service at the church in Chatham. The church was packed to overflowing. We had a great night of music, with the family presenting several numbers, and I had great liberty in preaching the Word.

Later that week we were invited to the local high school. There were over two hundred students there from grades seven to eleven. My wife and I sang some Norwegian songs as well as the national anthem of Norway. Then I gave a lecture covering the work that we did in Northern Norway and Lapland, including the culture and customs of the people. Then it was opened for questions. We valued this incredible opportunity, and the students and teachers were very responsive. Later that day we received a beautiful bouquet of flowers from the students and staff.

My brother and his wife ministered in Chatham, New Brunswick, for approximately five years. Let me share with you a bit of humour here, beamed at my beloved sister-in-law. They lived in the town of Chatham; however, they also had churches in three different rural areas where there was farming and lumbering. One of the elders, a farmer, had just recently been discharged from the hospital and was recuperating at home. One day, my brother and his wife decided to go out to the country and visit this farmer/elder. As their visit drew to a close, my brother read from the Bible and had prayer. When they were about to leave, my sister-in-law shook hands with the recuperating patient and said, "I know you've had a rough passage, but never mind, it's all behind you now." What she did not know was this man had just had a hemorrhoidectomy. Yes, the joys of pastoral calling.

17

My New Field of Ministry

On Thursday, March 8, 1956, we travelled from Chatham to Grand Bay to be introduced to the area of our first pastoral ministry in Canada. After a five hour drive, we reached our destination. Initially we stayed with Mr. and Mrs. O. Hoyt. She was the treasurer of the church, and he, a senior deacon. We stayed with this couple until such time as the church was able to provide a parsonage for us.

That first evening we had dinner with the chairman of our deacons' board and his wife, Mr. and Mrs. Darrell Liston. We became good friends with them over many years. After our meal, I had the opportunity to discuss the ministry in the churches in which we would be involved; they were all located along the Saint John River valley. These Baptist churches—Grand Bay, Browns Flat, Greenwhich Hill, and Oak Point—were all part of the then Maritime Baptist Convention, later to become known as The Atlantic Baptist Convention.

Grand Bay Baptist Church was ministered to by pastors who were from Saint John, New Brunswick. At this point the congregation was struggling. In fact, they were considering closing the church entirely. When I was called to be their pastor, it was with the provision that the church would either take on new life or be closed down permanently. The church itself consisted of people who commuted to Saint John, New Brunswick for their work. I would become their first resident pastor. By joining with three other churches upriver, they would become financially viable and be able to support a full-time minister.

The churches upriver were ministered to by a retired pastor from Fredericton, New Brunswick. These churches were made up of local people as well as those who had been relocated from the extensive area known as

Camp Gagetown. They had been forced to leave their homes, their farms, and their churches and reestablished themselves in the communities along the banks of the Saint John River. These four churches would then constitute one pastorate. It would fall to me to give the necessary leadership to bring it about. What a challenge! At the same time what an amazing opportunity. To merge one church made up of town people with three churches of primarily rural, farming, and lumbering people was a major task. Upon reflection, this was the Lord's doing and marvellous in our eyes (Psalm 118:23). However, one church was holding out from this merger. Interestingly enough, after I had the opportunity to preach in all four churches, they were unanimous in having this become one pastorate.

We were able to move into a rented house in Grand Bay. It was fully furnished, which was a blessing for us. It was agreed that I would receive a salary of $56.00 dollars per week. Some time was then spent on bringing about some semblance of organization. A field committee was formed comprised of two representatives from each of the two larger churches and one representative from each of the two smaller churches. The two larger churches would each provide one third of my salary, and the two smaller churches would each provide one sixth of my salary. While I was on the mission field I had been getting $56.00 per month, when the money was available. Now I would be getting $56.00 per week. When I accepted the call to the church, my brother expressed concern that I didn't know what my salary would be. The fact was I ended up getting $300.00 more than him for my annual salary. The Lord always provides.

For the first month that I was ministering in these four churches I had the use of a borrowed car. Now I needed to purchase a car of my own. I discovered that my brother in Chatham had a man in his congregation who had a car dealership, so on May 4, 1956, I bought a brand new Plymouth Savoy for $1200.00. That was a lot of money, but it was a necessary investment. The dealer asked me how much money I had in my pocket. I told him about $100.00, so he said to give him that as a down payment and pay off the balance as I was able. My first new car … no contract, no carrying charge … just good old fashioned trust. Now we would be able to get around at our own pace and in our own time.

In the meantime we had a visit from the immigration officer. We discovered that his sister was a member of one of our churches. I was able to express to him my appreciation for the way we had been cared for and dealt with through the whole process of immigration. In fact, the immigration department printed our story on a brochure. This was made available to other prospective immigrants to encourage them to come to Canada. By now we felt, beyond the shadow of doubt, that we were where God wanted us to be.

Once settled, we were able to sit down with the field committee and get some organization in place so that we could effectively minister in the Sunday services, Sunday schools, youth groups, and the work amongst the women. Our Sunday schedule meant that I had a service in each church every Sunday; we had two mid-week services of prayer and Bible study, four Sunday schools, and two ladies groups, for which my wife was responsible. With visitation, funerals, hospital calls, and other responsibilities, I had a very busy schedule.

From time to time we had special events. Since I had musical abilities, I would often train our choirs for special musical presentations. Every Sunday I preached four different sermons. Since many of the people travelled from church to church, they didn't want to hear the same sermon. This meant that I had to maintain a very strict study schedule. I spent at least two hours in my study before breakfast every morning. Then I would be back in my study right after breakfast until noon hour. Certainly in those days we didn't have the distraction of cell phones and emails like we have today. On Monday I would spend time visiting in the hospitals and nursing homes. This is also the day I would fast. Three afternoons per week I would spend visiting in the different communities.

My induction service on April 5 served to bring together the four congregations for the first time in a physical, tangible way, making them feel that they were one whole family. In time, numbers increased along with a deepening spiritual growth. This was accompanied by an increasing outreach into the surrounding communities. Along the way I became more and more involved in the Baptist Association meetings. I was increasingly involved in ministering at special rallies, especially when there was an emphasis on missions. In June of 1956, I was called to a special meeting of the executive of the Maritime Baptist Convention, along with the ordination council. I was to be interviewed regarding my training, my qualifications, and the standard of my ordination in Scotland. This interview went very well, and I was accepted as an ordained Baptist pastor, the committee having duly recognized my ordination credentials from Scotland. To God be the Glory!

It was very interesting to be involved in some special things in the communities where I was ministering. For the first time ever at Browns Flat, we had a special church service for all the school children, with special recognition of the graduates for that year. This was held in the Anglican church—it being the largest building in the community. The Anglican, United, and Baptist churches were all represented. The church was packed to overflowing. Later on one of the high school teachers in that community came to a personal relationship with Jesus Christ in one of our services. Later on I baptized her, and then she married one of our young men. She has maintained a strong, vibrant witness and service in the church there.

I also had the joy of speaking to the students in Grand Bay School at the closing of the school year. What a privilege and opportunity to influence and connect with the young people of the communities in which our churches were located. In July, the first two weeks after school closing, we conducted Vacation Bible School in the community hall in Grand Bay. This was an overwhelming success. The children were eager to hear the Bible stories, memorize scripture verses, and sing the choruses. This had never been done before in that community. It provided not only outreach, but also activity for the children during the summer break. It also brought many children into the Sunday school and impacted the entire community. The following two weeks we spent at Browns Flat conducting Vacation Bible School. Children from Greenwich Hill and Oak Point joined with the children in Browns Flat. We met in the community hall, and VBS was an outstanding success. Again this outreach served to benefit our Sunday schools and our youth programs in our churches.

18

Emotional Strains of the Ministry

To illustrate the emotional swings and diversity of ministry, let me share this incident and responsibility which fell to me, coming down from "a high" of success with our Vacation Bible Schools. I was at home one afternoon when a young RCMP officer came to our door inquiring if I were the local Baptist pastor. Assuring him that I was, I invited him in. He told me that he was the bearer of very bad news. Just a short way down the road from Grand Bay, the province was involved in building a by-pass road to divert the traffic from having to wind its way along the narrow river road, through several small villages, on its way to Saint John. This would be an incredible benefit, especially for the heavy transport trucks. The foreman on that project was Mr. Higgins, a member of Grand Bay Baptist Church, where I was pastor.

The police officer informed me that Mr. Higgins had just been killed in a tragic accident. He was about to wind up his day on the project and was heading to the little portable office when a heavy piece of equipment came along. The foreman decided to hitch a ride on the tractor that was hauling the unit that was used to pack down the gravel before the asphalt was laid. He jumped on to the tow bar, but his foot slipped and the heavy equipment rolled right over him, killing him instantly. The young RCMP officer, who was torn with emotion, said to me, "I'm supposed to tell this man's wife what has happened, but I can't do it, so I'm here to ask if you would please pass on this information to Mrs. Higgins."

Wow! This is when you draw upon God's enabling grace. One has to learn to "weep with those who weep." What a shock to this family, to this community, and to this church. One doesn't learn this in Pastoral Theology class. Mr. James

R. Higgins was only forty-seven years of age. For times like this we have to develop a heart of compassion like our Saviour. I learned the true meaning of this from the Norwegian language. The word for compassion in Norwegian is "medlidenhet," which literally translated it means "to suffer with." God grant that I may never lose that type of caring.

Another event comes to mind that involves bringing comfort to the bereaved. Our son, Ian, was born in the Saint John General Hospital on April 8, 1957. We were rejoicing in the gift of our new son; however, the day that I brought my wife and new son home from the hospital was also the day that I had the burial service for the new born baby of a young couple in the church. Oh, the highs and lows of emotions!

Over the years prior to my becoming the first full time pastor of the four churches, all four churches were more or less stagnant. Anyone who did serve these churches maintained mostly just Sunday services. Virtually they had maintained a "status quo." As one southern preacher explained: "That's Latin for 'the mess we's now in.'" Having just come from the mission field with a very positive outreach and burden for the unsaved, this was paramount in my ministry in the area served by these four churches.

On July 12, 1956, we had our first baptismal service in Oak Point Baptist church. We gathered on the shore of the Saint John River. It was a memorable day. I had ministered to Lloyd Hamilton and had the joy of seeing him come to a personal faith in the Lord Jesus Christ. The whole church, along with some of the people from the community, came to see him declare that faith as he followed the Lord in baptism.

Following his baptism, I said, "There may be others here today who should take this step of obedience. Will you take that step of obedience today?" One of the men in the gathering whose name was Stanley Patterson stepped out from the crowd and said, "I need to take that step of obedience now." There were many in the gathering who expressed surprise! I asked one of the deacons to have the people sing several hymns, and I took the opportunity to speak to the man to clarify that he knew exactly what this decision meant. I then proceeded with his baptism. He was dressed in his Sunday best, so he took off his jacket and his shoes and stepped into the water, where I baptized him. As I helped him out of the water, I noticed his tobacco pouch in one pocket and his wallet in the other. This was the end of his smoking habit and also the beginning of his commitment to support the church. Perhaps we need more of that kind of baptism today— the kind that takes care of bad habits and commitment at one time. Both men who were baptized that the day became very active in the church.

We had an interesting open door into many activities of the community organizations. Sometimes I was called upon to speak at their gatherings; sometimes they would come to the church service as a group. This gave us a great opportunity to share the Gospel with them. Another special activity that was common to our Baptist churches was the annual "Roll Call service." There would usually be a visiting preacher for the service. This service would normally be held in July, August, or September. During that service, the clerk of the church would call out the names off the members. Each member would then indicate their presence by quoting a verse of scripture or by giving a personal word of testimony. There was also the opportunity to give a special offering for some special project or for some special need.

My wife and I had the opportunity to attend the Baptist convention in Wolfville, Nova Scotia. It was a special time for us to enjoy fellowship and sit under the ministry of visiting preachers. Then it was back to our churches for a fresh season of service. While there we formed friendships that have been very dear to us over these many years.

September of 1956 was a significant month and year. Adaline, our eldest daughter, started school. For her this was a very exciting time and adventure. It was also a significant time for my mother. She had travelled with us to Canada and now, seven months later, was returning to Scotland. Leaving our children with friends, we drove my mother to Montreal, where she was scheduled to board a ship that would take her back to Britain. She had been such a help with the children and in helping us adjust to our new surroundings.

19

Growth and Changes

By the end of September, our churches and organizations were in full swing. Now there was more order and structure to our ministry within the churches and we better understood the needs and how we could meet them. The churches were beginning to realize that they were part of a much larger family and fellowship.

That fall I was appointed as the leader of the Christian Youth Fellowship. The youth rallies were held each Saturday evening in the church hall of one of our Baptist churches in Saint John. These gatherings attracted between four hundred and five hundred youth at each rally. Our youth choir spearheaded the singing for the rallies. A strong music program was developed amongst the young people. We always had special speakers—sometimes an evangelist, a missionary, or a pastor. Many of these young people came to personal faith in Christ, while others committed themselves to Christian service. This was very demanding for me since it involved my Saturday evenings throughout the Fall and Winter months, and I had always a full day on Sunday with four services in the churches.

There were many evidences of God at work in so many wonderful ways. There was numerical growth, increased financial giving, and organizational stability. But above all, there was real spiritual maturity. Many were coming to faith in Christ and expressing that faith through baptism. Because of this, in 1957 we had to give thought to planning major changes in the two larger churches, namely Grand Bay and Brown's Flat. In February of 1957, we launched a work up near Evandale Ferry. The arrangements were made to secure the use of the Evandale Public School. We organized a Sunday school for the children in that area, and every second Sunday we had church services there.

With the growth that was happening in two of our churches, we had to plan for major renovations and expansion of our facilities. In March, 1957, the first move to enlarge our facilities was taken at Grand Bay. Through the contact made by Darrell Liston, chairman of our deacons' board, we were offered a partially finished house for the sum of $10 on the condition that it be completely demolished This was a new structure, located at Petersville, that had never been completed and never lived in. We were interested in the new lumber, which would provide us with material to expand our facilities at the Grand Bay church.

Within two days a small team of men completely demolished the building and transported the material to the yard of the church. We now had the basic materials to enable us to expand the church facilities. Exercising my former training, I sketched the plans for the expansion. It was intended that we provide space for our youth and Sunday school rooms. One wall opening to the sanctuary would provide for overflow from our Sunday services.

We cut down some tall mature trees that were growing on the church property. This lumber would provide us with the necessary log trusses. These had to be custom cut and would require a lumber mill that could handle the extra long lumber. Even there the Lord provided a mill right in our own community. The mill was owned by Mr. Dan Usher. He actually did the work for free.

In the spring and summer of 1957, the foundation was dug, the basement walls were poured, and the extension was built. All the labour was donated by the men of the church. A carpenter was hired to do some of the finish work that required special skills. Windows needed to be replaced in the existing sanctuary. I learned that in the area taken over by Camp Gagetown, there were several abandoned Baptist churches. One of those churches had beautiful stained glass windows. I made contact with the government authorities at Camp Gagetown and indicated that we'd like to remove some of those windows and use them in the church at Grand Bay. We were informed that we should make a formal request by letter and also make a bid. We sent the letter and included a bid in the amount of $100. In due time, we received word that our bid was accepted and we could remove the windows. The stained glass windows were duly installed in the Grand Bay church.

The extension of the facilities served very well for several years. Over the years the community of Grand Bay-Westfield has developed into a major bedroom community for the city of Saint John, New Brunswick. As a result, there has been a major influx of new people into the community. The church likewise has grown into a vibrant ministry to these new people. What seemed like a failing cause when I arrived in March of 1956 has developed beyond all expectations, and the church now has its own fulltime pastor along with other staff.

Over time a parsonage was built, and since the first expansion another new sanctuary has been built. To give some idea of how the church has grown in recent years, I recall that in the first service I conducted in 1956 we had in attendance around fifty people, which included men, women, and children. The offering on the occasion amounted to $51. A recent article in *The Canadian Baptist Ministries* magazine reveals something of the growth of the church. This article stated that in 2010, Adrian Gardner, the associate pastor, reported that the children who attended the Vacation Bible School gave a special offering amounting to $581.61 towards a project in Bolivia. This gives some indication of the growth. It's worthy of note that a few years ago, a new community was developed at a place called Nerrepis, about ten miles away from Grand Bay. A Baptist church was established there with a senior pastor and an assistant. Now the church at Brown's Flat has its own pastor and the community there has also grown.

During my time there as pastor, it became evident that we had to consider enlarging the facilities is of the church at Brown's Flat, so plans were made and the church congregation voted to go ahead with the additions. It was decided to put in a basement and enlarge the entrance to the church to accommodate stairs that would provide access to the basement. We also wanted to add on a major part to the area behind the platform. This would provide a choir room space, along with a pastor's room that would serve also as a meeting room. This was a major undertaking, but we proceeded with enthusiasm.

A local carpenter was hired, and one of the deacons, Charles Moore, and I assisted as we had opportunity. Around the same time that the work began, plans were made by all four churches to have a major evangelistic outreach into the communities. The leadership of the churches felt that I should do the preaching at the evening services, so plans were made and the series of meetings commenced and lasted for six weeks. The meetings were held each evening, Monday through Friday, over the six week period. They were held in tandem with the work I was doing on the church building at Brown's Flat. My schedule was such that I would be in my study each morning around 4:30 a.m. seeking the Lord for a message that I would preach that evening. Getting my main points noted on a piece of paper, I would build on them throughout the day. Around 9:00 a.m. I would drive to Brown's Flat to work on the building. Someone always provided me with lunch and dinner. After six or seven hours working on the building (all the while mulling over my message and putting meat on the bones), I would wash, change into my suit, and get ready for the evening meeting at 7:00 p.m. Quite often I would lead the singing with the help of my accordion, and even sing a solo or a duet with my wife. In effect we were adding to the church—building during the day and adding to the spiritual church in the evening. Oh how the Lord truly blessed that ministry!

Almost every night the Holy Spirit worked in our midst. People were saved and backsliders were restored. Here I must share a very special incident. We started the evangelistic meetings at the Evandale schoolhouse. It was the second or third night of the meetings and the school had the usual school desks in place. To accommodate the people, we had placed planks between the desks and around the periphery of the room. One of our ladies invited a young mother to attend the service. She came and brought her three month old baby along. We'd been singing some gospel songs, and some of the Christians shared their testimony. In the middle of this, the young mother passed her baby over to another lady. She then stood up and said, "I'm not sure what you people have, but whatever it is, I want it." My wife led the congregation in a few more songs while I took time to pray with the young mother as she accepted Christ as her personal saviour. This was the beginning, and night after night, throughout the six weeks of services, we saw many come to a personal relationship with Jesus Christ. We also had the joy of baptizing some and receiving them into the membership of our churches. These were weeks of revival. To God alone be the Glory.

20

The Ups and Downs of Pastoral Ministry

By our third year in New Brunswick, we had visited households all the way along the river road from South Bay to Brown's Flat. The churches grew numerically, but more importantly, they grew in their commitment to the Lord. Grand Bay saw one of their young people train for the Lord's service and then come back to serve in the church. In Grand Bay we added a new deacon to the church in the person of Francis Mabey. He eventually trained for the ministry and became my assistant when I was serving in Sussex. He went on to serve in other churches in New Brunswick. For many years he served on the island of Campobello in the Bay of Fundy.

The second year of my ministry there, the field committee, made up of representatives from each of the four churches, decided to recommend to the churches that I should receive an increase in salary. The two larger churches should give me an increase of $2.00 each, while the two smaller churches should give me an increase of $1.00 each. This would make a total increase of $6.00. Each of the two larger churches voted to give me the $2.00 raise. One of the smaller churches voted to give the $1.00 increase, while the other smaller church discussed the proposal at their annual meeting. I was in attendance, and there was nowhere else to go, so I had to listen to the discussion. Everyone present had to have their say. Finally, one very outspoken lady stood up to speak to the motion. Remember, this was primarily a farming community. She made this statement: "I don't see why the pastor should have the cream when I have to drink the skimmed milk." That church voted against the proposed $1.00 raise. The joys of baptistic congregational government! However, one of the larger churches took up the slack, so I still received the $6.00 raise.

Sitting in the annual meeting of one of our larger churches one time, I was listening to the treasurer's report. Something did not seem to add up. I was convinced that more money had come into the church than was being reported by the treasurer. Here was a very delicate situation. I had to be very careful how I asked for some clarification so that I would not cast aspersions on the integrity of the treasurer. So when I did ask for an explanation, she said "Oh, I only keep a record of what is left after all the bills are paid." I asked where she kept the money for safe keeping, and was told, "In a tin box under the bed." There was no bank account. Well, I had to sit down with her and set up a simple bookkeeping record and also arrange for a bank account. This served well, because a short time later churches had to register as charitable organizations and provide an annual report to the government. At that particular church, the treasurer sat in the front pew at the end of the service and counted the offering for the day. Before I would leave, I had to check with her and she would give me the portion of my salary assigned to that church. It amounted to $22.00 and was given to me in quarters and dimes and nickels: *Let all things be done decently and in order"* (1 Corinthians 14:40).

One Sunday evening, I was preaching in one of the larger churches. Let me set the scene. It was winter; the snow was on the ground, and it was very cold. There was a very large attendance that night. With the pot bellied stove, filled with hardwood and generating lots of heat, plus the body heat from the large attendance of people, it was very comfortable and conducive to putting some of the congregation to sleep. One of the deacons owned two lumber camps and had a significant gang of men working for him. Six mornings of each week he would be on the go between 4:30 and 5:00 a.m., rounding up some of his men and taking them out to cut down trees and operate the mills. His day would end about 5:00 p.m. each day.

That evening it was so warm and comfortable that not too long after I started preaching I noticed that he dropped off to sleep. He always sat close to the front because he was rather deaf. I was warming up to my message; there was no sound system in those days, so I would increase my volume. To drive home a point, I brought my fist down on the hollow wooden pulpit. This startled my sleeping deacon. He jumped to his feet. Wide awake and looking around, he realized what had happened as the people muffled their laughter. He never again went to sleep in church. Today those churches are thriving with multiple staff and growing congregations. It's been my privilege to be back visiting and conducting evangelistic campaigns.

A highlight in our Baptist churches of Saint John and Kings County, New Brunswick, was a simultaneous evangelistic crusade over a period of ten days. Meetings were held each evening in all of our Baptist churches. A team of Southern Baptist pastors came from Virginia, U.S.A., to work with us as local Baptist pastors. The impact was incredible. Many came to personal faith in Jesus Christ. The ten days of outreach climaxed with a rally on the final Sunday evening. This was held in one of the movie theatres. It was a fitting climax, and many also professed faith in Christ. I served as the coordinating chairman of this crusade. As a result, I was invited to report to the statewide conference of the Southern Baptist churches meeting in Roanoke, Virginia. There I was made most welcome, and the delegates were thrilled to hear of the tremendous impact made by the Virginian pastors. I also had the joy of preaching at First Baptist Church, Roanoke, Virginia.

21

A Wider Ministry

During my years at Grand Bay/Browns Flat churches, I also had the joy of preaching at roll call services, conducting evangelistic crusades, and speaking at missionary rallies in Nova Scotia, New Brunswick, Prince Edward Island, and Campobello Island. I recall that at a week of meetings on Campobello Island (the summer home of the Rosvelt Family), the pastor and I went to visit in the community. We visited with a bachelor who was in his early sixties. After some general conversation, I asked him about his relationship with Jesus Christ. He made it very clear that he had never had much time for the Lord, the church, or religion. I asked him what he was going to do about it. This was his answer: "Well, I've lived this long without seeing a need to do anything about it, so I might as well let the tail go with the hide." Matter closed.

I preached at another evangelistic crusade on the South Shore of Nova Scotia. The meetings lasted for ten days. The pastor was single. He had obviously been a good student, which was evident by the number of degrees he had; however, he couldn't relate to the people. One day after making some key visits, followed by a wonderful meeting in the evening, he finally opened up to me. We talked and prayed into the early hours of the morning. His big concern was his difficulty in relating. I reminded him that it was important to communicate at the level of the people's understanding. After all, we're told in Scripture that this was what Jesus did and that *"the common people heard Him gladly"* (Mark 12:37).

The attendances at the meetings grew steadily night after night. Many stepped out to make their commitment to Jesus Christ. That was in the late 1950s. Now fifty years later, I'm sitting on a cushion that is a reminder of those memorable days. One of those who made a commitment to Jesus Christ was the principal of the local Consolidated High School. His wife, who had prayed for him for many years, was so excited. Before I left that community, she presented me with a lovely cushion cover. It has been on my desk chair all these years and is a constant reminder of God's faithfulness.

While ministering in Grand Bay, we developed a very close friendship with the Rev. Ken and Mrs. Morrison and family. We shared a lot of fun times together. In those days of limited finances, we even shared our Kraft dinners enhanced with tuna ... always making sure that our combined families got fed first and then we had what was left. We always had an exciting time getting our Christmas trees from the woods behind the Grand Bay parsonage. Then we had the fun of tobogganing and skiing on the hill. There were no computer games in those days; we made our own fun and games outdoors.

Sometimes, upon reflection, we recognize the enabling grace of God in trying to cope with all of the demands and responsibilities of a very busy, challenging, and growing pastorate. Some statistics may give some idea of just how busy we were. I had an average of seven preaching responsibilities each week. This was made up of four Sunday services where I preached a different message at each service, since a number of people would go from one church to the other. I also taught one Sunday school class and conducted two mid-week services. Then there were always extra committee meetings from time to time. During my four years of ministry there, I baptized forty-six people, and in addition we received thirty-one by transfer from other Baptist churches. I had thirty-five funerals and seven weddings. All of this kept me very busy. In addition to all of this, I had pastors' meetings and conferences. My wife was also kept very busy with the lady's ministries, conducting a Sunday school class, and speaking at missionary meetings in different churches. She also sang quite frequently on special occasions.

22

Our Move to the Dairy Town

In 1959, the pastor of Sussex Baptist Church invited me to come to the church to conduct a week of evangelistic meetings. The pastor of the church was Rev. M. Murray MacLeod, a fellow Scot. He had served as a missionary in India. While in Sussex, he had a very effective ministry as an expository preacher and pastor. The Lord was pleased to bless this evangelistic outreach in bringing many to faith in the Lord Jesus Christ. At that point in time, I didn't realize how much this week would redirect my ministry. One day I had a call from the chairman of the pastoral committee, extending an invitation to become the next pastor of Sussex Baptist Church. After giving it much thought and prayer, and in agreement with my wife, I accepted the call to that church. As has been the pattern of my whole ministry, I didn't know what my salary would be until after I had accepted the call. I have always been convinced that the Lord would take care of us at all times.

I would be moving from one end of Kings County to the other, but would still be part of the same Baptist district. Sussex is a beautiful small dairy town, famous for it is production of milk, butter, cheese, ice cream, and ginger ale. The town is located half way between St. John and Moncton, just off the Trans Canada Highway. One of the army headquarters was located in the town. It also had a hospital, which originally had been a part of the army camp. It had a primary school and a district high school. The RCMP was responsible for policing the town and the surrounding area.

Sussex had a weekly cattle auction, because it was the centre of large dairy farms. The local newspaper was called *The Kings County Record*. There was a large saw mill and also a furniture factory. Most of the businesses in town were owned and operated by members of the Baptist church. The principal of the high school was also the treasurer of the church. Many of the teachers were also members. The postmaster, the town clerk, and the veterinarian were all deacons of the church. The Sussex Baptist Church was the largest church in town, with something in excess of six hundred members and an undetermined number of adherents.

The church had a tall steeple with a bell. This bell not only called the people to worship on Sunday, but also served to warn of fire in any part of the town. As part of the church in Sussex, there was also a small country church a few miles outside of town. This country church had a unique feature. The women sat on one side of the church and the men sat on other.

Moving to Sussex from Grand Bay was a major change for us. The parsonage of the Sussex church was located right next door to the church building. It had a large double living room across the front of the house, a dining room, a very large kitchen, one large bathroom, and five bedrooms. Attached to the house was the pastor's study and church office.

A major problem was that we were leaving a parsonage that was fully furnished. There was the matter of finding sufficient and suitable furniture to furnish our new home. We decided to purchase new furniture for the living room, dining room, and master bedroom. We had heard of a family in a community next to Grand Bay who had a garage full of furniture they might be interested in selling to us. We decided to investigate, and what we found was incredible. There were beds, tables, chairs, dressers, and more. The question we now faced was that of cost. The people told us to pick out all the things we would like to have and then they would decide on a price. They asked for $120, and I offered $100 even, which was the price we paid. Again we had confirmation that the Lord makes provision. We were able to furnish the whole parsonage in Sussex. We bade farewell to our four congregations in Grand Bay, Brown's Flat, Greenwich Hill, and Oak Point, and moved to Sussex. This was the spring of 1960.

What a change it was to move from four smaller churches to concentrating my ministry in one larger church. One of the significant side benefits I discovered was the fact that I would be receiving a significantly larger salary and reducing the number of miles I would be putting on my car. When we moved to Sussex, however, it wasn't all plain sailing. In fact, one prominent lady, a member of the church who never went to business meetings, was appalled to hear that the church had called a "cowboy evangelist." She was used to the church having several pastors who had doctoral degrees. Now here was I, and my theology had never been doctored!

23

A Challenging and Exciting Ministry

When starting in a new ministry, my first messages set the tone for my ministry. That first Sunday morning I made it clear where I stood with regard to the Gospel. I preached from Romans 1:16: *"For I am not ashamed of the gospel of Christ, for it is the power of God to salvation for everyone who believes, for the Jew first and also for the Greek."* On the first Sunday evening, I shared about my call to the ministry based on Isaiah 6. There need be no doubt as to where I stood.

It was a busy time getting acquainted with various groups within the church, visiting the members and adherents of the church, assessing the strengths and weaknesses within the congregation, becoming acquainted with the pulse of the community, and measuring the spiritual tenor of the society as a whole. Some statistics will indicate just how busy and involved I became in that first year. This covers from March to the end of December, 1960. There were three hundred and ninety three meetings; I preached two hundred and fifty eight messages; had sixty-nine interviews, twenty funerals, and nineteen weddings; eight were received into membership; I made five hundred and seventy nine hospital calls, one hundred and thirty shut-in calls, and two hundred and thirty eight calls on members. I remember in our Pastoral Theology class in college being constantly reminded that "a home going pastor makes a church going people." In this way I was better able to minister to the needs of the people.

For the first nine months my wife did my office work and I had no assistant, yet I still managed to spend time with my wife and family. Some other changes were on the way. Around this time we discovered that my wife was pregnant with our fourth child. Little did we realize how this event would change a long time tradition at Sussex Baptist Church. For many years the Baptist and the United Churches had joint services during July and August. I was not too happy about this arrangement, and fully realized that breaking this tradition would not be easy or popular. However, circumstances were such that the Lord provided a way out. Our child was to be born in August of 1960. By July and August my wife was in no condition to consider travelling anywhere on vacation. This meant that we would be at home for those two months. Furthermore, our attendance at the church was growing significantly, and I felt that it didn't merit joining together with another congregation on the grounds of a summer slump.

I discussed the situation with the deacons and we concluded that we should continue our own services through July and August. This was to be announced at our quarterly business meetings in April. As expected, it met with some opposition: "We've always done it this way!" At the business meetings one elderly, unmarried lady asked why I wasn't going away on vacation. I explained that with our baby due in August we would be in town all summer, so I planned to keep preaching. So the pending birth of our daughter, Janilee Joan, forever changed history as well as a well grounded tradition.

That summer was one of great blessings. We had wonderful attendances, and our weekly giving was greatly improved. Our daughter, Janilee Joan, was born on August 24, 1960, in the Sussex Memorial Hospital while I was conducting the prayer and Bible study meeting at the church. It's hard to believe that she made such an impact at her birth and forever changed the history of Sussex Baptist Church.

The wider ministry of our Baptist churches in St. John and the Kings County was experiencing some significant developments. A major one was an increased concern for the children and youth of our area. Just prior to my leaving Grand Bay and moving to Sussex, a committee had been established to address these concerns. The committee was made up of three pastors: Rev. Kenneth Morrison of Edith Avenue Baptist Church, Rev. Ralph Galbraith of the Rothsay Baptist Church, and me, Rev. A. Morris Russell. Periodically the three of us tramped around the county checking various sites that might be suitable as a place to establish a camp ground, but without success. We expanded our committee and added a few laymen. After I moved to Sussex, I was a little closer to an area where there were potential sites that would be suitable for a youth camp. God, in His own time, introduced us to a property that has proved to be ideal in so many ways.

The property was located on the shore of Cassidy Lake, about fifteen minutes from Sussex and fifty-eight minutes from St. John. It consisted of approximately four hundred acres with a beaver pond, some woodland, and several open fields. There was a farm house, two large barns, several small sheds, and a drilled well. The whole farm, with all the assets, was for sale to cover back taxes. The price was approximately $1,200.00. Along the shore of the lake were three small cottages. The people who owned them didn't want to continue staying there, realizing there would be lots of young people in their back yard, so they were willing to sell. The price for the three cottages was $1,200.00. So for $2,400.00, we had an ideal setting for a youth camp, which eventually enabled us to serve the whole family.

In 1961, through the donations from our Baptist churches in St. John and Kings County, the property was finally purchased. Mr. Everett MacLeod, one of our deacons, and I spent several days cutting the lines on the property—in other words, marking the boundaries. Work began in earnest to prepare the property for the first camping season in the summer of 1961. The official dedication of the property was set for June of that year. The first building to be erected was the kitchen, complete with a commercial gas stove. Arrangements were made to borrow ten army bell tents, along with a large marquee, to serve as a dining and meeting area. A number of wooden platforms were made on which to erect the tents. Two large multi-cubicle outhouses were built to provide toilet facilities for the children.

Excitement was rising as we finalized the plans for the dedication of the campgrounds. We encouraged the churches in St. John to hire buses to transport children and adults to the dedication service. Our rural churches were encouraged to car pool and bring the adults and the children to participate in the grand opening. The dedication took place on a Saturday afternoon in June of 1961. We waited with bated breath, not knowing exactly what the response would be. On that special day under glorious sunshine the people started to arrive by bus and car. What a sight! About eight or ten buses lined up along that country road, cars were parked in the upper field, and some one thousand adults and children arrived to take part in that special occasion.

They enjoyed their picnic lunch and took part in the various games that were held. One of the major highlights generated exciting chaos amongst the children. One of our men in the Sussex church owned his own plane. We made arrangements with him to make several passes over the place where the people were gathered. With each pass he emptied bags of wrapped candies. There was a mad scramble by the children to get as many candies as they could. They had lots of fun. This was followed by the formalities of the day. Dr. Arthur Vincent, one of our senior pastors, spoke on this occasion. There was singing and a prayer of dedication. This was an outstanding success.

In the early days of organizing the camp, we decided that we needed a suitable name for it. Contest forms were sent out to all of our churches to solicit suggestions. Eventually we settled on "Tulakadik," which is a Mic-Mac Indian name for "camping ground." Tulakadik has grown beyond all expectations; at this writing, it has been in operation for over fifty years. To God be the glory. For further information on the camp, visit www.camptulakadik.com.

24

Pastoral Help

Around the same time as the camp opening, I received help with the addition of a pastoral assistant. Let me share with you how all that came about, and then I'll come back to the issue of the camp ministry. In the fall of 1960, I counselled Mr. and Mrs. Francis Mabey, who had felt the call of God to prepare for the pastoral ministry. While I was the pastor in Grand Bay, Mr. and Mrs. Mabey transferred their membership from the Victoria Street Baptist Church in St. John to the Baptist church in Grand Bay. They became a great asset to the church and very much involved in the ministry there. It was not too long before Mr. Mabey became a deacon in the church. Shortly after I left Grand Bay to become the pastor of Sussex Baptist Church, Mr. Mabey became aware of God's call up on his life.

On September 13, 1960, Mr. and Mrs. Mabey were "farewelled" from Grand Bay church. Mr. Mabey enrolled as a student at the Baptist Bible College in Moncton, so they moved as a family to Sussex Corner, and Mr. Mabey became my assistant. His primary ministry was to some of the rural churches, and he also conducted a Sunday school in their home. God had gifted him as a speaker and also blessed him with a wonderful singing voice. His wife played the organ and was a very capable leader. At that time they had two children. As my associate he also gave valued leadership at Camp Tulakadik.

Let me returned to the story of the camp. There was much work to be done for the opening of that first camping season. My wife and Mrs. Mabey spent time painting buoys to be used to mark off the swimming area in the lake. In the middle of all of this, Mrs. Mabey had to be rushed to the hospital where she delivered her son, Mark, two weeks early. She always claimed that travelling over the bumpy gravel roads to the camp was the reason for the early delivery!

We had one day of rain during that first week of camp. The rain was so heavy that the water ran through the tents. Not too many camps could boast of sleeping quarters with running water! Some interesting incidents bring back many memories. The original kitchen at the camp was ruled over by Mr. Mabey, who was our chef. He always did an excellent job of providing very substantial meals for the campers, and he was always very well organized. But even perfection has its flaws. One day he made a huge pot of beef stew. It was about thirty minutes before the time for serving dinner when I stepped into the kitchen to see if everything was on schedule. Just at that moment, he was transferring the pot of stew from the stove to the warming plate. Next thing we knew, Mr. Mabey had dropped the pot and the stew was all over the kitchen floor. He shouted to me: "Close the door, don't let anyone in!" While I stood guard, he hurriedly scooped the stew back into the pot and boiled it over again. Not a bit was lost. I chuckled when later I heard some of the campers say that it was the best stew he'd ever made! What the eye doesn't see, the heart doesn't grieve over!

Into the second year of Camp Tulakadik we built a large ridged frame structure lodge. This housed the large dining hall, the well equipped kitchen and cook's quarters, and later a basement. Churches around the association sponsored the building of individual cabins. A tuck shop and other facilities have since been added. Memories of campfires down by the lake still linger. Many life changing decisions were made there. Now children, youth, and families can enjoy what Tulakadik has to offer. The original vision of three pastors, later committee members, deacons like Darrell Liston and Dr. Eric Hicks, missionaries, leaders, and many others, has borne fruit in young lives. The initial investment of $2,400.00 has brought incredible results. To God be all the glory.

Office Help

As time moved on, the office work increased and my wife's work in the house and with the family demanded more of her time. This meant that she was increasingly limited in what she could do in the office. Eventually the church decided to acquire the services of a secretary. We were led to one of our own girls in the church, Edith Galley. She was very well equipped and understood the workings of the church. What a blessing for the church as she was able to relieve me of a lot of day to day office work to which I could not give proper attention. She fielded telephone calls, prepared the weekly bulletin, took care of correspondence, and spent endless hours bringing the church records and files up to date. We did a major overhaul on the church membership list by removing names of people who had died or moved away, and brought all the addresses, PO Box numbers, and telephone numbers up to date. To help with these major tasks, we developed an office help committee of ladies who did a wonderful job and also enjoyed a special fellowship.

Pastoral Changes

In 1962, Pastor Mabey received a call to pastor four churches in the Moncton area of New Brunswick. This included Berry Mills, Steeves Mountain, and The Gorge. He had a very good ministry there. He went to do some further study at one of the American Baptist seminaries. This involved a concentrated course of study. While there, he donated blood several times to help cover the cost of tuition. One can literally saw that it cost him blood, sweat, and tears! Later on he received a call to pastor a Baptist church at Wilson's Beach on Campobello Island, an island located in the Bay of Fundy just off the coast of Maine (it's well known as the summer home of FDR Roosevelt and family).

I had the joy of having a part in the ordination of Mr. Mabey. When I was the pastor of First Baptist Church in St. John's, I had him come to Newfoundland to conduct an evangelistic crusade. Pastor Mabey spent the rest of his days and ministry on the Island until the Lord took him home. At this writing, Mrs. Mabey and some of their family still live and work on the island.

25

The Continuing Saga of Sussex

Our work in Sussex continued and blossomed. I never did have another assistant there; however, I had a wonderful band of very capable laymen in the church, some of whom had come to know the Lord during my ministry. They were not only a great asset to the church in teaching and leadership roles, but their ministry reached out to the rural churches in the surrounding communities as well. They went out in teams Sunday after Sunday, conducting services in these small churches without pastors.

The church building in Sussex was a wooden frame structure. It had served well for many years, but it became evident that the building was deteriorating and showed signs of needing major repairs. Along with this, the sanctuary couldn't comfortably accommodate the ever increasing numbers that were attending. A stop-gap arrangement was made until a survey could be carried out and advice could be received from an architect. In the meantime, we installed an extensive sound system. Microphones were installed on the pulpit, and speakers were installed in the Sunday school assembly area. This was before the availability of closed circuit television. This area could comfortably seat at least one hundred people of an overflow congregation. Our deacons took turns overseeing the overflow. The architect brought in an estimate indicating what it would cost to renovate the existing building. In addition to the proposal to do major renovations, the architect brought in a proposal to tear down the old church and build a new brick building. In the meantime, during one of our morning services, a piece of the ceiling fell down and hit one of the trustees—a visible reminder that something should be done.

The deacons discussed all the pros and cons of the work. Their final, unanimous decision was to recommend to the church that we tear down and build new. At the business meeting of the church, this recommendation was presented. However, here we encountered a glitch. In spite of the fact that the deacons had discussed and agreed unanimously to recommend that we go ahead and demolish the old building and build new, one of the deacons stood at the business meeting and voiced his opposition to the proposal. The rest of the deacons were flabbergasted. This opposing voice resulted in splitting the vote of the church; however, the majority voted in favour of going ahead with the recommendation. Following the business meeting I called a meeting of the deacons. There I expressed my deep disappointment in the deacon who had originally supported the proposal and then changed his mind in the business meeting. He didn't appreciate the discipline given him by the board, so he stayed away from the next deacons' meeting and absented himself from Sunday worship for several weeks. Some of the deacons suggested that I should go and visit the said deacon, but I didn't agree. I explained that this should be done by the deacons. I discovered later on that over twenty years earlier, this same deacon had opposed the then proposal to build a new church!

On the day following this incident, a very interesting event took place. I was walking through the sanctuary when I noticed an offering envelope on the floor under one of the pews. Picking it up, I couldn't help but notice the name on it. It was the offering envelope of the deacon in question. The amount was clearly marked—-twenty-five cents. Enough said. Eventually two deacons were appointed to visit the recalcitrant deacon. I agreed to join them on that visit. Although he returned to worship, he did resign from the deacons' board.

The new brick church was eventually built. It also included a beautiful smaller chapel and offices. Eventually, a new Christian Education building was built, as well as a new parsonage. The work continued to grow.

Two major evangelistic crusades at that time resulted in many people surrendering their lives to the Lord Jesus Christ. One of those crusades was conducted by the Rev. D. Bruce Moore, who was serving as the convention evangelist. We had an incredible response. One evening I detected a bit of commotion in the choir behind me. A few minutes later a man from the choir came through the front door of the church and marched down the aisle. I came down from the platform to meet him at the front. As I shook hands with him, I asked him why he had come.

"I want to be saved," was his response.

I was startled by his answer. He had grown up in church, and his family was connected to the church. Some critics told me afterward that his conversion wouldn't last, as he was too big a sinner. But it did! He soaked up all the teaching he could get. He never missed prayer meeting or Bible study, and he became one of our most active laymen in the church. He even went out with the teams to minister in some of the small country churches. I remember one Sunday afternoon I baptized twelve people who had come to know the Lord through the ministry of our laymen in one country church. The evening after this man came to the Lord, his wife yielded to the call of Christ. She was an English war bride who had been brought up in the Anglican church. She was gloriously saved. Eventually she became a teacher's assistant, volunteering her time in our school for the physically and mentally challenged She was also a great help to my wife looking after the children, particularly our middle son who needed a lot of care since he had Legge Perthes disease.

While at the Sussex church, I was very much involved in the Leighton Ford crusades throughout the Maritime provinces, the Lane Adams crusade in Kings County, and the Billy Graham crusade in Saint John, which was the climax of all the crusades throughout New Brunswick. One Sunday afternoon over four hundred stepped out in response to the invitation.

26

Changes

We don't always find it easy to make or accept change, yet in the ministry and in the church we need to assess the immediate so that we can effectively deal with the ultimate. In this we recognize that we don't move from the centrality of the Word of God and the Lordship of Jesus Christ. It's self evident that we maintain the proclamation of the message of the Gospel while making a wise analysis of the methods. Shortly after I became pastor of Sussex Baptist Church, we became aware of the need to make some changes in our approach to the ministry of a rapidly growing church. Not only did this necessitate planning to provide more space, but also the need to plan some program changes. We were blessed with a beautiful Casavant pipe organ and a lovely piano, and we had a highly trained and talented organist. There were several trained singers in our choir, an incredible boys' choir (with several boy sopranos), and a very talented girls' choir. Both of these choirs were led by highly skilled leaders and musicians. I revelled in the incredible music of worship and praise.

We used the Baptist hymnal, which contained so many of the majestic hymns so full of sound theology with easy-to-follow accompaniment. We had a congregation that enjoyed and participated in the singing, making me feel that the whole congregation was a choir. I came from a very musical family where most of us played instruments and sang as soloists or in trios. I was playing the old pump organ in our home when I was only seven years old. I played several instruments, particularly the accordion and the guitar. Before I committed my life and talents to the work of the Lord, I also played Scottish dance music. In my younger years I sang in a trio, and while in college I sang in and played for our college quartet. In our home church I led our youth choir of some thirty voices. I say all of that to make it known that I do have an appreciation for "good" music and musical talent.

In the morning services, I largely preached in an expository style as well as using a series of themes, all geared to feeding the believer and fostering Christian growth. I also have majored on evangelistic preaching, largely in the evening services, thus following the injunction of Scriptures to the pastor to "do the work of an evangelist" (2 Timothy 4:5). My desire was to make the evening service more conducive to reaching the unsaved in the community, so the decision was made by the deacons to purchase a new Gospel song book for use in the evening service while still continuing to use the Baptist hymnal in the morning. This change needed to be approved at a congregational meeting, which it duly was. Our organist was furious at the change and told me that she wouldn't use the new hymn book in the evening. I reminded her that this was a church decision, and if she had attended the business meeting she could have voiced her objections then.

The first Sunday evening that we used the new books was a riot. Her objection was expressed in the way that she played the organ. The next day I took the opportunity to visit with her. I pointed out that since this was a decision of the church, and would enhance our evening service, we should really work together. From then on we became the very best of friends. After moving to Newfoundland I would occasionally visit back in Sussex, and she would insist that I make sure she was included in my visits. Later when she was diagnosed with cancer, I was one of the first that she wanted to see.

On our primitive television set in Sussex, on Feb 20, 1962, we witnessed John Glenn be the first man in space when he circled the earth three times in four hours and fifty-six minutes. It was also while in Sussex on June 13, 1962, that my mother died in Scotland. During my time there, I also had the opportunity to speak at many of the service clubs, school assemblies, and civic events, such as the dedication of the town council.

Mrs. Hicks, a nurse, made special pants for our son, Ian, which would fit around the casts he had on when he was being treated for Legge Perthes disease. I also had some medical issues at that time. While in Sussex I had four surgeries to repair hernias. Two were done in Sussex and two in Saint John. During one of these spells in hospital, my doctor, Dr. Russell Bryant, was absolutely puzzled as to why I was not recuperating. One day as he was making his rounds in the hospital, he stopped by my room and found seven preachers visiting me. I saw him standing at the door shaking his head and then turning away. A few minutes later, my nurse came in and said, "Gentlemen, doctors orders … you must leave at once." I wasn't allowed visitors for three days, and I experienced significant improvement.

I spearheaded the challenge to stop another liquor license being granted in town, and we were successful. We were blessed with having several retired pastors in our congregation. They were so supportive of my ministry and would preach for me when I had to be somewhere else. I always appreciated their wise counsel. At Christmas time the church always honoured them with a special gift.

We had the joy of welcoming two Norwegian girls who wanted to come to Canada to work and practice their English since they had trained as teachers in Norway. They were family to friends in Norway, so we were able to get them placed with a well known Baptist family in Saint John, New Brunswick. They would always spend time with us on their days off. Around this time we had the joy of arranging for and welcoming some more pastors from Scotland who wished to serve in Canada. Two young men from our church felt the call of God to the ministry, so they set about training to that end. At my time of writing they are serving the Lord in the Atlantic provinces. One of them was following several of his uncles and cousins who served as pastors and missionaries. The other left a very secure secular job and trained for the ministry. When God was working on his life he would call the parsonage and say, "I need to talk to you." We would get in his car and go out to a quiet country road and sit there and talk and pray about all the ramifications of such a decision. Since that time, I've conducted evangelistic crusades in two of his churches.

One of the trustees of the church had health issues and he was failing fast. I had a call from Dr. Bryant to say that I should come to visit him since he was failing very quickly. When I arrived I went upstairs to the bedroom. Gathered around his bed were the family and Dr. Bryant. We sang a hymn and I prayed. As soon as I finished praying, our dear brother sat up in bed, raised both his arms, shouted "Hallelujah," fell backwards, and went peacefully into the presence of his Saviour. What a testimony to all around.

One day I received a call to say that Mrs. Jonah had fallen while working in her garden and had fractured her hip. She was ninety-nine years old and from a very prominent family in town. She had been a teacher in a country school out near Fundy Park. Following her discharge from hospital, she was admitted to a nursing home. While there, she celebrated her one hundredth birthday. I went to visit with her on that occasion. Sitting by her bed, I did some reminiscing with her. In the course of the conversation, I said to her, "Mrs. Jonah, I'm sure that you must frequently think back to the 'good old days.'"

"What was good about the old days?" she retorted. "Main Street Sussex was mud; out at my school I had to pour hot water on the old pump before I could pump water. I had to light the stove to get the schoolhouse warm before the children came. What was good about the old days?" She was one amazing lady.

The year 1964 opened to a new world for me. I had a brother and sister-in-law who were deaf mutes. To many people these were handicaps. To these two people, these were challenges. My brother attended school in Edinburgh where he excelled. He loved sports. He was capped for cricket, and he won several swimming championships. After school he became West of Scotland champion wrestler, Cumberland style. He was never unemployed all his working days. His wife became an accomplished seamstress. Having them in our family made me very sensitive to the needs of children with challenges. My immediate response would be "What can I do to help?" While in Sussex, this concern led me to become involved with C.A.R.C., now known as the "Canadian Association for the Physically and Mentally Challenged." I was aware that there were several children in the community who had some of these challenges, and nothing was being done for them. I shared my concern with a few key church and community leaders. I was appointed the first president in Sussex. The outcome of all of this was that a teacher and helper were hired, and a school was started in our church facilities. This was a very rewarding investment. To see the children develop and reach their potential was most encouraging. Eventually two of the service organizations in town bought land and built a building. Part of the facility was made available to house the school. Eventually a sheltered workshop was provided and some of the teenagers were gainfully employed.

We enjoyed Sussex and the many beautiful surrounding areas, so we decided that it might be a good thing to build a cottage where we could find refuge periodically from a very busy life and ministry. We heard about a family who owned overnight cabins in the Norton area and had listed them for sale. A new by-pass highway had been put through that took the traffic from the old, well travelled road, so the cabins were no longer a viable proposition. In March, 1965, we went to investigate and ended up buying one of the double units for $300.00. It was complete with toilet, shower, and wash basin. It had two bedrooms, a living area come kitchen, and a full verandah. It was completely fitted with lights and electrical outlets.

With the help of one of my farmer friends from Poodiac who had all the equipment, we jacked up the cottage. I made arrangements with a friend who had a flatbed tractor/trailer to have it hauled where we wanted to locate it. After searching around various likely places, we settled on a site up the Dutch Valley. We talked with James Parlee who owned a farm and agreed on selling us about an acre and a half of land, which included a section of the Trout Creek. We gave the cottage the name "Solbakken," which was also the name of our place where we lived while we worked and ministered in Lapland.

We got all the necessary permits from the police and highways departments. In the early hours of May 10, 1965, we moved the cottage to the prepared foundation at Parlee's farm. By May 20, we had the electrical hook up taken care of by the hydro commission. By June, I had driven a water spike through the gravel to the water table, hooked up a storage tank, and buried a septic tank. Now we had running water and a flush toilet. Shortly afterwards, I installed a hot water tank. We had all the necessary conveniences. What a place to find relaxation and fun! Fish were caught in the creek, and the children from the farm and our children enjoyed the swim-hole. We had BBQ's and corn boils, and lots of visitors with trailers, tents, and RV's. We enjoyed it for about fifteen years, and then sold it for $4, 000.00. Some years later we saw it on the market for $12,000.00.

In September of 1965, Sussex Baptist Church celebrated its one hundredth anniversary. It was a wonderful time of rejoicing and reflection as we recounted the many blessings of God through the ministry of the church in the town and surrounding areas. Now we were on the verge of building new facilities. Several of the former pastors were able to return and share in the celebrations. Around this time, two of our young men committed their lives to serving the Lord in the pastoral ministry, and they are still serving Him today. It was also around this time that our middle son was diagnosed with Legge Perthes disease.

About this time some of my former classmates in college expressed interest in coming to Canada to the Baptist ministry. It was my privilege to help them realize their dream. In the Sussex church we were able to convene a missions conference. This had a great impact in having the church extend its ministry beyond our North American borders. We had no youth pastor, but we had a wonderful group of youth leaders and a strong youth ministry. We had retreats and both summer and winter camps. We often had toboggan parties. On one such trip, the guys talked me into racing them downhill on a toboggan. The snow-covered hill was slick and steep, so we lined up, and at a given signal we were off down the hill. I was the tallest and heaviest; therefore, I picked up a greater speed, outstripping them all. But hidden danger was ahead. What I thought was a large snow bank happened to be snow covered boulders. When my toboggan hit, it stopped, but I kept going. Flying off the toboggan, my knees caught the front and I ended up in the bushes at the other side of the road. I was crippled. The next day was Sunday, and I was scheduled to preach. To do this, I had to sit because my knees were in such pain.

One other time we were out to Tulakadik for a weekend retreat. We had a wonderful time; however, in such situations the leader is last to bed and first up in the morning. I came into church to preach at the morning service while other leaders stayed with the young people who closed off their retreat after lunch. I was feeling very tired, so when I got up to preach, I asked the congregation to forgive me if I fell asleep while I was preaching, in the way I forgave those who fell asleep each Sunday morning while I was preaching.

In my ministry in Sussex, I became involved with a fair amount of counselling. It was then that I appreciated the classes offered through Acadia Divinity School on "Pastoral Clinical Training."

As part of our congregation in Sussex, we had a very dear retired missionary lady, Mrs. Gullison, known to most of us as Granny Gullison. She was a prayer warrior. She wrote to scores of missionaries and kept in touch with many pastors. She rented an apartment from one of the other ladies in the church who bore testimony to Granny Gullison's prayer life. She would be on her knees every morning, praying for missionaries and pastors by name. I was included in her daily intercessions along with my wife and our family. How we missed her when the Lord called her home.

Close to the time of our leaving for St. John's, one of the prominent members in our church died very suddenly. This lady had been a very prominent leader in the Ladies Missionary Society of the denomination. In January of 1966, I had taken her husband to the hospital in St. John. He was in his nineties. Shortly afterwards, he was transferred to a long-term care facility. He was an amazing individual. From the age of nineteen he had served as a deacon in one of our large Baptist churches in the city of Saint John, New Brunswick. Upon his marriage to his second wife, he moved to Sussex. There he was soon added to the deacons' board, where he served faithfully.

In the meantime, his wife, in her late seventies, took ill and was admitted to the Sussex Memorial Hospital for urgent surgery. I visited her in hospital just a short time before she had surgery. We prayed together and committed her to the Lord, praying for God's wisdom for the surgeon. The doctor, a personal friend, said he would call me as soon as the surgery was over. Three hours after I had had prayer with her, the doctor called with the sad news that she had died during surgery. What a shock to me, to the church, and to the community. Neither she nor her husband had any family. With the help of the lawyer, my wife and I made all the plans for the funeral. Her husband couldn't comprehend what had happened, since he had a severe case of dementia. This was an extremely emotional time for all of us. Shortly afterwards, her husband also died. Two pillars of the church ... gone in one fell swoop.

As an aside to this story, let me share the following incident. The "Last Will and Testament" of the husband and wife were written, assuming that the husband would die first because of his age. His estate would then pass to his wife. The plan was that when the wife died, the combined estate would then be distributed to missions and to the training of pastors, with the remaining portion equally divided between the three men who had been their pastors while they were members of Sussex Baptist Church, of which I was one. However, that didn't happen. So the only chance of my ever being rich was lost forever. We are reminded, "*Do not lay up for yourselves treasures on earth, where moth and dust destroy ...*" (Matthew 6:19). So I have to be content with my treasures in Heaven. I must be content with such things as I have.

During this run up time to our departure for Newfoundland, we applied for our Canadian citizenship. We would move from being "Landed Immigrants" to Canadian citizens, with all its rights, responsibilities, and privileges. This is a step we have never regretted.

Our last days in Sussex were really hectic. Into the mix of packing and getting ready to move to Newfoundland were thrown farewell parties with the different church organizations, community activities, and the church farewell. This was an extremely emotional experience. The church presented us with a beautiful stereo cabinet and money. Oh, how we loved those dear people! Our second last Sunday was a great day of blessing. I had the joy of baptizing fourteen at the morning service. In the evening service I welcomed a total of twenty three into membership. To God alone is the glory.

Our middle son, Ian, was back in hospital to have his Legge Perthes' cast changed. Two of my deacons approached me and said, "Pastor you shouldn't be going to Newfoundland with your son requiring this treatment. They have such limited facilities."

"God never makes mistakes," I responded. "He has clearly called us to Newfoundland. In the light of this He will take care of the needs for Ian."

My final Sunday was charged with emotion. I was suffering from a very bad case of laryngitis and running a bit of a fever. However, in spite of that, with God's enabling grace and some medication, I had great liberty in preaching. The church was filled to overflowing. So ended a very fruitful and wonderful ministry in the dairy town of Sussex, New Brunswick.

27

Britain's Oldest Colony, Canada's Newest Province

The story of our move to Newfoundland unfolds. The details were fascinating each step of the way. We were on the move early since it took some time to co-ordinate our departure. Ian had to be picked up at the local hospital. We had secured the services of St. John's Ambulance to do the transfer to the airport. My wife and our youngest son, Erik, accompanied Ian in the ambulance to the airport in Moncton. We had secured two extra seats on the plane so that Ian could lie flat out. I drove to Halifax with the other three children. There the car had to be loaded onto the boat to be taken to St. John's, Newfoundland. We then boarded the plane in Halifax that was carrying my wife and other children. Everything went just like clockwork. In those days there was no problem with security. The weather was beautiful. We were on our way to Newfoundland.

The welcoming committee from First Baptist Church, St. John's, was there to meet us. We were whisked away to Hotel Newfoundland. By this time we were all very tired, and I had a temperature over 104 degrees. However, we were informed that there was a medical doctor who was a member of the church. He was called and prescribed medication and ordered me to stay in bed. The next day my wife and family went to the parsonage to supervise the unloading of our furniture. The day following we were able to move into our new home.

While standing in the living room and talking with the chairman of the board, I mentioned my son's problem with Legge Perthes Disease, and inquired as to the facilities for children's health care. He took me to the living room window and pointed out a large white building complex.

"That," he said, "is the new Charles A. Janeway Child Health Centre. It opened just a few weeks ago."

God's Word was proven true once again: *"Trust in the Lord with all your heart, and lean not on your own understanding; in all your ways acknowledge Him, and He shall direct your paths"* (Proverbs 3:5–6). God knew our need and met that need even before we needed it. But there is more. If we had stayed in New Brunswick, we would have paid for specialized treatment. Here in Newfoundland, the health care for children was free from birth to age eighteen years of age. This covered hospital, treatment, medicine, and therapy costs. If the child had lengthy hospitalization, special teachers were provided so that each child could keep up with his or her schooling. My son, in spite of long stays in the hospital, never missed a grade in school. Ian was transferred to the Children's Hospital right away. There he came under the care of Dr. Schapter, who at that time was Canada's top authority in the treatment of Legge Perthes Disease: *"And my God shall supply all your need according to His riches in glory by Christ Jesus"* (Philippians 4:19). We immediately got our children settled in schools that were operated by the United Church. The younger ones went to Curtis Elementary, and the older ones were settled in Macpherson Junior High.

During the first week in Newfoundland, I was introduced to radio and television. This would become a significant part of my ministry during the next ten years. It would give great exposure to the church and the Gospel, and the wonderful thing was that it would all be free.

On March 3, I was officially inducted to the ministry of First Baptist Church, St. John's, Newfoundland. The church was filled to capacity. I became the second fulltime pastor of the very first Baptist church in Newfoundland. Besides those representing the denomination, other pastors from the city and the Mayor were in attendance.

As I started my ministry, it was very interesting to note how young the congregation was. The church was located very close to the campus of Memorial University, so we were able to attract a significant number of university students.

Within the first year of my ministry there, we were blessed to have a number of medical doctors from several fields of medicine join our congregation. Some of them taught at the university, some were associated with different hospitals, and still others were in private practice. I used to jokingly say that they would diagnose my physical condition during the service and at the end of the service they would recommend treatment. In addition, we had several professors. Some of the doctors and professors became involved in the ministry of the church.

They led youth groups, taught Sunday school classes, served on the deacons' board, and became members of different committees working in co-operation with members from Newfoundland, mainland Canada, the United Kingdom, Europe, and the U.S.A. We had a very interesting blend of international members and a melting pot of cultures.

Special Ministries

Early in our ministry we introduced the bus ministry. Eventually we had a fleet of five buses, some owned and some hired. They would fan out over the whole city on Sunday mornings, bringing in children, young people, and parents to our Sunday school each week. We had an incredible team of adults and young people who went out every Saturday morning. They visited different areas each week, inviting children and adults to church and Sunday school, and following up on those who had attended the previous week. Many people came to know Jesus Christ as Saviour and Lord.

One summer we had a team of thirty to forty young people and their leaders from Word of Life camp, Schroon Lake, New York State. They were with us for about five weeks. Our members boarded them and fed them, while some stayed at the church. This team made hundreds of calls in homes, at the shopping centres, and on the streets, sharing the message of the Gospel wherever they had opportunity. They conducted backyard clubs for the children and participated in the regular services of the church on Sundays and during the week. Our Sunday school grew from a handful of children to around two hundred and fifty of all ages. We eventually had to bring in two portable units to accommodate the increase in attendance. This outreach ministry also impacted the growth of our mid-week groups, along with attendance at our morning and evening services. Early in my ministry, I met a Newfoundlander who was interested in meeting the "Baptist pastor." He proceeded to inform me that there were "no snakes, no skunks, no squirrels, and no Baptists in Newfoundland." We were happy to inform him that, while we were not anxious to introduce snakes, skunks or squirrels, we were happy to report that there was a very rapid growth in the Baptist population. At that time there were Baptist churches in Gander, Corner Brook, Placentia Bay, and two in St. John's.

In Newfoundland, I was introduced to a very worthwhile radio and TV ministry. I had regular ministries on VOCM, VOWR, CBC-Radio and TV, and CJON Radio and TV. These opportunities included broadcasting our morning and evening services, conducting chapel devotions, hosting Pastor's Study, and many opportunities for interviews dealing with many topics of current affairs: abortion, politics, religion, and community issues. I was also given many opportunities to host talk shows. I had the unique opportunity to do some training in the development of techniques for radio and TV broadcasting under the tutelage of Roy Bonasteel of CBC renown and his very effective program, *Man Alive*. This training stood me in good stead throughout my future ministry.

Our first Easter in Newfoundland was a great opportunity to reach out into the community. On Palm Sunday, I started a week of services focusing on the theme of Easter that climaxed on Easter Sunday evening. We had services every evening with an evangelistic emphasis. Throughout the week a number of individuals came to personal faith in the Lord Jesus Christ.

On Easter Sunday morning, the church was filled to overflowing. The service was televised on CJON-TV and carried right across the province. This brought an incredible response in calls and notes of appreciation. One woman wrote to say that she got so caught up in watching television and listening to the message that the turkey burned. A man called to say that when the invitation was given at the end of the message, he committed his life to the Lord. Others started to attend our services as a result of that outreach.

The telephone was a much used instrument in the Newfoundland home. The Lord laid a burden on my heart to start a ministry by using the telephone. After some discussion with the Newfoundland Telephone Company, we realized that this was a possibility. The company provided us with a suitable machine, a separate number, and a reasonable fee. So the "Dial-a-Devotion" ministry was launched. Five mornings per week I recorded a two to three minute message of comfort, salvation, and assurance. This included a scripture verse, and concluded with a reference to First Baptist Church and an invitation to visit with us. Cards were printed, the number was included on all of our literature, and it was advertised in the local newspapers. This continued for many years after I was long gone from Newfoundland. It became a ministry that I introduced to two other churches and it continues to this day, using more up to date machinery. As a result of this ministry, people would recognize my voice in stores and offices, which gave me wonderful opportunities to minister. Housewives, shut-ins, the elderly, and the lonely found it a great source of blessing.

We had a very strong music ministry with highly trained and talented musicians, a wonderful choir, a ladies trio, a men's quartet, and soloists. All of this provided great support for the ministry of the Word and the presentation of special programs throughout the year. Our proximity to the campus of Memorial

University enabled us to have a great outreach amongst the university students. It was a joy and a privilege to speak to school assemblies on a regular basis. We had a good rapport with the principals and teachers.

Our Vacation Bible School became a wonderful outreach among the children. The dedication of so many of our church members was highly commendable. We ran into a major problem, however, when we became overcrowded in our limited church facilities. Fortunately, the Lord provided us with excellent facilities at no cost to us. A new elementary school was built a very short distance from our church and located in a rapidly growing area. The principal of the new MacDonald Drive Elementary School was a personal friend. Through his good graces, we had full use of the school auditorium and classrooms for two weeks each summer. How we praised God for such opportunities!

Ministry at the Charles A. Janeway Child Health Centre

The Charles A. Janeway Child Health Centre had been the American army base hospital. When the base closed, the hospital was turned over to the Newfoundland and Labrador provincial government. The facilities were completely renovated and turned into a children's hospital. This hospital served not only St. John's, but children from all over Newfoundland and Labrador who came for specialized treatment. This was the hospital where our middle son received regular and specialized treatment for his Legge Perthes Disease and later his Oliers Disease.

This hospital caught my attention, and God laid a burden on my heart for the children there and their families. God has a habit of placing His people in key places. One of our deacons, Dr. R. C. Way, a native Newfoundlander born in Flowers Cove, had returned to Newfoundland. He had trained at McGill University and served as a physician at the Sir Wilfred Grenfell Mission Hospital in St. Anthony, Newfoundland. Now he was the pediatric cardiologist at the children's hospital. The hospital administrator had also become my good friend, so I spoke with him and some of the staff about my interest and concern for the spiritual needs of the children. The outcome was very interesting. We were able to start a Sunday school for the children on Sunday afternoons. My wife and I and one of our deacons (a professor at the university), along with his wife constituted the core workers, with others helping from time to time.

A large area was set aside for our use. The children were brought in wheel chairs and stretchers, while some could walk. Many times family members would join in and staff would also attend. Using flannelgraph, filmstrips, and lots of choruses, we were able to minister to these wonderful children. Many of them were there with terminal illnesses. As a result of this, I became the unofficial chaplain of the hospital. I had many wonderful opportunities to minister to the parents who were struggling to cope with the uncertainty that often surrounded the medical concerns in the lives of their children.

Because of my interest in the hospital, I became the chaplain to be called in the event of major accidents or natural disasters. This involved a number of rehearsals and practice runs. One time we were hit by an incredible snowstorm that lasted for several days. The city and the surrounding areas shut down completely, and our son, Ian, took ill at home. When we talked with our doctor, he concluded that he should be taken to the Children's Hospital and thought that he might have to have an appendectomy. However, the snowstorm was raging and there were drifts as high as the telephone wires. My car was snowed in, and ambulances were having major problems. I contacted the fire department, and they agreed to send out one of their large four-wheel drive vehicles. So my oldest son, Stuart, started to dig a path from the front door to the edge of the road. I had to follow close behind him carrying my son, because the path was filling in as fast as it was being cleared. The fire department vehicle arrived in good time and we were transported to the Children's Hospital. Upon arrival, my son was checked by a doctor who immediately admitted him to the operating room for an appendectomy.

While this was going on, there was chaos in the hospital. Injured children had been brought in and were lying everywhere. The staff couldn't get home and the new staff couldn't get in. The senior nurse saw me and said, "I'm so glad you're here. Can you stay on and help?" So I stayed on through the rest of the evening and on to the next morning. It was a real live emergency situation. I wheeled patients to x-Ray and to the O.R. I spent time comforting the children who were in pain and also ministered to some of the parents who were waiting anxiously for results from the doctors. Our ministry grew and impacted the community in so many different ways.

28

Planting New Churches

Sometime before I arrived in St. John's, the previous pastor had wisely encouraged First Baptist Church to purchase land in a rapidly developing area toward Mount Pearl in the west end of the city. The plan was to eventually develop a new Baptist work there at some future date. It seemed that the time had come to begin the work of establishing this outreach ministry. Plans were acquired for a new house to be built on the upper side of the large piece of land. The basement of the house was built in such a way that it would serve as a chapel for this new ministry. The dedication of the new parsonage took place on June 14, 1970.

In the meantime, a native born Newfoundland pastor was serving in a church not far from Sussex, New Brunswick. He was invited to return to Newfoundland and serve as pastor of West End Baptist Church. He accepted this challenge and moved to St. John's, serving under the Home Mission Board. Members were transferred from First Baptist Church to this fledgling church, and the new ministry was underway. Unfortunately, in a relatively short time, some problems developed in the new congregation. Along with a group of people who transferred from First Baptist Church with a desire to see a strong new witness established in the west end of the city, there were a few malcontents who saw this as an opportunity to leave because they were not happy with the strong Evangelical stance of the pastor and First Baptist Church.

Certain of the individuals began to flex some muscle. Two individuals, who were financially strong business men, began to dictate policy and demonstrate rather unspiritual, un-Christ like influences in the new church. They directed these attitudes against the pastor, partly because they didn't like his close friendship with me as well as his strong evangelical preaching, so they had a double reason for their unsavory actions. With a determination to assassinate his character and to further their own goals, they used every means to accomplish their desired ends. Because of their businesses, they were able to access the pastor's credit rating and account information at the bank and began to turn that information against the pastor. They contacted some of the denominational leaders and sought to defame the pastor and ridicule the fact that he had to borrow money to make ends meet.

What they should have been doing was paying him a better salary instead of trying to undermine his character and illegally access his private business. If anything were done like this today, these men would have been up before the courts. The pastor was called before the executive of the Home Mission Board, of which I was a member, so I accompanied the pastor to this meeting, which was held on the mainland. The upshot of it all was that I pled his case. I challenged the members present regarding their own private affairs. Almost all of them had to admit that that they borrowed each year to pay their taxes, and most of them didn't have the family obligations like this pastor in question. The conclusion was that I was appointed by the board to oversee and monitor the finances of this pastor and his wife. This was neither a pleasant nor an easy task for me, realizing that these men in this congregation were living up to the Deacon's Prayer of "Lord, you keep him humble, and we'll keep him poor." However, the Lord was able to overcome the situation. Another individual who had left First Baptist Church attended West End Baptist but would not become a member, because he wanted at some time to go back to First Baptist and vote me out. The Lord had other plans, however, and he died very suddenly: "Man proposes but God disposes."

The pastor at that time of Argentia/Placentia Bay Baptist Church moved back to the mainland, so the pastor of West End was able to move to this other pastorate away from this very unpleasant situation. As a result of this move, one of the pastor's sons moved in with our family in February, 1971, and has been part of our family ever since for these past forty plus years. He is now married and has children, who are included as our grandchildren. He serves as a very effective pastor in one of our Fellowship churches in Ontario, Canada.

29

My Mission and Passion

My mission and passion for outreach were challenged on every hand. In all of this, my wife was most supportive. Opportunities for the advancement of the Kingdom of God were constantly arising all around us. These became more and more evident through the impact of our radio and television ministries. A small fellowship of believers was started by my predecessor and was meeting periodically at Gander. Gander was known as "the crossroads of the world." It was at that time significant for international aviation. The trans-continental and trans-Atlantic flights made this their last and first point of reference and refueling base. This small group of believers was made up of RCMP officers, air traffic controllers, managers of well known mainland businesses that were established here, and many others. I had a burden for their spiritual growth and welfare, along with a desire to see a church established there.

One summer after we had finished our VBS at St. John's, my wife and I and the whole family travelled to Gander and had VBS there in the community hall. It was very successful and made a significant impact on the community. Many changes had been taking place that served to open up central Newfoundland. The last segment of the Trans-Canada Highway had just been completed across the province, thus linking the country from St. John's to Victoria, B.C. This highway just passed along the edge of the town of Gander. In July of 1966, during the week that we had VBS in Gander, we were able to attend a very special event. On the afternoon of July 12, we travelled to Grand Falls for the unveiling of "The Peak" that would mark the halfway point of the Trans-Canada Highway in Newfoundland. When it was completed, it stretched a distance of

7,821 kilometres, making it the longest trans-continental highway in the world. The Hon. Joseph R. Smallwood, Premier of Newfoundland, and the Hon. Lester B. Pearson, Prime Minister of Canada, both spoke at this very special event. It was special to be there.

A witness in Gander could have a significant impact upon central Newfoundland. To begin with, I made regular monthly visits to Gander to conduct Sunday school and a morning service of worship. I would leave St. John's early on Sunday morning, drive almost two hundred miles to Gander, and then head back to St. John's for the evening service. Within a short space of time, we began to consider building a parsonage and the church in Gander. The denomination had a piece of land in Gander that had been given to them by the local council; however, the government made an offer to exchange another piece of land for the one we had. This would give them space to expand some government facilitates, but it would also put the church location in a more visible spot. This worked out very well for the church and for the local authorities.

We then made contact with Central Mortgage and Housing Corporation so that we could purchase a set of plans. This enabled us to build a two-storey house with a full basement. We had two engineers in the church in St. John's who helped with some minor modifications to the plans that would make the house more suitable for use as a parsonage. All the necessary permits were acquired and the building was completed. The next step was to make plans for the building of the church.

I got in touch with a company in British Colombia whose services we had used in the building of the main lodge at Camp Tulakadik in New Brunswick. I also knew that they had developed plans for church buildings. Their specialty was the design of rigid frame structures. This meant that the buildings require no centre beams. This company was most helpful in offering suggestions that would help us reach our goal. The plans were received and again our two engineers made some modifications to make the plans more usable for a Baptist church. A date was set. Representatives from other Baptist churches, the denomination, and the town council were all invited to attend the sod turning ceremony.

Soon plans were underway for the construction of the new church. We even had all the furnishings we required. The Baptist church in Stephenville was closed because the American base had closed, so one Saturday we hired a large truck in Gander, and a group of us drove to Stephenville. There we took out the pews and all the other movable furnishings. We brought everything to Gander and installed all the furniture there. The Rev. Reuben Davis temporarily served as pastor there, followed by the Rev. Blois Crawford.

During my first year in Newfoundland, I had a recurring throat problem. This, of course, affected my voice. I would preach on Sunday, and on Monday morning I would have an elevated temperature. To counteract this, I bought some over the counter medication. However, it became obvious that I should do something about it. My family doctor recommended me to a throat specialist. Appropriately he was named Dr. Yap. He recommended that I get rid of all the patent medicine and drink honey and lemon. From that day on I have never had debilitating throat problems.

During our years in Newfoundland we always enjoyed the availability of plenty of fresh fish. We could buy salmon for fifty cents per pound. A large cod could be bought for one dollar each. One of the highlights of the year took place in the spring when the capelin were running and we'd take a fish net and go out to one of the small bays to fish. This small sardine like fish would come in to the shore and was easily caught

Rest, Relaxation, and Recuperation

One can tell by the record of our activities in Newfoundland that we lived a very busy life as individuals, as a family, and as a church. We were also involved in a very demanding ministry. There were challenges, opportunities, and many open doors. To get away for a trip 'around the Bay, or to Bowering Park or Cape Spear (the most easterly point of land in North America), was always a special family treat. A widowed lady in the church, sensitive to these challenges and demands, approached me one day with a proposal. She invited me to her home where she showed me a large wooden building out in the yard.

"I'd like you to have this building. If you could purchase a piece of land outside the city, you could move this building there and use it as a cottage."

Wow! Thank you Lord! One place that immediately came to mind was Pouch Cove, one of our favourite places to visit. We would sometimes go there to pick bakeapple berries or blueberries, or just walk along the shore. So the search was on. We identified a cleared piece of land surrounded by lovely trees just off the gravel road that led to the lighthouse. From there we had a clear view of the ocean, and it overlooked the village. An ideal location! Now we had to search for the owners. Eventually we tracked them down. They agreed to sell half an acre of land to us. We agreed on a price, and it was ours. Now plans had to be made to move the building.

We hired a flatbed truck, jacked up the building, got all the necessary permits from the police, and planned the move. The move went without a hitch. We had our cottage in place. I built a deck across the front of the building where we could sit, relax, and enjoy the breath-taking scenery. There were majestic icebergs drifting by like blue/white cruise ships. We could enjoy the cavorting mighty humpback whales blowing their water jets into the air. Then there was the cry of the gulls as they circled above the schools of fish and occasionally dove for their supper. No rushing traffic, no loud music, no cell phones, no intrusions of the modern world. Here we could enjoy unspoiled nature, contemplate God's greatness, and meditate on His majesty. It was the ideal place to recharge our spiritual batteries. We would pack a lunch and escape for a few hours. However, like other things graciously provided by God, we enjoyed sharing this place with others. Some of the groups from the church would go out to enjoy a summer evening campfire. Others would go for an afternoon of activities on a Saturday. Still others would go out for an overnight camp-out. There were times when I would exclaim, "All this and Heaven too!"

In all of my ten years of ministry in Newfoundland, with its busy, demanding, exciting ministries, I never had an assistant. The fact is, I didn't really need one. We were uniquely blessed with an incredible group of men and women in our membership. Our board consisted of four highly dedicated and well equipped men who were very supportive of me and had the same vision and burden for the ministry that I had. We also had an incredible band of men and women who gave themselves completely to the mission and ministry of First Baptist Church with a desire to glorify the Lord and see His kingdom extended. When asked to serve, there was no need to follow up on what they were doing, because they did it with dedication and enthusiasm. Therefore, I never hesitated to give my all since I had such a wonderful team in step with what was happening. We were labourers together with Christ.

30

All Things to all People that We Might Win Some

While in Newfoundland, I became significantly involved in the political life of the province.
I was always invited to the opening of the Provincial House of Assembly.
Sometimes when some controversial matters were up for debate, I would be a
guest in the Speaker's Gallery. This would often give me fuel for discussion on the
radio talk shows as well as significant material for some of my topical sermons on
subjects like abortion, women's rights, and family law. These were all very popular
topics at that time. One of my broadcasted messages was entitled "The Pope, The
Pill, and The Population Explosion." Interestingly, I was invited by the Roman
Catholic Archbishop of Newfoundland to speak on the subject of abortion. This
was a very large gathering of Roman Catholics and Roman Catholic clergy. Being
a little toad in a big puddle had its benefits.

I had a unique opportunity to meet a number of well known public figures
at this time, one being Malcolm Muggeridge, a onetime skeptic who had come
to faith in Christ. I also met Mother Theresa, well known for her work in India.
In both situations I sat on a panel when they were interviewed. It was significant
to meet the Queen Mother at a private luncheon in her honour at Government
House and later at a banquet. Sometime later I met the Queen at a reception
hosted by the Hon. Joseph R. Smallwood, and later at a banquet at Memorial
University. As a result of my political interests and concern for current issues,
I was invited by Dr. Raymond Gushue to participate in a family law study.
This resulted in some changes to some archaic family laws in Newfoundland,
along with moving toward more timely changes in the society of the twentieth
century.

Around this time, The Hon. Joseph R. Smallwood undertook the publishing of *The Books of Newfoundland*. He contacted me to help with the subject of the status of the Baptist churches and work in Newfoundland and Labrador. By this time, I was increasingly involved in the leadership of the United Baptist Convention of the Atlantic Provinces. I became president of the Pastor's Institute, served for a number of years on the Home Mission Board, was vice president of the Convention, served on the board of trustees of Acadia University, as well as being one of the several pastor/evangelists who conducted evangelistic crusades in all four of the Atlantic provinces. So while fulfilling my role as a pastor, I became more acquainted with the broader ministry. I had a bent for administration and enjoyed the challenges this afforded me outside of the local church. In addition, I was able to fulfill my passion for evangelism and missionary outreach.

As the city of St. John's expanded, so did all the services and the infrastructure. A very significant sign of this growth was the building of the Avalon Mall, the first of its kind in Newfoundland. Its location, its large parking area, and the fact that in those days shops were not open on Sundays, stirred a vision in me. God awakened me to the possibilities of what could be a significant outreach ministry to the community. This would enable us to take our ministry outside the confines of the four walls of the church.

After discussions with the church board and subsequently with the manager of the Avalon Mall in the summer of 1967, we launched our "Drive-In Church." We bought a portable organ, and I also had an accordion. We bought a sound system with horn speakers and microphones. Flyers were printed that included songs, information about the church, and a response section. The news media were out in full force; the CBC filmed the opening event on June 18, 1967. The parking lot was filled to capacity, and the mall security helped with the flow of traffic. It was estimated that we had three hundred cars and around one thousand people. The mall management provided us with space so that we could store our equipment. The men and young people of the church distributed the flyers as the cars pulled in to park. Our church choir gave support for the music, and someone would give a personal testimony. I then would preach a brief Gospel message and would give individuals the opportunity to respond to an invitation to accept Christ or talk to one of our counsellors who would be moving around the parking lot. Whole families would sit in their cars and join in. Over the years, many individuals made commitments to Jesus Christ, and others started to come to church. This ministry continued summer after summer through rain or shine or fog. Even during the Christmas season our choir and supporters presented

Christmas music inside the mall, which was greatly appreciated by the Christmas shoppers.

Going Into all the World

Because of my foreign missionary experience, and my burden for missions, I knew that I had to share this burden with our congregation. We were doing a relatively good job in reaching our Jerusalem, Judea, and Samaria; however, our "uttermost parts of the Earth" component was missing. While contemplating the extension of our church's ministry into the far reaches of the world, God orchestrated some very significant encounters.

The first one was with Ralph Borthwick, who worked with Wycliffe Bible Translators and was a pilot with Missionary Aviation Fellowship. He was ferrying a plane to Africa to be used there in support of missionary work. Aviation laws required that the plane be equipped with extra fuel tanks since he would be flying across the Atlantic, so he stopped in St. John's to have some modifications done to the plane. He was in St. John's for a week, and he made contact with us at the church. We had him share about his work, which began to awaken the church to an interest in world missions.

A short time later, in March, 1972, another missionary made an unscheduled stop over in St. John's due to inclement weather. The Rev. George Middleton had been a missionary in Ethiopia but had to leave there because of political unrest. He later established what became known as Emmanuel International. This mission not only preached the Gospel, but also ministered to the physical, social, and emotional needs of people around the world. His vision and enthusiasm soon captured the hearts of our people at First Baptist Church.

Our third encounter with overseas missions was with one of our Baptist denominational missionaries who had served in the Congo. The Rev. Charles and Mrs. Francis Harvey had lived through the terrible political upheavals in the Congo. They had a burning passion for missions, and they spent a week with us ministering in our Sunday Services, Sunday school, our ladies' fellowship meetings, and our youth meetings. As a result of our exposure to these missionary challenges, we were soon assigning a significant portion of our income to the cause of missions at home and overseas.

We became involved in a very significant and unique ministry called Christian Literature Crusade. My contacts with CJON-TV served us well. This ministry involved on camera, live presentations of Gospel and literature work around the world. A number of our people were on hand at the station, manning the phones, taking pledges, answering questions, and praying with some who had personal needs. The response was incredible and made an impact throughout the area covered by the TV station.

As missionary interest grew, our missionary contact increased. One of our favourite missionary visitors was Bishop Gus Marwheh from Africa. His father had been a cannibal and their tribe was constantly at war. However, God in His grace and mercy had used missionaries to bring the Gospel, and their lives were gloriously transformed. Bishop Marwheh was an incredible influence on our congregation. During one of his visits, he brought with him a national pastor called Philip Pajebo. He had such a radiant testimony to the grace of God in his life. He was the youngest of a very large family. While sharing his testimony he said, "I was so bad, I was the white sheep of the family!" He had very little English, so Bishop Marwheh had to translate for him. Sitting down to eat dinner one evening, we had a very embarrassing moment. My wife had cooked spaghetti and meatballs. We gave thanks for the food and started to eat. All of us were enjoying the meal, when suddenly I noticed that Pastor Pajebo was staring at his plate. I asked Bishop Marwheh if there was a problem.

"Oh yes," he replied. "The spaghetti reminds him of stomach worms, and he cannot eat it."

My wife very quickly boiled some rice to go with the meatballs. Problem solved. We learn so many lessons through cultural encounters.

31

Blessings and Benefits

The significance of radio and TV ministry can't be fully measured; however, from time to time we would hear from individuals, many in isolated areas, who were reached and impacted by this extension of our ministry. RCMP officers posted to isolated communities and school teachers teaching in small country schools were amongst those who wrote to express appreciation for the music and ministry, while at the same time speaking of me as their pastor.

In October of 1970, a number of Evangelical churches banded together to hold a community wide evangelistic crusade. Our evangelist was Dr. Barry Moore. This was very successful and resulted in many coming to a saving faith in Christ. There were outreaches into colleges, university, schools, and other community organizations. Many interesting contacts were made because of international fishing vessels coming in to port.

Another time, we had an American evangelist at the church for a week of meetings. Amongst other things, we were invited on board a Russian vessel to have lunch with one of the officers. We distributed some Russian Scriptures, and then took several of the officers on a tour of the city.

One day I received a call from the hospital. A Norwegian factory ship was in port and one of the fishermen was a patient at the hospital and couldn't speak English. Somehow the hospital knew that Norwegian was my second language, so they asked me to come and interpret for him. He had been involved in a terrible accident on board. He had slipped and fallen on to a conveyer belt that pulled him into a fish processing machine and had mangled his left arm. He had to have his arm amputated, so I spent time explaining what the surgeon had to do. The other problem was getting in touch with his family in Norway. It so happened that his family in Norway knew me. They lived on an island near the town of Harstad, in northern Norway, where I had had meetings on several occasions, so I was able to pass on the information to them. Then I was able to make arrangements for his transfer to Montreal, where he was to be fitted with prosthesis and then sent back to Norway. While he was in the hospital, my wife baked some Norwegian goodies and made some coffee Norwegian style and took it in to him. God was pleased to use some of what I had learned in my missionary service in Lapland.

Our Christmas Eve family services were very special. They were always conducted by candlelight. The service consisted of traditional Christmas carols, interspersed with scripture readings covering the whole Christmas story. This was highlighted by scenes from Bethlehem projected on the screen. Of course, I highlighted the fact that my Christmas gift to the entire congregation was that the service would last only fifty- nine minutes.

One of the precious memories of one of our Christmas Eve services was the fact that a young man came to personal faith in the Lord Jesus Christ. Shortly afterwards, his wife came to personal faith. Then along the way their family came. He became involved in fisheries research at the Fisheries College. He travelled to many parts of the world developing fisheries programs. His son now has two doctorates in theology and works overseas

Each New Years Eve we had an Open House at the parsonage. This gave us an opportunity to have informal fellowship with our members and adherents. At 10:00 p.m. we started our New Years Eve service, which went on to shortly after midnight. It consisted of singing favourite songs and choruses and providing opportunity to share personal testimonies. I would give a brief devotional and then we would close the service around the communion table and spend the last few moments of the old year and the first few moments of the New Year in the attitude of prayer. Precious memories!

A Dream Come True

In 1968, along with the Rev. Freman Fenerty, the former pastor of First Baptist Church in Newfoundland, I received a wonderful gift from one of the members of our church. It was a five weeks, all expenses paid trip that took us to the U.K., Italy, Jordan, Israel, Egypt, Turkey, and Greece. We were able to arrange a stop off in the U.K. for a few days. My former pastor in my home church in Scotland was now serving in London. He met us at Heathrow airport and gave us a whirlwind tour of London. I ministered at the mid-week service. The following day we were able to fly up to Scotland, where we stayed overnight with my wife's folks in Edinburgh and I was able to take Pastor Fenerty to the historical highlights of the city. My home church very kindly arranged a service that evening, so a number of my family and friends were able to gather. It had been twelve years since I had been in Scotland. What an incredible evening! Many of the young people were there; I conducted the youth choir and ministered the Word. The following day we flew down to London and then on to Rome, Italy.

In Rome we joined up with an American Express group. They had been on a 'round the world tour and the last leg of that tour would take in the lands of the Bible. This group of people consisted of wealthy, successful business and professional people. We learned later that they were not at all enthusiastic when they learned that two preachers were going to be joining them; however, that attitude changed very quickly. They learned that because of our knowledge of the Bible, we could augment what the guides were saying about each place that we visited. In addition to that, we often spent hours with them at the end of each day, answering their questions and ministering to their spiritual needs. We literally became their personal chaplains and counsellors. They also soon learned that we enjoyed fun, and they were not slow to play some tricks on us.

What a thrill it was for us as pastors to follow the steps of our Lord, walk in the paths of the prophets, and trace the missionary journeys of Paul. I came back spiritually enriched and with a greater understanding of the places and the people in the Scriptures. We had the joy and privilege of worshipping at First Baptist Church in Jerusalem. We arrived just minutes before the service was about to begin and were ushered to the very front pew. Two spaces were available, but not together. As their service went on, we made an amazing discovery—that evening was a baptism service. Then I discovered that I was sitting next to one of the candidates—a converted Jewess. My friend was sitting next to another candidate—a converted Arab. That evening both would be expressing their oneness in Christ as they followed the Lord in baptism. We are all one in Christ.

Shortly after the Six Day War, I was leaning on a fence that stretched along the edge of a large open area in front of the Wailing Wall in Jerusalem. I had two guides with me—one, an Israeli who had been an officer in the Israeli army, and the other an Arab who had been an officer in the Arab army. Here we were standing together, enjoying a pleasant conversation. It's hard to understand.

We had the joy of seeing one couple open their heart to the Lord. I kept in touch with them for years until the Lord took them home. Then when we were in Greece and travelling back from Sounion one afternoon, I sat with our guide and talked to her about the Lord, and she expressed faith in the Lord Jesus Christ.

This tour provided me with greater enlightenment for my messages and a greater source of information for my teaching in churches where I pastored and also during the time when I taught in a Bible school. It also stirred up a desire to share this experience with others in churches where I ministered. As a result, I became involved in leading eleven different pilgrimages to the lands of the Bible over the ensuing years, along with other tours to Europe and Britain.

Learning Lessons in the School of Experience

My mother, who had just the very basics of schooling, would often say that she had gone to the school of hard knocks and graduated from the university of experience. How foundational and valuable. The pressures and demands of the work in Newfoundland took their toll on my health. I suffered a heart attack that laid me low for some time; however, I had wonderful support from the congregation and my doctor friends. I was really privileged to receive the best of care from my heart specialist, plus I learned the benefits of learning to walk two miles per day.

My deacons planned to send me away for a time of rest and recuperation. They booked my wife and me on the Portuguese Airline to London, England. At no extra cost we could get a Portuguese flight from London to Lisbon, Portugal. We were booked into a hotel at Estoril/Monte Estoril, right on the beach, at a ridiculously low price, with all meals included. What an ideal place for me since I was worn out physically, emotionally, and spiritually.

Personally I was not aware of what had happened. What I know of what happened between leaving Newfoundland and arriving in Portugal was told to me by my wife. That first week I ate, slept, and walked the beach. The weather was glorious, the sun shone every day, and I breathed in that pure invigorating air. Each day my wife read the Scriptures, and she did the praying. Gradually I felt refreshed, revived, and renewed. I learned a life-changing lesson during those very special days. When we get to the place where we seek to do the Lord's work in our own strength, with our own abilities, we will eventually run out of steam. God finally brought me face to face with the truth of Isaiah 40:28–31. The reality is that *the everlasting God, the Lord, the Creator of the ends of the earth, neither faints nor is weary.* Then He reminds us:

Even the youths shall faint and be weary, and the young men shall utterly fall. But [and here is the secret for those of all ages in the service of the Lord] those who wait on the Lord shall renew their strength; they shall mount up with wings like eagles, they shall run and not be weary, they shall walk and not faint.

The lessons learned at that beach side resort in Estoril, Portugal have stayed with me to this very day. When I feel I'm running on empty, I take time out with the Lord. During our stay, the hotel staff was so good to us. The economy in Portugal at that time was not very good, so the staff was so grateful for anything extra that we did for them. Even my wife's used pantyhose were grabbed up by the cleaning ladies. On the Sunday of the second week we decided to seek out a church. We found an English speaking International Church within walking distance of the hotel. The fellowship was just what we needed. We were so blessed and strengthened by that time of worship.

Retreat to Recuperate

The second week of our stay we decided to hire a car so that we could visit some of the special places around us. We soon learned that when driving in Portugal, two things were an absolute must—good brakes and a very loud horn. How we enjoyed Sintra, which was located inland from where we were staying. Then we went north on the beautiful coastal road all the way to Nazare. The picturesque village and colourful fishing boats were captivating.

We also went to Lisbon one day. There we visited the large Romanesque Cathedral with its almost fortress like bell towers, the more Gothic like monastery, and then down by the harbour the amazing monument honouring the Portuguese explorers. It was from here the Portuguese fishermen, for centuries, had been travelling to Newfoundland waters to fish. In fact, in St. John's, by the Confederation Building, is the larger than life statue of Gasper Corte-Real, the Portuguese navigator who reached Terra Nove (Newfoundland) in the beginning of the fifteenth century. This was the era of the great discoveries. This statue was a gift from the Portuguese Fisheries Organization in gratitude for the friendly hospitality extended to them by the people of Newfoundland.

Over those two weeks in Portugal we were greatly refreshed. For our final week we flew back to London. From there we travelled up to Edinburgh to visit with my wife's parents. It was a joyful time with them. Then we travelled back to Newfoundland and right back in to the Lord's work.

32

Concerns for the Maturing Population

Our next major adventure came about because of a growing concern for the aging population in our city. Through my extensive pastoral visitation ministry, this concern grew in our hearts and minds. Several guiding factors began to fall into place. We developed a committee with the goal to investigate the feasibility of such a project. It was not too long before we realized that God's hand was gently guiding us along step by step. Around this time the magnificent and historic building that was The Newfoundland Hotel was being sold. Could this building be modified to serve as a seniors' residence?

At this point, I was introduced to a leading entrepreneur in the community, namely Mr. Andrew Crosby—one of the well known, high profile members of the Crosby family in Newfoundland. I was led to believe that Mr. Crosby had a similar thought in mind. Trusting my memory, this property belonging to the Canadian Railway was priced at less than $500,000.00. I immediately set up an appointment with Mr. Crosby so that I could get his opinion on such a project as this. The day arrived for the appointment. I remember so clearly the events of the day. I parked my car on the side of the street just outside the Crosby office building. I put my hand in my pocket to get a quarter for the parking meter, only to discover I had no money. Here I was about to discuss a project that might initially cost a half million dollars, and I didn't have the money for the parking meter! Oh well, *"Now faith is the substance of things hoped for, the evidence of things not seen"* (Hebrews 11:1).

Upon entering the elegant office, we made the initial introductions. I then shared my vision with Mr. Crosby. He swung around on his desk chair, opened his filing cabinet, pulled out an inch thick file, and laid it on his desk.

"Pastor Russell," he said, "this file contains the results of a study done by my project manager, Mr. David Cook. It covers the very same ideas that you have for the remodeling of the Newfoundland Hotel, to be used as a seniors' residence.

Wow! Someone had already done the work. He called in the project manager, Mr. David Cook, with whom I eventually became very good friends. Together they shared with me the conclusions they had arrived at on the basis of their study. Because of the age of the building, its downtown location, and its limited outdoor space, it was concluded that this might not be a wise plan. Then they offered this advice: get a substantial piece of land on the edge of the city and build a brand new building so that we could plan a building that would better serve its purpose. Before I left there that day, I knew the Lord's hand was in all of this. Mr. Crosby pledged his support and offered the services of Mr. David Cook as our project manager.

It was not long before I became acquainted with Dr. Timothy Starr. He spearheaded the Home Mission Board of the Fellowship of Evangelical Baptist Churches in Ontario. I discovered that he had been involved in developing seniors' residences in Ontario and Quebec. He in turn introduced me to Mr. Tibor Vandor, who had worked with Dr. Starr on the research and funding of such projects. Step by step, God was opening doors and leading us along. In this whole process, I had to make a few trips to Ottawa to consult with government agencies. Our main contact was the CMHC (Central Mortgage and Housing Corporation). Seed money was provided by CMHC in the amount of $30,000 00 to cover preliminary costs.

1. A survey had to be taken to determine the need. Ads were placed in the different newspapers, announcements were made on radio and television, and the relevant provincial and municipal departments were consulted.

2. The results showed that a three level care facility was needed in the city. CMHC then indicated that it would fund the project under the conditions that the total amount would be provided, ten per cent of which would be free, and ninety per cent would be amortized over a period of fifty years at four per cent interest.

3. A suitable piece of land had to be secured from the city. A very suitable lot was provided at the corner of Portugal Cove Road and MacDonald Drive for the generous sum of one dollar.

4. Mr. David Cook was secured as the Project Manager. Architects' plans were drawn up, the services of Mr. Tibor Vandor and Dr. Timothy Starr

were secured as consultants, bids were secured, contracts were handed out, and the work got underway.

The structure would be in the form of a "T" and would provide three levels of care. One wing would provide a variety of apartments; another wing would provide partial care. The third wing would provide full care. A chapel was provided where regular services would be held, conducted by the local clergy. A contest was set up to have the general public participating in providing a suitable name for the complex. It was won by one of the staff on the CBC radio and TV station. The name "Escasoni" was chosen, which is Mic-Mac Indian meaning "Green Boughs."

On September 3, 1976, I had the joy and privilege of participating in the official opening ceremony and unveiling of the corner stone that bears my name. Members of the provincial and municipal government were there, along with the Lieutenant Governor of the province.

The work continues, and many local seniors have been well cared for in their maturing years thanks to many who made this possible. To God be the Glory!

33

Ongoing Family Concerns

Earlier in my saga of Newfoundland, I made mention of my middle son, Ian, who received wonderful care and treatment for his Legge Perthes disease. The day finally came on December 20, 1971, that he was scheduled to have what was expected to be his last visit to Dr. Schapter. It was expected that this would give Ian the all-clear. No more casts, no more therapy, no more hospital stays, In addition to this, there would be no more carrying him in and out of the car, and no more carrying him upstairs to his class room in school. That day the doctor shared the good news that the x-rays showed as close to a one hundred per cent complete healing that he had ever seen. Praise the Lord! How thankful we were that God had brought us to Newfoundland.

Just before we left the doctor's office, I expressed my concern about another issue with Ian. I pointed out that a small lump had developed on the ring finger of his left hand. I saw the expression on the doctor's face change. He immediately sent us to the x-ray department to have a complete skeletal survey done from head to foot. In those days no other scans were available.

Two hours later we were called back into his office. He had a panorama of x-rays displayed on the screen. He then started to point out tumours in the long bones of Ian's legs, in his fingers, and other places. These tumours were located in areas where there would normally be marrow. He explained that these tumours were benign, but as Ian grew the bones would weaken and result in multiple fractures. This is a developmental disease called "Ollier's Disease," and would require ongoing multiple surgeries to remove the tumours and replace the cavity with bone shavings taken from other parts of his body.

This was a bit of a downer. Ian's response to this news was, "So really what you're saying is that now I have cancer." The doctor assured him that it wasn't cancer, and then told us to go home and think about the surgery. We not only went home and thought about it, but we also prayed about it.

One week later, Ian told the doctor that he was willing to get started on a program of surgery. The doctor said that this would mean that he wouldn't be able to be involved in contact sports. This was not good news for Ian, since he was looking forward to playing hockey. I spoke to the doctor privately and asked him what he would do if it were his boy. He told me that he would let him play anyway. That was good enough for me.

The surgeries that followed dealt mainly with the weight bearing bones first, and then his hands and other smaller bones. In total he had eighteen bouts of bone surgery, yet he still graduated from high school right on schedule. Just like he started grade one with casts on, so the night of his graduation from high school he sported a cast on his arm as he walked across the stage to receive his diploma. Now in his fifties, he does very well but struggles with some health issues.

We experienced God's enabling every day. My wife was always involved in my entire ministry and the needs of families associated with the church. She spent quite a bit of time counselling the women and teenage girls. As an accomplished secretary, she took care of all my correspondence and the secretarial work associated with the church and the variety of projects in which I was involved.

Our home became a haven for several teenagers. There was always room for one more at the table. For several years we had students boarding with us. One was the nephew of our family doctor. He was a student from Hong Kong, and our doctor wanted him to stay with us so that he could improve his English. Another student was from Grand Manan Island in the Bay of Fundy. His parents wanted him to be in a good family environment while he attending Memorial University. A young lad from Sussex, New Brunswick came to live with us for several months. He had some difficulty during his last year in high school and needed to catch-up on a few subjects. Then there was an older teenage girl who was having problems with her father who was aggressive and abusive. She fled from her home one day and found refuge with us. She has since been counted as one of our adopted children, and her son as one of our grandchildren.

Our eldest son did the janitorial work at the church for several years. By and large he did a great job; however, he's always remembered for one big mistake.

We were to have a baptismal service, so part of his responsibilities was to fill the baptistery. It took a few hours to accomplish this, so while it was filling he went about some other chores. Then he forgot to check on the water level. When he finally remembered he went in through the basement door, only to discover the water pouring through the ceiling of the basement. The big mistake was that there was no safety overflow. There was a major cleanup job to do. It did not happen again.

While in Newfoundland, our eldest daughter was able to go to Glasgow, Scotland to study. This was made possible through a grant from the provincial government. She was there for only one year. After returning to Newfoundland, she married and moved to Ottawa. Now she lives in B.C. along with her children and grandchildren.

After high school, our eldest son went to apprentice as a printer at the printing office of one of our newspapers. Printing became his career, and he eventually owned his own business

Needling the Preacher Got Results

Somewhere along the line I sustained a back injury, which at times gave me excruciating pain. Eventually I was hospitalized. I lay on a striker bed, sometimes facing up, sometimes facing down. It became chronic. I had consultations with a neurosurgeon. Suggestions were made that I could have surgery with no guarantee of success. To walk was extremely painful. I wore a neck brace for over two years. I went through several therapies for several weeks several times per week. I had a halter (almost like a hangman's noose) that went under my chin. The cord then went through a pulley attached to the top of the door with a ten pound weight attached. This would take the pressure off my spine.

At one point I contemplated leaving the ministry and going on disability support. My family doctor, who was Chinese and a member of our church, treated me with pain medication. This had no lasting effect. One day he said to me, "Pastor why not try acupuncture?" This was something new. My initial response was to talk to my neurosurgeon about it. His response was that if it didn't help, it at least would do no harm." With that I agreed to have my family doctor start acupuncture treatment.

After about an hour of needles being inserted at key points in my body, and feeling a burning sensation along the nerve lines of my body, I began to feel relief. I walked out of that office pain free for the first time in many months and I remained pain free. Thank you, Lord! Others heard of this and got similar results.

The question then was raised about how acceptable acupuncture was as a medical procedure and therapeutic treatment.

By this time, acupuncture was increasingly in use across the country. It became obvious that action needed to be taken to regulate its use provincially and nationally so as to protect it from misuse. To give this issue some publicity, I invited my neurosurgeon to join me on a TV interview session. This proved to be very enlightening. One of the issues raised by the neurosurgeon was that they really didn't know why or how it worked. To this I pointed out that we have other treatments of which we can say the same thing, but through their use have proven to be very effective. One case in point is the use of Digitalis. To this he agreed. The outcome was that we organized an Acupuncture Society, with the goal to protect patients from being victims of unskilled and untrained use. This has been accomplished.

A Loving Congregation

While in Newfoundland, we celebrated our twenty-fifth wedding anniversary. The people of the church were very kind and generous. They put on an incredible banquet and showered us with so many beautiful gifts. It was a very memorable evening.

I was never content with maintaining the status quo. One country preacher used this phrase in his sermon one Sunday morning. After the service, some of the people asked him the meaning of "status quo." He answered with, "That's Latin for 'the mess we's now in.'" A very apt description.

I've never been content with maintaining the status quo. We need to have the courage to ask the Lord for a fresh vision. Be constantly open before the Lord to seek His will and be ready for new enterprises. The fields are white to harvest. This is an ongoing challenge.

One pastor always enjoyed going to a conference. Besides being challenged in his personal life, he always enjoyed picking up new thoughts, new phrases, and new words. At one such conference the speaker used a new word quite frequently. The pastor had never heard this word before; the word was "phenomenal." He didn't know how to spell it, so he wrote it out in phonetic form: "feen-o-meenal." Upon returning from the conference, he decided to use it in his message that first Sunday. The only problem was that he didn't quite remember how it was pronounced, so he practiced it in its phonetic form. Reporting on the conference he said, "The fellowship was feen-o-meenal, the preacher was "feen-o-meenal, and the blessing of God was feen-o-meenal." At every opportunity through his sermon he used the word "feen-o-meenal."

After the service some of the Deacons approached him and said, "We know you must have been really blessed at the conference, but could you tell us what this word 'feen-o-meenal' really means?"

The pastor thought for a moment. "Let me explain it to you this way," he said. "Suppose you were walking along a country road and saw a cow grazing in the field. That's not feen-o-meenal. Then suppose you saw a beautiful thistle growing by the side of the road; that's not feen-o-meenal either. Then a little farther on, if you were to look up into the sky and saw a lark and heard it singing … that's not feen-o- meenal. But, if you ever saw a cow sitting on a thistle and singing like a lark, now that would be feen-o-meenal."

Some of the things we saw happening and which we experienced while living and working in Newfoundland were "feen-o-meenal." It was all by the grace of God and in the power of His Spirit. Truly He did *great things for us whereof we were glad*" (Psalm 126:3, KJV).

34

Dealing With Convention Conflicts

During the time we were serving in Newfoundland, some major issues were being raised in the United Baptist Churches of the Atlantic Baptist Convention. I had spent twenty years in a very active role in the convention. Those years were spent in pastorates in New Brunswick and Newfoundland. I served on the executive, ministered in evangelism in the four Atlantic provinces, served on the ordination council, was an active member of the Home Mission Board, served on the district and association level in both New Brunswick and Newfoundland, and was the president of the Pastor's Institute. I was also vice-president of the Atlantic Baptist convention (I missed being President by one vote). I was also elected Trustee of Acadia. This may give some idea of my commitment to the denomination.

A number of us as pastors were having some grave concerns over what was happening at the Convention level as well as in some of our churches. A group of concerned pastors began to meet regularly to pray and work toward bringing our influence to bear to bring the churches and Convention back in line with the original basis of faith and practice. Issues were discussed and concerns were expressed to the governing boards; however, many of the issues remained unresolved.

In the last convention that a number of us attended, some very clear lines were drawn. Some of the concerns evident in the Convention were voiced by the leadership in the assembly. Concerns included being desperately short of funds for the work, needing more young people to offer themselves for service overseas, the shortage of men offering themselves for the pastoral ministry, and the practice of some of our churches encouraging "open membership."

One of our concerned pastors was selected to speak on behalf of the concerned group. He spoke to each of the issues, and then he clearly stated that what we really needed was to get back to preaching the Word of God as the inspired, inerrant Scriptures. We needed to recognize the sovereignty of God and the Lordship of Jesus Christ, and have our membership made up of born again, baptized believers. If we did this, all of these so-called problems would be solved. At that point a significant number of the delegates booed and shouted him down.

That day a number of us walked out of the convention assembly, and we have never been back. This was a significant price to pay for our conviction. I had spent twenty significant years of my ministry in The Atlantic Baptist Convention churches. I had made many friendships and memories, and had seen many churches grow and ministries expand. These things could not be taken lightly.

When I returned to the church in Newfoundland, I reported on the happenings at convention. Not wishing to be accused of splitting the church, I immediately resigned from the pastorate of First Baptist Church, St. John's. In turn, I resigned from all the positions I held on boards and committees of the Convention. I let the church decide what they were going to do about their relationship to the Convention. The board called a meeting of the membership and unanimously decided to withdraw from the Atlantic Baptist Convention.

Later at a meeting of the Council of the Baptist Federation of Canada, I was vilified. One of the well known leaders sought to assassinate my character and charged me with misappropriation of church funds, since I had influenced the church to leave the Convention. This I had not done. One of my dear friends and brother pastor who served on the Federation Council stood to my defense. He made it clear that this was not so and had the individual withdraw the charges. This was a very difficult time for me, but I thank God for friends in high places. In spite of this, we left the First Baptist Church still the recipients of their love and support, and many of those people are friends still as I write.

Let me share some statistics from my ten years of ministry:

June 17, 1975, was a very significant Sunday. We had eleven baptisms, and twelve people were received into membership. God was still at work. Around this time I observed some significant anniversaries. On June 25, 1975, I celebrated the twenty-fifth anniversary of my ordination. Already I had the joy of serving the Lord in three countries and two provinces in Canada. That Sunday in First Baptist Church we had the joy of seeing seven people make a public commitment to Christ. Some were first time decisions, and some desired to follow their Lord through the waters of baptism. Five days later, on June 30, my wife and I celebrated our twenty-fifth wedding anniversary. What a special time of reflecting on twenty-five years of marriage, with five children, having served in three countries, and ministering in four pastorates. The Lord had done great things for us, and we were glad.

That evening, Dr. and Mrs. Way took us out for dinner. Upon returning to our home, we were actually ushered into the church, where we were greeted by a large gathering of people. What a wonderful time. There were many gifts, a purse of money, and an outpouring of incredible love. What a memorable time. I had already tendered my resignation to the church, and things were happening in an amazing way.

We had planned a vacation back to family in Scotland as part of our twenty-fifth anniversary celebrations. At the same time, a church in Ontario was prepared to extend a call to us strictly on the recommendation of fellow pastors. We thought that it would be better for me, however, to fly to Toronto to meet the people and confirm whether this was the right thing for us to do, so I made the four day trip to Toronto. I met with the board and preached at the Sunday services and mid-week service. It was a hectic time, but very profitable. Their call to me to be their pastor was confirmed. Tentative plans were made that we should move there in the early part of November.

On Monday morning I travelled back to Newfoundland, arrived home on time, and had just four hours to unpack my suitcase and repack for our trip to Scotland. Later that evening we flew out of Gander to Scotland. There we would visits with family and friends, I would preach in our home churches, and we would continue our twenty-fifth anniversary celebrations.

Upon our return to Newfoundland, it was decided that my wife should join me on a trip to Toronto so that we could check out the housing situation and allow my wife to see where we would be moving to. This trip we made in early September. Upon our return to St. John's, we got confirmation that we had bought a house in Mississauga. Everything was coming together.

On October 26, the church had a farewell gathering for us. This was a very emotional evening. The following day would be our last Sunday, and on October 28, 1975, we were on our way to take up residence in Mississauga, Ontario, and begin our ministry at Long Branch Baptist Church in Etobicoke, Ontario.

Travelling across the Island we visited pastors and friends along the way. It certainly was a time of mixed emotions ... leaving behind so many wonderful people and anticipating a new ministry. Now ends a significant chapter of my pastoral ministry. We enter upon new adventures in the work of the Lord. Could it be "hats off to the past, coats off to the future, the best is yet to be"? Without a doubt, my years in Newfoundland made a significant impact on me and my approach to the ministry. This would serve me well in the years to come. It has been our joy to be able to return from time to time and breathe that fresh Newfoundland air, as well as enjoy that unique Newfoundland hospitality.

35

The Future is as Bright as the Promises of God— Our Move to the Metropolis

At the very outset of my commitment to serve the Lord, I stated two reservations. First, I really didn't want to serve in a warm climate. Well, He took care of that—I started my fulltime ministry three hundred miles above the Arctic Circle. Secondly, I really didn't want to serve in a large city, as I'm a country boy at heart. Now here I was, in the process of moving to Canada's largest metropolis—Toronto.

I learned a long time ago to not put any qualifications or reservations on my commitment to serve the Lord. The centre of God's will is the safest and happiest place to be—whether it's the white wilderness of the Arctic, or the centre of the hustle and bustle of a great cosmopolitan metropolis. The motto blazoned above the fireplace in our mission headquarters in St. Leanards in England still holds true: "Dare you go where the Holy Ghost leads and leave the consequences with Him."

The church at Long Branch was part of the Fellowship of Evangelical Baptist Churches in Canada. We were looking forward to becoming a part of this great fellowship, though the move would not be easy. The culture would be very different both geographically and within our family. Our eldest daughter had already moved to Alberta, and our eldest son had gone west as well.

We arrived in Toronto on November 4, 1975, after travelling two thousand miles. We got the keys to our new home two days later. For the first time in twenty five years of marriage, we owned our own home. Our furniture arrived on November 13, and we were able to move in. The house was located right next to the elementary school where our youngest son would be attending. The Cawthra High School, which our two middle children would be attending, was within walking distance of our new home. We were also only fifteen minutes by car from the church. We were very conscious of the Lord's guidance in providing us with our new home.

Little did we realize the significant changes that would be brought to our family as well as to the future of our ministry. Truly we know not what the future holds, but we know who holds the future. This will become more evident as we shall see in the unfolding of the future chapters.

This was a major change. The GTA (Greater Toronto Area) is a conglomerate of many boroughs brought under one administration. It extends north, east, and west, but is limited by the shores of Lake Ontario in the south. What was once known as "Toronto the Good" has melted into a cosmopolitan mix. At one time it was a gathering of Scottish, Irish, English, and Welsh immigrants. Now it has become a multi-racial, multi-cultural, multi- religious, multi- lingual hodge podge of people from every corner of the globe. From a spiritual perspective, going into the entire world and preaching the gospel to every creature has been made easier. The world and every creature are right on our doorstep. It was into this environment that we as a family had moved and were being called upon to minister.

We soon realized that our exposure to other cultures and other language groups would serve us well as we ministered through Long Branch Baptist Church to this multi-cultural group right on our doorstep. At one point, the church considered relocating to one of the newer growing communities; however, the big question was who would minister the Gospel in this area. Our church was the main centre of Gospel ministry in the Lakeshore area. A move would mean that they would be left without a witness, so it was decide that we should stay and upgrade our facilities. This was accomplished through those with building skills and interior decorating abilities. This course of action proved to be a wise one. Some years after I had left, the church made further changes …this time modernizing the accesses to the building, and relocating and upgrading the office facilities and pastor's study. The main entrance to the church was redesigned, giving it a higher profile in the community.

One of the main thrusts into the community was an extensive visitation program, in which we distributed information about the church and its various ministries. One incident comes to mind that demonstrates the apathy and attempt at anonymity in the community. I approached a man, probably in his sixties, sitting on his rocking chair on the front porch of his house. I offered him the information about the church, which he accepted. Trying to engage him in conversation, I posed the question: "Do you attend church?"

"Oh yes," he replied.

Probing a little further, I asked if he attended regularly.

Again he answered in the affirmative.

"How regularly?" I further asked.

"Christmas and Easter," was his response. What a challenge!

Two or three days after we arrived and were getting things organized in our new home, I received a phone call from one of the ladies in the church. Apparently she had been visiting a lady in an apartment building whom she had met through the visitation program and had been ministering to her. This lady had requested that the new pastor come to visit her. I agreed to visit her that afternoon. Right after lunch, I prepared to go out and make this call. As I was getting into my car, it seemed as if the Lord prompted me not to go alone. I went back into the house and suggested to my wife that she come with me on this visit. To this she readily agreed.

Arriving at the apartment complex, I rang the buzzer. The lady answered and I immediately identified myself, so she buzzed me in. I made no mention of my wife being with me. When I got to the door of the apartment, I knocked and the lady immediately opened the door. I was absolutely shocked. There she stood, welcoming me with obvious pleasure. All she was wearing was a very transparent, see-through negligee! I stepped aside and introduced my wife. At that the lady's countenance changed! Welcome to the big city. For the short time we visited we realized that she had serious problems. As she tried to share them with us, she kept turning to my wife saying, "Of course, you wouldn't understand." Well, we never did go back. A lesson learned. How thankful I was that I had responded to the prompting of the Lord. From then on my wife visited with me on such visits.

During my time there I introduced my "Dial-a-Devotion" ministry. The response was immediate and incredible, ministering to the many throughout the area. The church was not without its problems, but they were relatively minor. Largely there was a great response to the proposed innovations and changes in some areas of the church's ministry.

We had a significant number of seniors associated with the church. Many of them had been very active in days gone by, but now they were more or less on the side lines. I became greatly burdened about the fact that they represented a vast resource of talent that was not being used. After consulting with some other churches that had very successful ministries to seniors, we finally launched our ministry, calling it "The Young at Heart." My wife and I and another lady gave leadership to this group. From time to time we called on others to help out.

We met once each month and had games, travelogues, visitors, and trips. The highlight was that we had a meal at lunch time. This was very special for those who normally ate alone at home.

Each Christmas our youth at the church planned, prepared, and served a special Christmas dinner for our seniors. The young people dressed up—girls in long gowns, fellows in black pants with white shirts and bow ties. They also put on a program for the seniors. This was a highlight of the year. Every two months the seniors would conduct the evening service. Someone played the organ, another played the piano, and still another played the violin. Several would give testimonies, and I usually brought an appropriate message. How they enjoyed their opportunity to minister! This reached out to the community, and some of them became members. This ministry continues today with a whole new generation of seniors.

While we rejoiced in what God was doing amongst our seniors in the church, it should also be noted that God was blessing in other departments. In the summer months we had a very effective Drive-In Church ministry, and our Vacation Bible School was most encouraging. We had developed weekly home Bible study groups in different areas, each one being led by one of our deacons. Our missionary outreach had grown significantly, as had the financial giving. It was encouraging to see how God was blessing with souls being saved, others obeying the Lord by being baptized, and of course new members being welcomed in to the church fellowship. Overall our ministry at Long Branch was going very well.

Outside of the church I was serving on a committee that was working on plans to build a seniors' residence that would eventually become known as "Fellowship Towers." This would be located on Yonge Street in Toronto near the intersection of Bloor Street. I was also serving as the chairman of "The Toronto Spiritual Life Convention." This was a very effective Evangelical ministry that organized a week of deeper spiritual life ministry held in January each year. Well known conference preachers came to minister primarily to Christians with a goal of developing a deeper Christian life, while challenging many to give themselves in full-time service.

It was a joy and privilege to be a part of such a vibrant, effective ministry within the church and the general community in Canada's largest metropolitan area. This was especially significant since I had made it clear to the Lord in the beginning of my ministry that I never wanted to serve in a big city. However, I soon discovered that God had other plans for my life and ministry. Little did I realize just how this would come about.

36

1980–A Year of Challenge and Change

The January, 1980 Toronto Spiritual Life Convention would play a significant part in the future of my ministry. Dr Stephen Olford, whom I had known for many years in the United Kingdom, was our convention speaker. God used his ministry in a mighty way. A goodly number responded to the challenge to offer themselves for God's service wherever He would lead. As I was closing that final meeting, I was very much aware of the fact that God was working in my life and had plans for changes in my life and ministry. My wife and I spoke about it afterwards, and she shared that she had felt the same urging of God. We concluded that we would allow God to lead in whatever way He chose. At that moment we did not realize the total significance of that commitment, but God did!

In the meantime, God provided an opportunity for us to relax and contemplate what He had in mind for us. One of the ladies in the church invited us to spend two weeks at her place in Hollywood, Florida. They were very special days that were refreshing to the body and the soul. Little did we realize how significant this would be as we soaked up the sun and enjoyed the sandy beaches and the sea in our first trip to Florida. We returned north refreshed and rejoicing in what God provided through His servants.

We came back to the church at Long Branch looking forward to an outstanding week of ministry by Rev. A. Larson and the Global Outreach Quartet. What a time of blessing night after night. Individuals came for salvation and others for renewed dedication. Not least of all was an incident that would bring about a radical change to my ministry. It took place on the Thursday evening of that week at the close of the service. Most of the people had gone, and I made my way back to my study where I found Pastor Larson waiting for me. He then asked me if I had thought of moving from the church where I was pastoring. I indicated to him that I hadn't, but I said nothing about what had happened earlier in the year at the Toronto Spiritual Life Convention. Then he said that God had prompted him to speak to me about a church that was in need of a pastor, and he told me that I would be an ideal candidate.

Wow! Obviously I asked him where the church was. I was startled by the answer—Nassau. I was not even sure where Nassau was located. He then indicated that he was going to submit my name. I said that if he felt led to do so that would be fine. Shortly afterwards I received a letter from Calvary Bible Church in Nassau, Bahamas, inviting me to come for two weeks of ministry from April 18 to 30, 1980. I responded in the affirmative. This would be a new experience for me, since I'd never ministered in a warm climate.

My wife and I made our way there, open to the Lord's leading yet with no personal desire for a call. Besides all of this, had I not said to the Lord that I would do whatever He wanted me to do and go wherever He wanted me to go, except I didn't want to minister in a warm climate?

We were met by the chairman and secretary of the church board at the airport in Nassau on April 18, 1980. They took us to the church parsonage, where we stayed for the time we were there. From then on we were engaged in a whirlwind of activity. That first Sunday I spoke at the adult Bible class and then preached in the morning service, which was broadcast over the local radio station covering most of the islands in the Bahamas. That morning there were two hundred and seventy-five in the Sunday school, four hundred and seventy in the morning service, and over five hundred in the evening service. We were also well supported by a wonderful choir, organ, and piano.

Throughout the week that followed, we were kept very busy with meetings, looking in on the various programs of the church, and getting acquainted with the city and the island, as well as visiting some of the beautiful beaches, and enjoying the hospitality of several families.

The second Sunday we were there was incredible. The morning and evening services were packed to overflowing, and we sensed God was at work in a very significant way. The congregation had a meeting that we didn't attend; however, the church board informed me that they were prepared to extend a unanimous call if I would consent to come as their pastor. I couldn't give them an answer since I had no plans to leave the church where I was, but I would certainly give it prayerful consideration.

As my wife and I travelled back north, we talked about all that happened during our visit to Nassau. Then we recalled what had happened when God spoke to us at the Toronto Spiritual Life Convention. We then wondered if this was the move that we should make. When we returned home, we continued to pray for God's guidance. By May 2, 1980, we became convinced that God would have us accept the unanimous call to Calvary Bible Church, Nassau, Bahamas.

That evening I called the secretary of the church council to inform him that I would accept the unanimous call to the church. It was announced to the church on Sunday morning that I had accepted the call. Our youngest daughter was on vacation in Nassau and attended the church the Sunday morning that my acceptance was announced. She told us later that the church erupted in sustained applause; however, when I gave notice of my resignation from the pastoral ministry at Long Branch Baptist Church, they expressed regret at our leaving. I realized that I had helped heal some wounds and also helped the church recover from some divisions, and now I could move on. Before that could become a reality, however, there was still work to be done.

In July of 1980 there was a large gathering in Toronto of Baptists from around the world. My wife and I decided to go to the place where they were meeting to see if we might see some folks we knew. We had the joy of meeting up with some of our friends from Norway. What a happy reunion! We invited them to come and worship with us at Long Branch, and then to our home for a BBQ. There were twenty-seven Norwegians who came along with some friends from the church, making forty in all. We had such a wonderful time of fellowship. This is one of the joys of the Christian family that bridges languages, cultures, and countries.

Preparation, Planning, and Packing

By the end of July, 1980, we had to start thinking about our major move. We felt it necessary to make a trip to Nassau to meet up with the church council, assess the details of our move, and make a decision as to when we would actually begin our pastoral ministry there. So we spent two weeks at the beginning of August working out all the details. A major change was that our youngest son would register at a school there. We enrolled him at St. Augustine's School, where he would start at the beginning of the school year in September. Other young people from the church were students there.

Back in Canada we had our first garage sale on August 23. It was a beautiful day, and the sale was a huge success. I gave about one third of my books to Central Baptist Seminary. In the middle of all of this activity, we had the wedding of my eldest son. Being the parents of the groom was one demand on our time, but I was also the officiating pastor at the wedding. Two weeks later we had another wedding of two of our young people at the church. This was followed by another garage sale, this time to dispose of the furniture our family didn't want, as we couldn't take furniture with us to Nassau.

One major blessing was that the church in Nassau would provide me with a car, so I had to sell my relatively new car in Canada. A local businessman admired my car and was willing to pay exactly my asking price. The problem was that I needed the car for the remaining two weeks before leaving.

"I'll give you a certified cheque for the car, and you can drive it for the next two weeks," he offered. "On the day before you leave, deliver the car to me."

The deal was sealed and two weeks later I delivered the car. Oh, how the Lord takes care of the details when we leave the issues to Him! The son of one of our friends in the church was a real estate agent, and he took care of the sale of the house. We got a few thousand dollars more than we paid for it—thank you, Lord! All that remained to be done was the packing of my books and personal belongings.

The mover came and loaded our stuff into a container ready to ship to Nassau. Through the courtesy of one of our deacons and his wife, and our eldest son and his wife, we could stay with them until we had to fly south. Our church people were so kind and generous to us at our farewell gatherings. The deacons and their wives treated us to a sumptuous meal and time of fellowship. The church as a whole treated us to a lovely meal following our last Sunday service on October 5, 1980, and presented us with a generous cheque. Upon reflection, I believe that we had left the church in a numerically and spiritually healthier condition than we had found it. To God be all the praise and the glory.

During our final week in Canada, we took care of all the final details. Three of our family members were moving with us, so they had a lot of good bye gatherings to deal with. The Bahamian Immigration Authority required that we all should have health certificates from our family doctor. We were all required to have a character reference from our local police department.

At the Bahamian end, the church had to secure work permits and residence permits for us. Eventually we set forth on what would prove to be a very rewarding and fruitful ministry that would have world-wide implications. What a life and what a ministry! From a little cottage in a coal mining community to a sub-tropical paradise—something only God could graciously plan and execute. All of this came about only by the grace of God. By October 11 we flew to Nassau and were warmly welcomed by our Bahamian church family.

37

Bahamas—The Islands of the Shallow Seas

The very mention of the Bahamas brings visions of sun, sand, and sea. It speaks of the exotic, the dramatic, and the romantic. The Bahamas is an island nation made up of some seven hundred islands stretching from a line off West Palm Beach in Florida in the north to almost Cuba in the south. There are some relatively large populated islands, while many are mere clusters of coral rock. Only thirty to forty islands are populated to a greater or lesser degree.

This is a sub-tropical archipelago largely influenced by the Gulf Stream. Because of their location, they're very vulnerable to tropical storms and hurricanes. The highest point in the whole island group is located on Cat Island, and is sixty-three metres high. In days gone by, some islands had large stands of timber. However, very little is now left.

The capital of the Bahamas is Nassau, which is located on the island of New Providence. That Island is twenty-one miles long and seven miles wide. The second largest city is Freeport, which is located on the island of Grand Bahama. In Freeport there is the largest container port on the Eastern Seaboard, and a dry dock that can accommodate the largest ocean going cruise ships.

Originally these islands were largely populated by Lucayan Indians, a branch of the Arawakan speaking Tainos. Between 500 and 800 AD, they began migrating to the Bahamas from other Caribbean Islands, and the population grew to around 40,000. Evidence of the Lucayans is noted in some of the larger islands.

In 1492, Christopher Columbus set out to discover America. His goal was to spread the Christian faith and hopefully discover the "Fountain of Youth." On October 12, 1492, he set foot on the island of San Salvador. A cross and a plaque mark the spot today. The explorers spoke of the islands as being lushly forested and in Baja Mar—meaning shallow sea. These islands were of very little interest to the Spanish because they found no gold and no Fountain of Youth; however, they did find the peace loving Lucayans—a great source of slave labour. So over a period of about thirty years, some 40,000 of them were deported. Some were taken to Spain, but most of them were taken to Hispaniola as slaves. The islands were depopulated for one hundred and thirty years.

In the meantime, the Spanish claimed the islands until the Treaty of Versailles in 1783. Then came the Eleutheran Adventurers from Bermuda to establish a British colony. This was followed by the age of wreckers, privateers, and pirates, the most famous of all being Edward Teach, known as Black Beard. Later the islands became victims of rum running during the days of prohibition in the United States of America. Following this, Woods Rogers was appointed Governor of the British Colony. Then on July 10, 1973, the Bahamas got its independence from the United Kingdom. Since then there has been a marked increase in the development of this island nation. Although very British in character, its economy is very influenced by the United States of America. Realizing that the country has only eight per cent arable land, most things have to be imported. There is also very little manufacturing done in the country. Again, there is great dependence upon imports.

There are three major influences on the economy. The top of the list is tourism, which accounts for sixty to seventy per cent of their economic activity. The bulk of the service industries and labour force is directly related to that. Next is offshore banking, followed by insurance. Much of this is tied to the North American market. More recently, there has been increased Asian influence, primarily from China.

As of the 2000 census, indications are that the population stands at around 302,000. Seventy-five to eighty per cent of residents are descendants from the days of the African slaves. Some of them came from the local plantations, while the larger numbers came from the time of the abolishing of slavery in the U.S.A. The balance of the population is made up of white or Asian people.

Regarding the religious life of the people, the census indicated that thirty-five per cent are Baptist, fifteen per cent are Anglican, thirteen per cent are Roman Catholic, eight per cent are Pentecostal, seven per cent are Assemblies of God, and the balance is made up of the independent groups.

The educational standards have improved considerably over the more recent decades. The College of the Bahamas has played an important part in the ongoing education of teachers and business majors, and has helped with preparation for transfers to other colleges and universities in Britain, the U.S.A, and Canada. The government-operated schools care for the education of the bulk of the children from kindergarten through high school. Christian schools have also been established. Some are multi-denominational, while others are operated by Anglicans, Roman Catholic, and Methodist churches.

The Bahamas has had a democratic government since its independence from Britain on July 10, 1973. It also has a Governor as a representative of the Queen. Perhaps the better known one and least liked was the Duke of Windsor. He had reigned as King of the United Kingdom for barely eleven months. In order to separate him from the German and Nazi influence during the war, George VI posted the Duke to the Bahamas until after the war, when he returned to France. One of the incidents in which he was implicated, and as a result was conveniently absent, was the murder of Sir Harry Oakes. His and others' behaviour at that time is still the subject of "Sip! Sip!" (gossip) in the country. So along with the attraction of the pristine beauty of the islands, the clear waters, and the pink sands, there is a checkered history that always makes for an interesting conversation.

The focus for one in the ministry of the Gospel is the people. They are friendly, open, and always ready to express their faith. Becoming the pastor of Calvary Bible Church enabled me to minister to these dear people, and also have a significant voice in the affairs of the nation. I was a big toad in a little puddle.

That Special Call

Throughout my ministry, there have been two principles that have been very important to me as I have sought God's guidance regarding my decision making in any sphere of service.

1. I have never sought a call to any church or ministry. This was no less true of our move to take up the ministry of Calvary Bible Church in Nassau, Bahamas.
2. I never wanted to know what my salary would be until I knew beyond the shadow of a doubt that this was where God wanted me to serve and I had accepted the call. Only then would I sit down and discuss some of the details. I believed that following God's call was primary, and that God would then honour my commitment by meeting my needs. In my well over sixty years of service, I have proved that God is no man's

debtor. So in this move to the Bahamas, I proved God to be unfailingly faithful.

My wife and I and three of our children arrived in Nassau on Saturday, October 11, 1980 to take up our ministry at Calvary Bible Church. This was the weekend when Discovery Day is celebrated in the Bahamas. A group of the leaders were at the airport to welcome us, and then at the parsonage we were welcomed by a group of the ladies who were there and had a meal all ready for us. What a welcome!

Sunday, October 12, was our first Sunday at Calvary Bible Church. The Sunday school that day had four hundred and sixty-nine in attendance, and the morning service had well over five hundred. The choir led us in our music, and what a spirit was in the service! My opening message was one that I had preached on the first Sunday of every new pastoral ministry. The message is taken from Romans 1:16: "*I am not ashamed of the Gospel of Christ.*" That morning several responded to the invitation to accept Jesus Christ as their Saviour and Lord. One of the special things in that service was the dedication of the daughter of the secretary of the church board and his wife. This young lady is now married with a family of her own. That first week was extremely busy getting acquainted and oriented.

Now that we were in a sub-tropical climate, the bugs that go with the territory had invaded the parsonage, which had been unoccupied for some time. So the exterminators were called in to do a cleanup job.

38

The History of the Calvary Bible Church

Calvary Bible Church began on September 16, 1962, under the leadership of Pastor and Mrs. Earl Weech. It was clearly evident that God's hand was on this ministry from the very beginning. With Pastor Weech as the spiritual leader, supported by outstanding laymen, the work started in a very humble way. One of those laymen was Mr. Frank Pinder. He was a very successful businessman. Each Saturday, Brother Pinder would move the cars out of the showroom of his car business and prepare it for services to be held there the next morning. At the first service there were four hundred and thirty-two people in attendance. Then a large tent was brought in from Florida and erected on the car lot. Due to a very bad storm in January, 1963, however, the tent was completely destroyed, so they reverted back to the show room.

In time, a parcel of land was bought on Collins Avenue, and in February, 1963, there was a ground-breaking ceremony and the plans for a new building were underway. In the meantime, God was at work in the heart of one man who eventually would become very important in the growing work of Calvary Bible Church. Mr. Merlin W. Albury, husband of Mrs. Vivian Albury, came under the sound of the Gospel one evening while sitting in the car waiting for his daughter, Anita, who was one of the church pianists. Merlin heard Pastor Weech's message and came under deep conviction. The following week he gave his heart to the Lord. Merlin Albury, an outstanding architect, was then used of the Lord to draw up the plans for the beautiful church building that now stands on Collins Avenue, Centerville, Nassau. God has His own way of drawing people together to accomplish His purposes. By December, 1963, the rapidly growing congregation was now able to move into the new church building, even though it wasn't completely finished.

The men of the church worked very hard night after night after they were finished their regular day's work. They would often finish the day washing off the dirt and perspiration with a swim in Montague Bay. The ladies kept the men supplied with food and drinks and ice cream. This was a community miracle as men and women of the church and community and business world donated man power and materials to help raise the beautiful church and Christian education building to the glory of God. The growing congregation was able to move into the new church, even though it wasn't completely finished.

The dedication of the completed building took place on October 25, 1965. From August of 1963, the church was managed by an executive board comprised of Pastor Weech as chairman, Carl Moree as treasurer, Jasiel Thompson as secretary, and Redith Roberts, John Pinder, John Lowe, and Raymond Thompson as board members. This board was expanded to form the church council in 1966. The Articles of Association were unanimously approved and signed on March 14, 1969. In 1970, a parsonage was built in High Vista. During this time, *Echoes of Calvary* was established on ZNS radio

Pastor and Mrs. Earle Weech, who were the founding pastors, served from 1962 to 1970, at which time they went back to the United States to serve the Lord there. Pastor Jasiel Thompson served as interim pastor from 1971 to 1972. He was much appreciated as an able preacher and Bible teacher. For many years he ministered on *Calvary Bible Time* each Sunday morning on ZNS 2 Radio.

Pastor and Mrs. David Cole, natives of England, served at Calvary from 1972 to 1978. They left a very significant legacy in the church. Missionary interest was a very significant part of the church since the very beginning; however, under the leadership of Pastor and Mrs. Cole, the missionary vision became much greater. With the help of some of the staff from Peoples Church, Toronto, Canada, an extensive missionary program was launched. This included the Faith Promise Offering Plan. The first year (1973), $47,500 was promised for missionaries and mission projects at home and overseas. This was a significant contribution to the effective fulfillment of the Great Commission. This increased steadily each year, and Dr. James Blackwood of Global Outreach Mission made a significant contribution to this ministry at the missions conference for many years.

During the time of Pastor and Mrs. Cole's ministry, there was a significant development—the Awana Clubs were introduced as a ministry amongst our children and young people. Mrs. Cole and Mrs. Barbara Sawyer, along with others, spent much time giving direction to this ministry. Eventually we had some four hundred kids involved in the Awana clubs, making it one of the largest in North America. After six years of ministry at Calvary, the Coles returned with their family to England.

39

A New Country, a New Church, a New Culture

When I arrived in October of 1980 to assume the pastoral leadership of Calvary Bible Church, the church had been without a fulltime pastor for two years. The ministry had been maintained by Jasiel Thompson, Dansbury Hudson, and visiting pastors and missionaries.

This ministry lay before us as an incredible challenge with limitless opportunities. We were convinced that all of our previous ministries—from mission work in Lapland to rural communities and towns in New Brunswick, to pastoral ministry and extensive radio and television ministry in Newfoundland, to the Metropolis of Toronto—had equipped us for this major move to the sub-tropics of the Bahamas and the Caribbean. What a contrast from the Arctic snow to the island sun. With our wide experience in cross-cultural exposure, we readily adapted to our new field of service. God would use us to take the church to new levels of ministry and a diversity of impact. As one of my teachers used to say as he breezed into our morning class, "Hats off to the past, coats off to the future, the best is yet to be."

We launched into our new ministry with a renewed vim, vitality, and verve. It was an extra blessing to know that my wife, who'd had major cancer surgery, had recovered fairly well. As a result, she was able to submerge herself in ministry amongst the women, the children, and the youth. She was also involved in visitation with me, along with conducting a very effective counseling ministry. By pooling our resources, we were able to have a very effective ministry together.

A Snapshot of Ministry and Family

A look at my journal of daily activities from October 12 to October 31, 1980, more or less gives an introduction to what my ministry would be like in the next ten years, and how busy I would be in this new sphere of service. In those first twenty days, I had twenty-seven meetings. At that time I prepared and presented thirty-one messages. My wife and I made six visits to members of the congregation. During that time I had six interviews/counselling sessions and conducted three dedications. I had twelve radio programs and eight television devotionals. Our Sunday school had classes from kindergarten to adult, and the average attendance for the three Sundays was four hundred and eighty. Our Sunday services averaged around the five hundred mark. During that time, twenty-five people made personal commitments to the Lord Jesus Christ, while others expressed their desire to follow the Lord in baptism. We enjoyed the fellowship of evangelical pastors and missionaries who were serving the Lord in the Bahamas. This was always a great source of encouragement. These ongoing demands were relatively characteristic of my ten years of ministry there.

Three of our children came down to Nassau with us. Our youngest son was still in school, so he completed his formal education at St. Augustine's College. Our middle son also travelled down with us. He was already in the work force, but couldn't be employed in the Bahamas since he didn't have a work permit. However, we discovered that he had been badly bitten by the "love bug" just before leaving Canada. Within the first month, he headed back north as the only cure for his malady. Our youngest daughter stayed on with us in Nassau for quite some time. Although she could not be gainfully employed, she was kept busy. She was quite helpful around the house, thus giving my wife more time to be involved in the church, in the women's work, and visitation with me. Our daughter did quite a bit of volunteer work and developed some lasting friendships in Nassau. Eventually she was able to return to her place of employment in Canada, where they had kept the position open for her. However, it wasn't too long before both our middle son and youngest daughter married and settled down in Canada.

Very soon my regular schedule included eight to ten meetings per week, plus my time in my study at church, which usually started at 7:30 each morning. If I didn't get to my study at this time, I would have to fight very heavy traffic along Bay Street. In this way I could get a good one and a half hours of work in before the rest of the staff arrived and the telephone started ringing. Four afternoons each week my wife and I would spend time visiting in hospitals and senior homes and with shut-ins. We also made follow-up pastoral calls on members of the congregation. Throughout my entire ministry I was very much convinced that "a home going pastor makes for a church going people." Visitation enabled me to sense the needs of the congregation, and this would guide me in planning my teaching and preaching ministry. In this way, as a shepherd I could better tend to the sheep.

My wife had a significant ministry amongst the women. In addition to this, she exercised a strong ministry in spiritual counselling as well as to those who made a commitment to the Lord Jesus Christ. She had a powerful ministry through prayer, and from time to time she also ministered to women's groups in other churches in the city.

It was not too many months before we identified needs that impacted some of our people within the church family as well as those in the community at large. Visiting one day with the Arnett family, I discovered that Pastor Frederick Arnett, leader of our street meeting team, Ambassadors for Christ, was also ministering to the physical needs of a number of people with whom they had come into contact. In the course of our conversation, we discovered that he was personally contributing to the needs of those less fortunate. I expressed my concern that the whole church should really be involved. Around this time my wife had been involved with the ladies who were studying that portion of Scripture in Matthew 25 where we find these words in verse 40: " ... *inasmuch as you have done it to one of the least of these My brethren, you did it to me.*" We felt it appropriate that we should call this ministry "Operation Inasmuch." This was duly approved by the board of the church.

Two large wooden bins were built and placed by the main foyer of the church. The congregation was encouraged to contribute non-perishable grocery items and place them in the large bins. A number of our men in the congregation were in the wholesale grocery business and made significant contributions to this ministry, along with substantial financial gifts. Eventually a retired layman volunteered his time to take on the management of this ministry along with other helpers. Later we acquired a building on the site of the new church property and we expanded this ministry to include clothing and household item, all of which were housed in this building, which was used as a distribution centre. Over the years since this ministry started, some sixty to one hundred packages are distributed each week.

The Ambassadors for Christ team was a group of men and women who reached out to the community with street meetings, evangelism, singing and preaching, and visitation. Many have been won to the Lord through this important and significant ministry. One very precious story follows. The team was witnessing in one of the streets through testimonies, singing, and a short gospel message. Unknown to the team, there was a lady who was listening to this witness. This lady was confined to bed, unable to move. She could barely turn her head, and had very limited movement of her hands. She heard the singing and the brief gospel message and called her grandson to tell him to go out and tell the preacher to come in because she wanted to talk to him. That evening she committed her life to the Lord Jesus Christ. What a change took place and what a witness she would give to anyone who came in. My wife and I started to visit her regularly. She was such an inspiration. Unable to care for herself, twenty for hours a day she lay on a double bed. Her whole world was confined between the four walls of a room approximately eight feet by ten feet with one window, one door, and one chair. We visited her to bring some brightness to her day and blessing to her heart. I always read from the Word of God and had prayer with her. Now here was the moment of inspiration. Just as soon as I finished praying and said "Amen," she would immediately wax eloquent in prayer. Her prayer consisted of thanksgiving and praise, but never a word of complaint or a plea for the Lord to take her out of her misery. What a challenge to those of us who have it all.

40

Raising our Sights—Expanding our Boundaries

The year 1982 was shaping up to be a very busy year. By this time my ministries at the church were placing greater demands on my time and energy. Increasingly I was becoming more and more significantly involved in more and more enterprises in the community and country at large. God had earlier instilled in me a sense of vision and mission for concerns that reached out in concentric circles, touching other countries, cultures, and situations. All of these grew out of the fact that I had been privileged by God's grace and enabling Spirit to be exposed to so many areas of service over my preceding years of ministry. I had developed a wealth of knowledge and experience. To not put this into practice, and not encourage others to do likewise, would be a serious failure on my part and would in the end fall short of my calling and burden to spread the good news of the Gospel wherever I encountered open doors. In Calvary Bible Church itself my calling was to be their pastor. This meant feeding the flock of God, shepherding the people of God, equipping them to do the work of God, and seeing them in turn reproducing in the place where God had called them to serve.

The following statistics will help to indicate something of my involvement on the local scene. It's my prayer that they may serve as a challenge to young men contemplating the pastoral ministry in this twenty-first century. We need to keep in mind that we serve God by ministering to people, not by being slaves to programs.

My 1982 records reveal the following, and on average represent each year of my ministry in the Bahamas. My preaching ministry is represented by the fact that I prepared and delivered two hundred and ninety messages in 1982.

I prepared and delivered eighty-one radio messages and twelve television programs. In all, I had five hundred and eleven meetings. It was encouraging to note that during that period of time there were one hundred and five first time decisions for Christ. These were counselled by trained counselors, and then they became part of our new converts Class. Throughout the year, either I, or my wife and I, made three hundred and twenty-seven visits to hospitals, shut-ins, and members of our congregation, some of whom were facing special challenges. I conducted six funerals and seven weddings. Some of these were held in early morning hours to avoid the heat of the day. For each couple I conducted four to six pre-marital counselling sessions. In addition to this, I was deeply involved in family counselling and ministering to families who had been impacted by drug problems, which were rampant at that time. During the year I had the joy of baptizing twenty-one individuals.

All of this was very demanding and challenging, as well as physically, emotionally, and spiritually draining. I had to pause and take inventory and determine if my exhaustion was due to the possibility that I was doing so much in my own strength. Then I would pause and reflect upon those precious words from Isaiah 40:

> *But those who wait on the Lord shall renew their strength, they shall mount up with wings as eagles, they shall run and not be weary, they shall walk and not faint.* (Isaiah 40:31)

Around this time a relatively new Christian, a well known business man, had a concern for my wellbeing. He realized the need for me to uncouple from time to time; however, where does one go while living on an island seven miles wide and twenty-one miles long. There were other islands, but how does one get there? So he talked with a number of other men in the church, encouraging them to share in his concern. Together they presented me with a beautiful boat, complete with outboard motor. Wow! This would enable my wife and me to escape to Rose Island or one of the other cays to relax rest and renew with no cell phone (of course in those days Facebook, Twitter, and I-Pads were not available). It meant also that we could, from time to time, take family and friends out with us. Many times I walked that pink sand beach, soaked in the azure seas, baked in the sub-tropical sun, and looked up to the clear blue sky to shout: "All this, and Heaven too!" This prompted me to write the following poem of gratitude and praise.

All This, and Heaven Too

The islands of the shallow sea,
Is surely where I want to be.
With sand so pink and sea so blue,
It's ours: "All this, and heaven too!"
The sun that warms each beautiful strand
Brings many to Bahama land
Its wonders to enjoy and view,
And cry: "All this, and heaven too!"
God's handiwork we do behold,
Whether in reef or hidden shoal;
We see His hand in all 'tis true;
Ah, yes: "All this, and heaven too!"
The birds that fly, the fish that swim,
They all indeed belong to Him;
Who had ideas, not a few?
And promised: "All this, and heaven too!"

So, visitor to our island shore,
Enjoy this Paradise and more;
It's all on loan to me and you,
So take care of: "All this, and heaven too!"
But remember also what God has planned,
There's more to life than Bahama land.
He died on the cross for Gentile and Jew,
To provide: "All this, and heaven too!"
So trust Him today, my visitor friend,
You'll enjoy a life that will never end;
Be assured of this, that when you do,
He will give you: "All this, and heaven too!"

After two or three hours I would return to my ministries refreshed and invigorated. Our Lord repaired to a desert place, and I had the joy of repairing to a deserted island. How many times I have thanked the Lord for loving, caring, thoughtful, and Godly men.

Extending My Ministry

One of the great joys I had was having the opportunity to teach at Day Star Bible School. This was operated by one of the Evangelical missions operating in the Caribbean. It was a great privilege to have a part in equipping young potential leaders. I taught primarily from the Epistle to the Ephesians and the Epistles of St. John. Along with these, I taught some of the principles of leadership in the local church. At least two former students are now successful pastors in local Bahamian churches.

Around this time I had the joy of getting acquainted with some of the members of the Billy Graham Ministries. One of them had extensive knowledge and experience with sound systems. A growing congregation and a need to replace and improve our sound system in the main sanctuary caused us to seek some expert advice. The result was a greatly improved sound system that enabled those who attended our services to sit wherever they wished and hear clearly the music and the ministry of the Word.

Changes and Growth

Growth always comes with challenges as to how best to cope. Our Sunday school records at this time showed that our attendance was around the five hundred and fifty mark. We needed more space to take care of the increase in numbers. Our sanctuary was packed to capacity on Sunday mornings. Church growth principles show that when attendance fills eighty per cent of available space, one needs to consider enlarging or having a number of people hive off to start another church in another location. This situation gave rise to an immediate solution to the situation.

We decided to expand our junior church ministry by running it concurrently with the morning service. This took the children out of the main sanctuary, thus freeing up quite a bit of space there for the adults. Then we divided up our junior church into three different departments, which operated just like church services.

At that time I drew rough drawings of what could be done to make better use of the space in the sanctuary. Then we called in the services of an architect who would help to implement these plans. This would involve redesigning the platform and pulpit area to provide space for our forty-voice choir. However, upon checking the beautiful panelling on the back and side walls of the platform, we discovered some major problems.

What appeared to be rich and beautiful looking on the surface was not so. Some unseen creatures had been hard at work. We had become victims of one of the unseen hazards of a sub-tropical climate. The termites had been hard at work destroying those panels on the back while the surface was left intact. All of them had to be replaced. Some of the windows had to be replaced, new carpeting was installed, and the pews were upholstered. What a transformation!

With the increase in attendance, particularly on Sunday mornings, we were running out of parking space. People were having to park on neighbouring properties, particularly across the street. The church was located on Collins Avenue, which presented a major safety hazard for people crossing this major thoroughfare. We approached the owners of the service station located right next to the church. They weren't open on Sundays, so they kindly agreed to allow us to use their facilities for overflow parking. They agreed to let us cut a gateway through the wall to provide easy access to the church. This was a good, temporary solution to our parking problem.

(41)

Reaching Beyond our Shores

While rejoicing in what God was doing in our Jerusalem, we also realized that we had to keep our global vision in perspective. The mandate from the Lord of the Church was to make sure that we were not negligent in including the "whole world." We became aware of a major need in Haiti, so my wife and I began to make plans for a trip to Haiti.

We set out on February 19, 1982. We wanted to visit our missionary to Haiti, Miss Phyllis Newby. She was a native of Jamaica who had been working in Haiti for many years. There was also a need for a major building project. The third thing we wanted to do was minister to the national pastors, as well as to the teachers who were working in the mission schools that were serving in rural communities, some of which were located in remote areas.

The first thing we did was have the pastors and teachers gather at the mission centre in Port au Prince, the capital city. My wife and I both ministered during those days. Some of our ministry was geared to providing material that could be used by them in the community where they served. We also shared some inspirational teaching to provide encouragement in their personal life. They were so appreciative of the time that we were able to spend with them.

Next came the ministry to some of the Haitian congregations. It was very special to observe how God had worked in the lives of so many people. Their simple, yet genuine, devotion to the Lord, and their limited, yet whole hearted, service in His kingdom was certainly worth emulating.

There were also some interesting and unique experiences. There are two experiences I should share with you at this time. Both of them took place in the evening service of two different churches, both of which were rather primitive buildings. In one church, there was a single light bulb hanging from a rafter. It was the only source of light and probably only twenty-five watts strong. I was preaching through an interpreter. Suddenly I was aware of some commotion at the back of the church. I realized that the commotion was making its way gradually towards the area where the interpreter and I were standing. I could see some of the people on each side of the aisle reaching out with their foot and stomping. Then, as the object of their activity came within the circle of light created by the twenty-five watt bulb, I identified it as the biggest cockroach I'd ever seen, making its way towards me over the earthen floor. Here I was preaching, the cockroach was coming forward, and I hadn't even given an altar call. One quick stomp and I disposed of the creature and went on preaching.

On another evening in the same building while I was preaching, my wife was sitting in the congregation just on the edge of that ring of light produced by the single light bulb. In the midst of my message, I noticed my wife moving her head from side to side. At first I thought she was disagreeing with my message. Then I realized that her eyes were fixed on the rafter above me. After the service was over I immediately asked her what was going on. She informed me that all the time I was preaching a rat kept running back and forth on the rafter above me. She was concerned that it might fall on me at any moment. These were exciting interludes in what are sometimes very harsh circumstances.

After surveying the situation in several areas, we finally settled on Thomazeau as the place where we would erect the building. This building would be planned to house the church, the school, and the clinic. Having made this decision, we returned to Nassau to draw plans, raise funds, and challenge some of our people to form teams and make the trip to Haiti to make this project a reality. My wife and I were absolutely overwhelmed by the desperate needs and the abject poverty of this amazing nation. Let me take a few minutes to give some background to this nation and people, so that we may better understand the people and the land.

Haiti is part of the island known as Hispaniola and is over 10,200 square miles in size. The official language is French, but the common language of the people is Creole.

At one time, the people were in slavery to the plantation and land owners. In the eighteenth century, under the leadership of one of their own, they staged a massive revolt against their masters. Their owners were murdered indiscriminately, and the vast sugar plantations were set ablaze. The mansions were burned to the ground, and the slaves were free. The Haitian people were the first in the entire world to be freed from slavery, but the foundations of their economy were destroyed. They have lived largely in poverty ever since. It continues to be the poorest country in the Western hemisphere. It's still suffering under unscrupulous politicians, and in recent years has suffered under the widespread devastation caused by natural disasters. My wife and I couldn't forget the desperate need that we saw everywhere we went and were determined to alleviate some of that suffering ... at least in one given community.

The smells coming from the open garbage dump just outside of Port-au-Prince were pungent and overpowering. People lived on that dump in shacks made from whatever pieces of material that could be salvaged from the refuse. In Haiti, arable land is in short supply. Two major crops were grown, namely tobacco and sugar cane. Neither of these crops contributed much to the nourishment or wellbeing of the people, and they were foreign owned. The hillsides were denuded of trees. They had been cut down to make charcoal for cooking fires. Because there were very few trees on the hillsides, the soil was washed away during the heavy rains of the rainy season. Wages were very low. Education facilities were scarce. In the largely rural areas, most of the buildings were made from crooked branches interwoven with palm branches. Some had mud walls and corrugated metal roofs.

During our days there, the country was ruled by Jean Claude Duvalier, commonly known as "Baby Doc." It was a tyrannical dictatorship. His reign was brought to an abrupt end as a result of a massive revolt of the people. He fled the country, taking with him millions of dollars, and found refuge in France. At the time of this writing, he has returned to Haiti and is presently on trial for his terrible, brutal treatment of the people.

Working Together, Advancing the Kingdom

Miss Phyllis Newby, whom we had supported for many years, was our representative in Haiti. She had established schools, churches, clinics, and orphanages, largely throughout the remote rural areas of the country. These were all led by national pastors, teachers, and workers working under extremely primitive conditions with very limited support. Formidable opposition was experienced from voodoo and the voodoo priests. One of the great triumphs was to see some of those priests coming to personal faith in the Lord Jesus Christ, and to see the power of voodooism forever broken by the power of the Gospel of the Lord Jesus Christ. He and He alone can break the power of cancelled sin and set the prisoner free.

I know of one village where the voodoo priest was gloriously saved and scores of the villagers came to personal faith in Jesus Christ.

Upon returning from Haiti to Nassau, I immediately secured the help of a friend who was an architect. Together we came up with some simple plans that would serve as a guide for the proposed building. Two things were now very important—we needed to raise the finances and we had to recruit teams. About this time we had our missions conference. We dedicated one evening when we would take up an offering for the project in Haiti. Following a presentation of the project in Haiti, we took up an offering. That one offering brought in over $7,000.00. Eventually our people gave over $30,000.00 towards this project. This was over and above the faith promise offering of our missions conference. In addition to this, people began making plans to take one or two weeks off from their work or their business. We stressed the fact that no building experience was necessary, but certainly would be helpful. One building contractor, Brother Isaac McKenzie, took several weeks off from his business to head up this project. He and I were the only ones with any building experience, and we offered on the job training for any who would come. We had a variety of people, men and women, who made up the team. One worthy of mention was a Lieutenant Commander from the Royal Navy who was in Nassau for a time training members of the Bahamian defense force. He learned very quickly and became a very proficient cement block layer.

Before all this was put in motion, my wife and I made a second trip to Thomazeau, Haiti. With building plans in hand, our goal was to get some of the local people to select a plot of land, measure for the foundation, and get everything ready for the first team to come down and start building. In due time, we assembled the first team, which included the building contractor, myself, and twelve others. Each member was to carry two suitcases. One would contain their personal clothes and whatever work gear they needed. The other suitcase would contain used clothing, t-shirts, and other items that would be made available to the people. We also carried non-perishable food items as our personal food and sufficient extra to provide lunch for the children of the village where we were doing the building. We had to fly from Nassau to Miami and then from Miami to Haiti. The airlines, the airport authorities, and the customs officials all along the way were so helpful and co-operative.

We were about to make our plans become a reality. Our first day on the job was very exciting. We were out bright and early so that we would get started ahead of the heat of the day. On average, at the high sun it was around one hundred degrees. We finished in early afternoon to try to avoid the hottest part of the day. Our building materials were unloaded by the edge of the highway. From there we hauled the sand, cement, blocks, and lumber and plywood by ox-cart to the job site, about one kilometre away, since there was no road in to the village.

The building contractor and I set up the corners of the first long wall and then showed the team who were going to be laying cement blocks how to mix the mortar and start laying the blocks. The building was to be thirty-five feet wide and seventy-five feet long. Within the walls would be housed the church, the school, and the clinic. Good progress was made that first day. Everyone was very tired, and those who were not used to physical labour had many aching bones and muscles. A shower, a hearty meal, and an early bedtime were all most welcome.

While the building contractor and I were travelling back to the mission headquarters that afternoon, I raised an important question. In our eagerness to get started, we'd omitted one serious matter. We had not checked to see if the foundation had been laid to the correct measurements by the local men. We agreed that first thing the next morning we'd check the measurements. This we did, only to discover a terrible mistake. The long wall we'd started on was exactly right. The front foundation was also correct. Very good so far. However, upon checking the back foundation, we discovered that it was only thirty feet long— five feet short of what it should have been. Thank you, Lord, for prompting us to check. This was promptly corrected and we were able to continue laying the blocks. Wondering what gave rise to this error, I asked the local men what they'd used to measure the foundation. They proudly showed me a twelve inch school ruler. Someone obviously miscounted.

Two other teams came down from our church in the Bahamas and the work continued. There was no electricity in the village, so we needed to get a generator to give us power to operate saws and drills. One of our men flew down from the Bahamas in a private plane and brought a generator for our use. This was something new for the village and attracted much attention. When the job was completed we left the generator to be used by the people of the village.

We had a few weeks' break from the work, and then we brought down one final team. Their job was to install the doors and also the decorative blocks in the window openings. One of the blessings of having the teams come down was that on the Sundays our teams split up into several groups and spread out to other villages where they gave testimonies, sang, and ministered the Word of God. One day I met a pastor on his way home from church, and he was carrying a live chicken under his arm. I discovered that this was part of his pastor's salary.

My wife sometimes helped in some of the clinics. Some of the children were seen with distended stomachs, a sure sign of malnutrition. A number of them also had reddish coloured hair. One realizes how many of them are denied the basic necessities of life, so we provided the children of the village with lunch every day, and this was very much appreciated.

Finally the day came when we were to hand over the building to the village. That morning, the primitive school building made of wooden framing, woven palm branches, and a metal roof, collapsed. It had become the victim of the ever present termites. No need to worry, though—they had a beautiful building that they were now calling "le palais."

There was a great celebration. The school children were gathered as a group and sang the national anthem and some other songs, saluted the flag, and gave God thanks. We then gathered inside the building to give out gifts of clothing to the children and others. We offered thanks to God for His enabling grace and goodness.

That same day a very beautiful and emotional event took place, one that I will not soon forget. While standing outside talking with the senior pastor, who was also one of our interpreters, I noticed an elderly Haitian lady approaching us. She had on a very simple dress, obviously made from cotton, probably a flour sack. I noticed that she was carrying a large melon. When she came in front of me, she got down on her knees in the dust and offered the melon to me, all the time speaking in Creole. I was not quite sure what was happening, so I turned to Pastor Andre for an explanation. He indicated that this lady was offering me the melon as a thank you gift to me and the team in appreciation for all that we had done for the village. I indicated to Andre that I couldn't accept this gift, since she and the villagers had so little. The pastor said that I must accept it, or else she would be very offended and feel rejected. I thanked her graciously and profusely with tears in my eyes. I remembered the story that Jesus told of the widow and the rich people. This lady gave out of her "want," while we had given out of our "abundance." Hers was the greater gift. Sometime later my wife succumbed to her cancer and the Lord took her home. Then the villagers dedicated the medical clinic in her honor.

42

Twenty Years of Faithful Ministry

In September of 1982, we celebrated the twentieth anniversary of Calvary Bible Church. We had a whole week of celebrations from September 11 to 18. We kicked off the celebrations with a formal banquet at one of the hotels on Cable Beach, Nassau. It was a memorable evening in which leaders and pastors were honoured for their contribution to the ministry of the church over the years. On that Sunday morning the service was broadcast. Pastor Earle Weech, the founding pastor, preached the morning message. We were honoured to have in attendance the Governor General of the Bahamas, Sir Gerald Cash and Lady Cash. Also in attendance was Lady Pindling, wife of the Prime Minister of the Bahamas. I may note here that Lady Pindling was also a faithful listener to our radio program *Echoes of Calvary*.

All through the week we had evening gatherings highlighting the different ministries within the church. Friday night was a special night of history. The ladies of the church put on a wonderful banquet in the Earle Weech Auditorium with some five hundred people in attendance. As a highlight of the evening, we commissioned a chef at one of the hotels to bake an anniversary cake in the shape of the church building. It was a masterpiece. The cake weighed over four hundred pounds, and it took four able bodied men to carry it into the auditorium. My wife had the honour of cutting the cake. What a memorable week!

Following the week of celebration, we planned a number of special events that would impact the life of the church as well as reach out into the community at large. We planned an evangelistic crusade with Dr. Ralph Bell, a native of St. Catharines, Ontario, and an evangelist with the Billy Graham Association. God really blessed in that significant outreach. On the Friday night we held a youth rally in the local arena with about four thousand people in attendance, and over one hundred made personal commitments to Jesus Christ.

Late that fall we had Rev. Arthur Larsen with us for a series of Deeper Life meetings. We also enjoyed the music ministry of James Barlow. During that week one hundred and twenty-five people rededicated their lives to the Lord, and fifteen made first time commitments to Jesus Christ. Later that year we had the opportunity for a very unusual, unexpected outreach touching not only all of Nassau but our family islands as well. "The John Templeton Award" was awarded to Dr. Billy Graham and the Billy Graham Evangelistic Association, acknowledging the impact of this incredible ministry around the world.

Arrangements were made for Dr. Graham to come to the Bahamas to receive this award. Realizing this, a number of us felt that we should make the most of this visit. I was asked to become the chairman of a planning committee to arrange for a great evangelistic rally at the sports stadium featuring Dr. Graham and his supporting team. This was an exciting time. The event was planned for November 24, 1982. There would also be a choir led by Cliff Barrows. Sessions were organized to train counsellors and ushers, and prayer meetings were planned throughout the city. Plans were made to enlist the support of the churches through the different denominational leaders. This was to be a major event of the year.

God was very gracious in granting us wonderful weather, which was so important since it was to be an outdoor event. Over 25,000 people crowded into the sports arena. The sound of that great song, "Blessed Assurance," echoed through that tropical evening. Dr. George Beverly Shea's baritone voice carried a wonderful message in song. Then to a resounding welcome, Dr. Graham rose to deliver a powerful, yet simple, gospel message. When the invitation was extended to the people to accept Christ and the choir stated to sing the hymn "Just as I Am," over two thousand people came forward in response. This was worth it all. To God be the Glory.

This was an eventful year in so many ways. What reassuring joy it is to know that the Gospel is still the power of God unto salvation. Later we were able to attend the Evangelism Explosion Conference at Coral Ridge Presbyterian Church in Florida, pastored by Dr. James Kennedy. There my assistant, his wife, my wife, and I became certified trainers. Upon our return to Nassau, we were able to set up training sessions there.

43

Involvement in Government, Country, and Community

In 1983 I became involved in speaking at school assemblies in government schools as well as denominational schools and private Christian schools. As a result, we had a church parade of the teachers from these different schools. This gave us an incredible opportunity for outreach into different levels of society.

One ministry that was developed resulted from a visit from the very well known American, Dr. Charles Colson. As a result of his involvement in the Watergate scandal in 1973, he had been sentenced to prison. He served seven months of his sentence. While he was in prison, he became a born again believer. His life was completely transformed. As a result, God gave him a great burden for those who had been sentenced to prison. From this, he founded Prison Fellowship. He was invited to Nassau to receive the Templeton Prize for progress in religion. While in the Bahamas, he launched the Prison Fellowship Ministry in Nassau. It was a real joy to work with him and to see this ministry established. One of the laymen in our church committed himself to this ministry. Over the years he's had the joy of leading many of the prisoners to personal faith in the Lord Jesus Christ. The Lord continued to open doors of opportunity and gave us the wisdom and strength to take advantage of these opportunities.

Ongoing Challenges

In January of 1984, my dear wife was admitted once more to McMaster Hospital in Hamilton, Canada. She was always very insistent that I remain in Nassau to be faithful in my ministry. She assured me that she was being well looked after in the hospital and by the family in Canada. However, this visit to Canada revealed that the cancer was spreading. It was now in her leg bones, pelvic area, ribs, and vertebrae. The doctor determined that my wife should have radiation as well as chemotherapy.

At this point I decided that I should make a quick trip to Canada to have consultation with my wife's caregivers. I left my youngest son in Nassau in the care of some friends at the church. I was in Canada only a few days when I received word from one of our board members, who was also our pharmacist, that Erik had been involved in an accident with his motorbike, was in the hospital requiring surgery. The surgeon required my authority to be able to go ahead with the surgery. This I was able to give over the phone. Here I was in Canada, with my wife in hospital in critical condition, and my son in Nassau in hospital going through knee surgery. Where could I go but to the Lord? In times like these, we prove that God's grace is sufficient in every circumstance.

Before I returned to Nassau, my wife was discharged from the hospital and was cared for as an outpatient. When she came out of the hospital, I had to get medication for her that cost $180.00. All the flying back and forth, plus medication costs, put stress on our finances; however, God graciously provided for all our needs. Realizing the cost of medical care, I put in motion plans to provide our staff with medical insurance. This was duly done. My wife returned to Nassau in time for our missions conference that year.

While in Nassau, my wife came under the care of Dr. Lunn, who gave her excellent care. She became a regular patient at the Cancer Clinic at the Princess Margaret Hospital where she received excellent care. Getting blood transfusions, chemotherapy, and radiation seemed to restore my wife's strength and mobility. As a result, with the doctor's permission, I was thrilled to have my wife to join us on our group tour of the Bible lands. We had forty-four people on this tour that included Jordan, Israel, Greece, and the Greek Islands. This was a very special time in so many ways.

In July of 1984 our eldest daughter was married in Toronto, and we were able to be there. My wife expressed a great desire to see her parents and family in Scotland, so arrangements were made for a Jamieson family reunion in Edinburgh. This would prove to be her last visit with family. Her cancer specialist made plans with a hospital in Edinburgh for her to continue with chemotherapy and also blood transfusions. This worked out very well.

I was able to preach in my wife's home church, Spurgeon Memorial in Edinburgh. I also preached in my home church, from which we were commissioned to go to the mission field back in 1950. From there we were able to go to Drogheda and minister with our Global Outreach missionaries. Then it was on to Switzerland to speak at the Global Outreach conference. This was where we always had our conferences when my wife and I worked with the mission in Lapland and Norway. On our way back from the conference, we stopped in Wales where we had fellowship with our former missionary co-workers, Betty and Vivian James. While there I preached in the Norwegian church in Swansea.

Upon our return to Nassau, my wife developed a wonderful ministry to cancer patients. She was often called upon to counsel with patients at the cancer clinic as well as privately. She was able to help them both emotionally and spiritually.

Over Christmas and New Year we had a wonderful time with family and friends. Over a period of three evenings we had different groups in from the church to the parsonage. We served them a wonderful festive meal followed by a time of singing and games. This was a very special time.

Multiplication for Expansion

At the meeting of our church council in February, 1985, we made two very significant and major decisions. These decisions involved increasing our staff. Up to this point I was alone on the ministry staff and depended on some of our lay people to fill in when I had to be away. With a heavy preaching schedule of five messages weekly, plus weddings, funerals, and visitation, it became evident that I very much needed assistance. We were giving thought to securing an assistant to the pastor and also a youth pastor.

We had in mind a young man to be an assistant to the pastor. He had come to personal faith in Christ through the reading of a Gideon Bible in a hotel room. He was a very valued employee of Batelco, the national telephone company; however, following his life changing encounter with the Lord Jesus Christ, he became involved as a leader of our evangelistic team. He'd also had some Bible school training at the Baptist school in Nassau. He and his wife were incredible witnesses and workers in our church. It was only after much prayer and many interviews that he finally consented to become my assistant. What a blessing to me and to the church as he led in evangelism and visitation.

Next was the question of a youth pastor. We found out that Clint Kemp, grandson of the founding Pastor, would soon be graduating from Moody Bible Institute. We made contact with him and extended to him a call to become our youth pastor. He accepted and became a vital part of our staff. He did an outstanding work amongst the youth of the church.

Eventually both of these men, Pastor Arnett and Pastor Kemp, were ordained to the Christian ministry at Calvary Bible Church. We were convinced that we were moving in the right direction.

Growth in Numbers Required Expansion of Facilities

With the growth in attendance, we not only had problems finding parking space, but we also needed room space to accommodate growing Sunday school and adult departments. We needed more space to accommodate administration as well as our two new pastoral staff. We were in the time when the growing drug problem was wreaking havoc in our society and impacting many of our families.

Around this time we became aware of certain properties on two sides of our existing property. Upon further investigation, we discovered that all properties on both sides were up for sale. There was a large vacant lot next to another lot with six cottages on it. Then there was a two storied apartment block containing six apartments. Facing the main street, parallel to the main church building, was a ranch style bungalow. We believed that this was not just coincidence, but God's timing for us to move forward and take action.

Our church council immediately appointed an ad hoc committee to further investigate this possibility. Mr. Brian Moree, one of our lawyers in the church, was appointed to chair this committee. These combined properties were valued at two million dollars, but we could purchase them for $446.000.00. Our Association, the legal entity of our church, was apprised of the properties and the cost. They were the only ones who could negotiate the purchase and the finances. A short time before all of this we had burned the mortgage we had on the Earle Weech Auditorium, so we were now free and clear to move ahead with the plans for this new purchase.

A businessman and long time friend of the church, upon hearing of our plans to purchase these properties, immediately wrote a cheque for $200,000.00, with no strings attached. We negotiated with the bank for the balance of the money. Eventually the small cottages were demolished and the lot used for extended parking. The apartments were renovated to accommodate the radio broadcasting studios, and the balance of the space was used to accommodate some of the groups of the church. The ranch style building was designated to house the counselling centre. An extra $50,000.00 was spent here in renovating the building. My youngest son and his wife worked for several days cleaning out garbage and debris so that the work of renovating could be accomplished. Initially the main thrust of counselling was dealing with the drug problems at that particular time. Now the centre covers every sphere of counselling. It has also become a training centre for other counsellors. The Billy Graham Telephone Centre was also established here to handle the telephone calls resulting from the Billy Graham TV specials aired in the Bahamas.

44

Respite and Retracing Steps

Toward the fall of 1985, my wife had a period of renewed energy and was able to participate in a number of things. Feeling this way she expressed a desire to make a visit to Lapland and Norway where we had started our life and ministry together in 1950, with a desire to make one last visit to Scotland. It was most encouraging to think that she felt this might be possible.

Immediately we got in touch with the specialist in McMaster Hospital in Hamilton, Ontario. He assured us that if her blood count could be stabilized and some treatment administered, he was sure this could be done. He agreed to supply us with a printout of what he was doing. This would be helpful in the event that she might have to be admitted to hospital somewhere along the way. So trusting God for His enabling grace and daily strength, and not even taking out health insurance, we set out to help fulfill my beloved wife's earnest desire.

We boarded British Airways 747 in Nassau and flew to London. Because of the kindness of the British Airways manager in Nassau, a personal friend, we were privileged to travel in the comfort of the upper deck. We were the only passengers there. God is so good. We arrived safely in London. We stayed there to take care of the jet lag. While in London we took a bus tour and visited some of our favourite and famous sites. We then flew out to Oslo, Norway, where we stayed over for a couple of days. This gave us an opportunity to visit with Knut Andersen and the Ruud family.

From there we flew north to Tromso. When we first went to Norway in 1950, this trip took us four days by road. Now we did it in less than four hours. Upon our arrival in Tromso, we were met by Birger Ruud, former hospital manager in Nordreisa, where our eldest daughter was born. We were also met by Hulda Wangberg, who had taught us the fine points of the Norwegian language. What a wonderful reunion and such a flood of memories. We checked into a hotel and I picked up a rental car.

Oh the memories! It was here in Tromso that our eldest son was born. On Sunday morning, July 21, we visited Tromso Baptist Church where I had been the interim pastor in the 1950s. It was a real joy to share with them from Psalm 46. I had great liberty in preaching in Norwegian. How wonderful to meet so many of our long-time friends. However, it was sad to see that the church was not prospering. It would seem that the spiritual life of the North was severely reduced. Since my time in the North there had been some significant changes.

There was now a university in Tromso, and one of the young men who works in the university library is from Espenes where we used to live. The economy had improved considerably, and there was evidence of prosperity on every hand. The off-shore oil drilling brought significant changes to the country.

As we travelled to Sommeroy, Tromsdal, Andenes, Narvik, and Harstad, it was good to see so many to whom we had ministered some thirty years earlier going on with the Lord. We had such a wonderful time visiting in Espenes where we had lived when we started married life together. While there I ministered in the chapel. I played the organ and preached. Wherever we went, our friends were so generous with their hospitality and also their monetary gifts.

We then drove to Nordreisa where our eldest daughter was born and where I had worked in Bethesda, the mission hospital. We visited Birger Ruud, one time mission hospital manager and now manager of a farm. This farm was very unique. The workers at the farm were made up of patients who were struggling with schizophrenia and other emotional challenges, so this was a form of therapy for them.

Since we were there in the summer time, there were many of our Sami friends (Laplanders) there with their reindeer. Arrangements were made to have them gather at the farm for a time of fellowship. Some of them were from the Logjje and the Eira families, who were amongst our best friends from Kautokeino. I had attended the wedding of one couple. Another individual was happy to show me the Lappish New Testament I had given to her to help her grow spiritually. Of course we had to have a meal of Lapskaus—a stew made from reindeer meat. My mouth is watering even as I think of it.

From there we travelled back south to Oslo where I preached at First Baptist Church. Then we flew back to London and on to Edinburgh where we spent just a few days with family. By this time my wife was running out of energy, and we were sure that her blood count was down. I took her to the hospital and there they gave her three units of pac-cells. They were so kind and helpful, and she felt so much better.

We got back to Nassau on August 28, 1985. Considering we had travelled 3,500 kilometres in Norway, 1,200 miles in Britain, plus about thirty hours flying time, and we were travelling for forty-five days, my wife held up very well, and she was able to fulfill her dream. All that time, all that travel, and there were no mishaps or medical upsets. We were surely grateful to the Lord for His watch and care over us.

An Exciting Fall of Ministry

Back in Nassau, things were beginning to gear up for a very exciting fall with a pastor's assistant in place, a youth pastor organizing our youth ministries, and the purchase of our new properties being finalized. We saw the hand of God multiplying our members and expanding our ministries.

Because of the increase of the drug problem throughout our country, the government established a Drug Council to seek to find ways to deal with this major problem. I was invited by one of the government ministers to join this council. One of our church members, a lawyer, was also asked to join. More will be said about this later. All of these issues presented their own challenges and opportunities. Then we moved into our Christmas season with all its exciting activities. There was the nightly live manger scene at the front of the church, the Sunday school programs, and the choir's presentation of their Christmas cantata. During the Christmas season we had over one hundred of our leaders and members at the parsonage for Christmas fare and fellowship. It became increasingly clear, however, that this would be the last Christmas my wife would be with us

45

The Month that Changed our World

By the first week of January, 1986, very serious action had to be taken. Between Dr. Lunn in Nassau and Dr Clarke in Canada, they made it very clear that my wife would have to get ready to go north to Canada. The day before this happened, I went back to the house just after noon. When I arrived there I found several ladies from the church sitting in the living room. I asked them if they had spoken to my wife yet, and they told me they had not, as she was in the bedroom counselling a young lady. This was unbelievable. You see, by this time she had to make her way to the bathroom on her hands and knees, yet here she was deeply concerned for the well being of this young lady.

The following day, January 9, 1986, my wife flew up to Canada where she was admitted to McMaster University Hospital. In the meantime, I had a very busy weekend at the church with Dr. Elmer Towns conducting seminars and also preaching at the church that Sunday. Finally, on the following Thursday, I was able to fly north to Canada. The ticket cost only $291.00. I was upgraded to first class, and what a blessing it was to relax in comfort.

My eldest son met me at the airport and drove me to the hospital. What a shock to see such changes in my wife. She was very weak and very tired. Obviously the cancer was spreading. Dr Clarke explained what was happening. The cancer had spread throughout her body and had invaded all the major organs. She was in much pain and had nose bleeds as well as bleeding in her eye, and she was throwing up blood clots.

At the beginning of the year, my wife had chosen Isaiah 41:10 as her text for 1986—how appropriate:

Fear not, for I am with you; be not dismayed, for I am your God. I will strengthen you, Yes, I will help you, I will uphold you with My righteous right hand.

That evening I stayed with her until 11:00 p.m. As I left she said, "Let me go home to Heaven." Those were the last words I heard her speak. Dr. Clarke said if family members were coming they should come right away. We had made it clear to the doctor and the head nurse that there should be no heroics, and that they should let her go peacefully. That evening before leaving for Brantford, I read the wonderful words from 2 Timothy 4:7–8:

I have fought the good fight, I have finished the race, I have kept the faith. Finally, there is laid up for me the crown of righteousness, which the Lord, the righteous Judge, will give to me on that Day, and not to me only but also to all who have loved His appearing.

My wife responded in a very weak breath, "a great text." On the way back to Brantford that evening in the car I sang that great hymn "It is Well with My Soul," and also my wife's favourite hymn, "I know not why God's wondrous grace … but I know whom I have believed."

On the morning of Wednesday January 22, 1986, I awoke at 4:30 a.m. and sat on the edge of the bed. It seemed as if the Lord said to me, "Today is the day." I was deeply convinced that my wife would not make it through that day.

I made my way to the hospital around 9:30 a.m. There I was met by the head nurse who informed me that my wife had lapsed into a coma around 4:30 a.m. I sat beside her bed and read Scripture and prayed. I was joined by Mrs. Way at 11:00 a.m. and at 11:15 a.m. my wife slipped peacefully into the presence of her Lord.

How I thanked the Lord for His goodness and grace and for the privilege of being able to serve Him together for thirty-six years: "*Thou wilt keep him in perfect peace, whose mind is stayed on thee*" (Isaiah 26:3, KJV). I will never forget standing at the window of that room on that bleak winter's morning, gazing across the valley, seeing the leafless trees, the snow and the frost, and being reminded of that truth … we know not what the future holds, but we know who holds the future.

The only part of my wife's body that was not invaded by cancer was her eyes, and these were donated that someone else might receive sight. Family and friends came from Scotland, the Bahamas, the States, Newfoundland, New Brunswick, and all over Ontario. The funeral service was set for Saturday, January 25, 1986, at Long Branch Baptist Church, Etobicoke, Ontario. The church was filled to capacity. We honoured not only Adaline Betty (Jamieson) Russell's life, but also honoured her Lord. Only the family went to the graveside for the burial. It was a blustery, snowy, very cold day and not soon forgotten. Our married life together ended as it had begun. We started married life in the far north, three hundred miles above the Arctic Circle—lots of snow and very cold. That day as we lowered the casket into the grave it was bitterly cold with driving snow stinging our faces.

After the funeral I spent some time taking care of some business and then headed back to Nassau. My wife's sister and my youngest daughter joined me to help take care of some of my wife's personal things. We received such a loving, caring welcome back to the church, but it was also a very emotional time. That first Sunday we were back in Nassau we had a memorial service for my wife. It was a powerful testimony to my wife's life and ministry.

A Month of Missions and Memorials

As usual, the month of March was dedicated to missions and missionaries. Our Festival of Missions was a highlight of the year. It would be the first one without the help and support of my wife; however, many of the ladies of the church rallied around to help with the planning. It was an outstanding conference, with over $90,000.00 in our first Sunday of Faith Promise offering, and more came in later in the month.

This was the church's fourteenth missions conference, and over the years $1,000,000.00 had been given to thirty to forty mission projects and missionaries. Considering the fact that our nation had third world status, we had the joy of seeing such a response to the work of the Gospel around the world.

In the wake of our missions conference, we had a very special time on Sunday, March 16, 1986. My brother, Rev. Henry Russell, and his wife were visiting with me in Nassau. I had him preach in our morning and evening services when the church was packed to overflowing.

Following the morning service, a very special event took place. There was a service of dedication for our new Christian Counseling Centre. This was dedicated in honour of my wife, Adaline Betty Russell, recognizing her involvement in the ministry of counselling. Our church choir led in the singing, and Pastor Arnett and Brother Jasiel Thompson took part. My sister-in-law, Mrs. Mae Russell, cut the ribbon, Ian unveiled the name, and Brian Moree read the statement and purpose of the counselling centre. This was the official launching of this ministry that had been very dear to my wife. This ministry continues today and has made a great impact on the community.

On the same property as the counselling centre is another building that is used as the distribution centre for the Operation Inasmuch program. This provides food and clothing for the needy in the community. As I write, the ministry of the counselling centre has been extended to Marsh Harbour, Abaco.

Ministry and Memory

Since I was now alone I thought it wise to change my approach to my visitation ministry. I always had my wife with me in visitation, so I never had any problem. Now, however, I hesitated to visit a woman when I was alone. Therefore, in such cases I always made a point of having someone else with me. If I were visiting in the hospital or a nursing home I would continue to visit by myself. I was always more cautious in my interviews and counselling ministry. When in my study at the church, I always had an open door policy. In some cases, I would prefer to refer people to our counselling centre. One principle that was always shared amongst widowed pastors was, "Be very careful. The choir may turn into a band of hope." It was safe to avoid all appearance of evil.

That first Easter without my wife was very significant; however, it also took on new meaning as I was reminded of the promise that comes with the resurrection. It reminds us of the fact that one day we will be reunited with loved ones.

Mother's Day brought with it some deep emotions. This was a day that was very meaningful to my wife. She always spoke at the special Mother's Day service, and always did a Mother's Day broadcast on our radio program. This Mother's Day service was dedicated to the memory of my dear wife. The church was packed to overflowing.

The following week I flew up to Canada, where along with family we made arrangements to have a memorial stone inscribed and installed at my wife's grave. Then I travelled to Scotland to visit with my wife's parents and other members of her family. This was a bit of an emotional roller coaster as I shared memories and photographs with family and friends. It was so different not being with my wife. It was so different being alone after thirty-six wonderful years together in marriage and service for the Lord. We had been on the mission field in Lapland then in four pastoral ministries. Life was not always easy, but we had great joy and satisfaction in seeing many come to a saving knowledge of Jesus Christ. We had experienced incredible growth in churches where we had served. Our five children, plus two adopted kids, were all married, and we had five grandchildren. We ascribe all glory and praise to our wonderful Lord and Saviour Jesus Christ. Let me say here at the time of this writing that I now have twenty-two grandchildren and ten great-grandchildren. And still the family circle grows as another great grand is on the way!

The summer of 1986 was so busy. The highlight was our daily Vacation Bible School. This was always a great outreach, and it made a great impact upon the community. We had over four hundred pupils and teachers. A number of the children professed faith in the Lord Jesus Christ. The closing program on Friday evening brought out many parents, and the church was filled to capacity.

46

A New Direction and a New Relationship

As the months rolled by, it became more and more evident that I couldn't go on indefinitely seeking to minister in a growing congregation with an increasingly diversified program while at the same time trying to take care of personal responsibilities at home. I was burning the candle at both ends. If this went on indefinitely, then the light would eventually go out. My fifteen to sixteen hour days were taking their toll, and I didn't want to jeopardize my primary task, namely my pastoral ministry. I needed someone in my life that could share in my ministry and provide needed support. There were possibilities within the church, but at that time I didn't think it wise to foster a relationship there, since it might create complications.

In the meantime I was fostering a relationship with a lady in Canada. Sarah (Morag) Forrester had been a friend dating back many years. We first really met in middle school, and she was part of the youth group in the church where we had both become Christians. She was also a member of the youth choir, which I conducted. She and I were part of a group of nine young people who were baptized and received into membership the same evening at the Baptist church in Larbert, Scotland, which her grandfather had helped to start.

Her goal in life was to become a nurse. In those days in Scotland if you were a nurse you did not marry. If you married, you had to resign from the nursing profession. This being the case, she didn't develop relationships that would jeopardize her career. Morag's mother and my mother were the only two widows in the church, and they were very close friends. So Morag pursued her nursing career, which lasted for over forty years. Twenty one of those years she taught nursing. In 1968 she moved to Canada where she helped to open the new Centenary Hospital in Scarborough.

Over the years, my wife and I maintained contact with her. In fact, she attended the weddings of several of our children. And now here we were developing a relationship that would lead to marriage. Along the way I discovered something very interesting. Apparently my wife had indicated to the family that I would likely re-marry, and she would not be surprised if I married Morag. So unknown to me, this was a family foregone conclusion. This made it so much easier for me, knowing that this is what the family expected. How the Lord orders the steps of the righteous!

We became officially engaged in June and we planned to marry on November 1, 1986. Most of our planning was done by long distance telephone. I think Bell Canada went into a financial crisis mode after we got married! Back in those days we didn't get special deals or discounts.

The wedding day was soon upon us. The venue would be Churchill Heights Baptist Church in Scarborough with the reception at The Prince Hotel in Pickering. The pastor of the church, the Rev. Ian Bowie, and my brother, Rev Henry Russell, conducted the service. No wedding is complete without a few incidents along the way, and ours was no exception.

My wife made her own wedding dress. One half hour before she was due at the church she was still sewing on buttons. Her dear mother of ninety years of age walked her daughter down the aisle with pride and regal style. At last her only child was getting married. The ceremony went very well, with every effort to make it God honouring. The reception was graced by family, friends, and relatives, including some of our pastor friends. There were the usual toasts and roasts followed by a sumptuous meal. We had ordered strawberries and cream for dessert; however, there were no strawberries to be found that time of year. The chef, however, had a bright idea. Since there were lots of Scottish people amongst the guests, he would make trifle. This was where the problem arose. Of course the head table where the bride and groom were seated with the attendants was served first. Well, one had to accept the "spirit" in which the dessert change was made. The problem was the dessert was laced with liquor. Given the fact that the greater number of our guests was teetotalers, it was embarrassing. Otherwise the reception went very well. Upon retiring to the hotel suite, with my feet so sore in beautiful patent leather expensive Italian shoes I was glad to kick the shoes off. It was then that I discovered why my feet were so sore. I had omitted to remove the cardboard support from inside the shoes! Oh well—love bears all things! We had to leave for the airport at 4:30 a.m.

We were so glad that we were heading towards a warmer climate for our honeymoon. We were heading for Orlando—it was a Mickey Mouse deal! We spent a wonderful week in that part of Florida before returning north to pack and get ready to move back to Nassau.

In the meantime, my new wife and I visited my brother and his wife. On the way from their place we walked toward the parking area to get the car, and my wife tripped and fell and broke her wrist. This meant a visit to the hospital where my wife had taught nursing. Some of her former students took care of her. Of course they enquired about what had happened, so I told them that we were married ten days earlier, and I had told her that if she didn't do what I said, I would break her arm. A good joke, but of course not true.

My wife now had to watch while I and some others took care of getting ready to go to Nassau. My wife's mother was going with us since we didn't want her to be by herself in Canada. Upon our arrival in Nassau, we received a wonderful welcome, and with the help of the ladies in the church, a reception was planned. On Sunday morning, November 16, we were welcomed to the church. My wife's mother who was soon known to everyone as "Grandma Forrester."

Of course I couldn't pass up the opportunity to share a bit of humour. I reminded the congregation that although my wife's name was Sarah, I was not Abraham and there weren't going to be any Isaacs!

Christmas Traditions, Celebrations, and Complications

Before we knew it, the Christmas season was upon us. This would be a real initiation for my wife as she became acquainted with some of the traditions, celebrations, and complications of Christmas. This was a busy, exciting time in church and amongst our families. The introduction to the festive season was the entertaining we did at the parsonage. We set aside several evenings, and each evening we would have twenty-five to thirty people from the church. We served a full dinner, sang carols, played games, and had good fellowship.

For three consecutive nights before Christmas, we had the live manger scene on the front lawn of the church. This was complete with people playing the part of the people in the Christmas story, including a real live baby with live animals. Each evening we sang carols, read the appropriate scripture, and acted out the scenes. On Christmas Eve we always had a very large Christmas service that lasted for only fifty-five minutes. I always reminded the people that this was my Christmas present to the entire congregation.

The first Christmas Day that we had together in Nassau was a never to be forgotten experience. We woke that morning to the horribly inconvenient fact that the electrical power was off over the whole island, and it stayed off until the early hours of Boxing Day. This meant that we couldn't use the oven or our gas stove, since it required electricity to ignite the gas. Fortunately, I had cooked the turkey the night before so that we could cook the potatoes and vegetables on the top of the stove.

Without electricity our water pump couldn't work, so we had to get water from our neighbour who had an emergency generator. We had no air conditioning, and the temperature in the kitchen was ninety-six degrees. After our Christmas dinner, we all went out in the car for a drive to get the benefit of the air conditioner. What an experience for my wife and some of the family who had come down from Canada. On Boxing Day forenoon we were all swimming just off Paradise Island, where the temperature was about ninety degrees.

On Boxing Day evening we were invited to Lyford Cay, an exclusive resort built by a Canadian, Mr. E.P. Taylor. We were guests of the manager, a fellow Canadian who was also very actively involved in Calvary Bible Church. While having dinner our host said, "Don't look now, but Robert Redford has just sat down at the table behind you." My wife, not being well versed on celebrities, innocently asked who Robert Redford was. She very quickly learned that Lyford Cay was a gathering place for celebrities of every stripe.

A. Morris and Sarah (Morag) Russell -we married on Nov. 1. 1986

(47)

Family Complications

On February 18, 1987, a mishap suddenly changed our family life. My wife's mother was living with us at High Vista, Nassau. Grandma fell just outside the parsonage and fractured her hip. She had to be admitted to The Doctors Hospital in Nassau. After x-raying her hip, Dr. Rassin concluded that she would have to go to Canada to have it fixed since they did not have the facilities to repair the fracture.

Dr. Rassin was the medical officer for Air Canada, which meant that he could very quickly make the arrangements with Air Canada to fly her back to Canada. In the meantime, he was able to secure her hip by applying a large plaster cast. Plans were put in place to transport Grandma by Air Canada on the following Saturday. We had to organize an ambulance to take her to the airport in Nassau, and also one to pick her up in Toronto and take her to the hospital in Scarborough. We had to pay for three seats on the plane to accommodate the stretcher. Then we had to have two seats for us. So we had to have five seats altogether. This was amazing since it was the busy tourist season.

Getting Grandma on the plane was a bit complicated. Because of the stretcher and the size of the cast, we couldn't get her through the main door of the plane. But even in this the Lord provided. The plane we were taking had a door with steps that dropped down in the tail of the plane. We strapped her securely on the stretcher, turned the stretcher on edge, and carried her straight into the plane. Since my wife was a nurse, we didn't have to hire another nurse to travel with us. It was a perfect flight with an ambulance waiting for her in Toronto.

She was checked in at the Scarborough Hospital on Sunday at 5:30 p.m. and the fracture was repaired; however, she was never able to walk again. She also had many other complications. My wife went north every month to visit her mother. This was a great strain, as I had to return to Nassau to make final preparations for our missions conference.

1987—A Year of Blessing and Change

Our missions conference was outstanding. We were able to host over forty of our missionaries. Dr. James Blackwood was our speaker, and the Three Sons trio brought special music. It was a great time of blessing and challenge. Over eighty-five people made decisions, some for salvation and some for service. The Faith Promise offering was around $170,000.00, with some one hundred and eighty-nine families participating. This was the highest Faith Promise offering ever in our fourteen years of conference.

On April 21, 1987, Pastor Earle Weech, founding Pastor of Calvary Bible Church, went home to be with the Lord. Pastor Weech was a choice servant of God. For many years he had ministered throughout the islands of the Bahamas, doing evangelism and establishing churches. In 1962 he founded Calvary Bible Church in Nassau, Bahamas, and in 1985 he established Calvary Bible Church in Freeport, Grand Bahama. He was a man of slight stature, but a giant for the cause of Christ. He was loved by many. I was privileged to share fellowship with him over seven years, and it was always a joy to have him preach when he visited.

In July of 1987, my wife and I accompanied by Pastor and Mrs. Kenneth W. Morrison on a tour of England and Scotland. Our primary goal was to have a reception in our home church in Larbert, Scotland, so that we could meet with many family and friends who could not get to our wedding in Canada. This was a memorable time.

When we returned to Canada we went to visit Mother, who was still in hospital. She was critically ill, but still holding on, but on October 27, 1987 she went home to be with her Lord at the age of ninety-two. We arranged for the funeral service to be held that Thursday in Scarborough, and later that day we flew to Scotland where we had another funeral service and burial on the Saturday at her home church in Larbert, followed by a reception for around sixty guests. In short, we spent our first wedding anniversary taking care of my wife's mother's funeral. However, Mother got her long time wishes fulfilled. She had longed to see her daughter married, and then she enjoyed her adopted children and grandchildren. She also got to see where her daughter was living, and got a little taste of the beauty of the Bahamas and its people.

By now we were caught up in the final preparations for the Barry Moore Crusade, which was set to begin on November 29, 1987. We had a wonderful week of blessing with forty-eight decisions for Christ. Wrapping up the year, I noted that I had made one hundred and ninety-four visits, conducted seventy-seven counseling sessions, participated in three hundred and sixty-four meetings, preached or presented messages and studies, and recorded one hundred and ninety-nine decisions for Christ. This was a year of very mixed emotions, but through it all we knew the truth of Psalm 46:1–2: *"God is our refuge and strength. A very present help in trouble. Therefore we will not fear ..."*

In two other churches where I had served we used a ministry that we called "Dial-a-Devotion." A new message was recorded every day, and people could call in and get a devotional message. These proved to be worthwhile and very popular, so we started this ministry in Calvary Bible Church, Nassau. It became very popular and was maintained for many years.

48

International Impact and Ministry

Being located in a place to which tourists were attracted, it was not surprising to find that many of them found their way to Calvary Bible Church to worship with us. Since Norwegian is my second language, it was always very special to welcome tourists and visitors from Scandinavia, and particularly Norway. One time we had two men from Norway who were attending the Baptist World Alliance Conference meeting in Nassau. One of them was the principal of the Baptist college in Oslo. We discovered that we had many mutual friends, since I had preached in many Baptist churches in Norway.

One evening it was so exciting to have around twenty five Norwegian tourists attending our evening service. They had enquired at the information desk in the hotel if there was a church where they might worship. The hotel clerk indicated that they would be very happy attending Calvary Bible Church. She didn't know that Norwegian is my second language. How happy they were when I greeted them in Norwegian. More than that, how amazing that God had directed them. I had chosen for the opening hymn that evening, "He the Pearly Gates will Open." This is a very popular hymn in Norway, where it's entitled "Han Skal Opne Pearle Porten." They sang it heartily in Norwegian while we sang in English.

On another occasion I got word that Dr. John MacArthur would be arriving in Nassau on a cruise ship with a group of his people. We made plans for him to speak to a group of pastors. This was followed by a public meeting in our church. We had a full church and a great time of blessing through the ministry of one of God's choice servants. We often jokingly commented that we had more visitors from around the world because of our location rather than when we lived in the Arctic.

Special Ministries to Special People

In April of 1989, we had a very remarkable baptismal service. Our counseling centre staff worked very closely with the staff of Teen Challenge, a ministry with a very interesting program. Their focus was working with recovering drug addicts and teaching them some skills so that they could become gainfully employed. A number of those men came to personal faith in the Lord Jesus Christ. As they were discipled, they came to realize the need to take the step of obedience by being baptized. I had the joy of baptizing nine of them one Sunday evening. Some of their old buddies were there to hear their testimony and witness their baptism. All of them were much bigger than I, and all of them were muscle bound because they had been "pumping iron." I said that evening that I would not like to meet them in the dark. All of them were trophies of God's grace. Such is the joy and privilege of being in the ministry.

Deteriorations and Discouragements

Along the journey of life, one becomes very much aware of the fact that this temple of clay begins to deteriorate. Hearing loss was quite common to members of my family. The brother next to me was a deaf mute. In my late fifties I became increasingly aware of the fact that my hearing was getting worse. In April of 1988 I went for hearing tests. These tests revealed that I had sixty-five per cent hearing loss in my right ear and sixty-nine per cent hearing loss in my left ear. I was immediately fitted with two hearing aids. The first day I wore them I could not believe the difference. I could hear the birds singing—something I had not heard for years. Of course, there were some things I would rather not have heard.

The full realization of the difference shattered me on the first Sunday I was back in Nassau. As usual on Sunday morning I walked onto the platform, the choir stood, the congregation stood, and the organist struck the opening cord of "The Doxology." At that point, I nearly went through the roof. The noise was deafening. I had to quickly adjust my hearing aids. Just think of how much I had been missing all those years.

Around this time we encountered some discouragements. There were those who were trying to sow discord in the church. When God is blessing, Satan is not one bit happy, and he seeks to find someone or something through which he may distract from our God given goals. The principle we had adopted in our church council was that we should have unanimity in our decisions before we would move forward; however, there was one individual who made an ongoing effort to frustrate our efforts by his consistent negative votes.

At one of our council meetings this happened, and I immediately felt prompted to confront him. I openly and boldly said, "I believe that you have some sin in your life that needs to be dealt with. You consistently vote negatively in all that we discuss, and I believe this sin needs to be dealt with." He immediately stepped down from the council and very shortly thereafter it became known what was going on in his life.

Family Sorrows, Sickness, and Celebrations

On June 27, 1989, in the middle of our Vacation Bible School at church, I received a call to say that my dear friend and fellow pastor, Rev. Kenneth Morrison, went home to be with the Lord that morning. What a shock to hear of his sudden death from a heart attack while still in his fifties. Our youth pastor took over the leadership of the VBS for the balance of the week, and my wife and I made immediate arrangements to fly to Ontario to conduct the funeral service. It was an extremely emotional time for me having had this friendship for thirty-three years.

In February of 1990 my wife went north to Ontario to have surgery. It was discovered that she had a very large lump in her breast, and it was felt that she should have this removed as soon as possible. This was the way in which my first wife had started with her cancer, so this was causing great concern. The lumpectomy showed, however, that there was no malignancy. For this we were very grateful. She was able to be back in Nassau in time for our Festival of Missions held during the first week of March.

While I was in Nassau I had the first and only burial at sea. A ship's captain, father of one of our very active young men in the church, died in Nassau. Following the cremation, I was asked to go out in a boat with some of the family members and scatter his ashes at sea.

In May 1990 I held a baptismal service on a Wednesday evening in which fourteen were baptized. The candidates ranged in age from nine to fifty-eight. It was an incredible evening of testimony, praise, and thanksgiving. It's wonderful to see the fruit of one's labours.

49

Decisions, Decisions, Decisions

In June of 1990, I celebrated forty years as an ordained missionary/pastor, having served in Norway, Lapland, New Brunswick, Newfoundland, Ontario, and the Bahamas. I served in the Arctic, rural New Brunswick in four country churches, Sussex, New Brunswick, a busy dairy town well known for its ice cream, St. John's, Newfoundland, a busy sea port boasting a rapidly growing Memorial University, and Etobicoke, part of the bustling city of Toronto. And now here I was in Nassau, Bahamas. Once a colony of Great Britain, it was now a fledgling independent nation, finding its way in the world, scattered on seven hundred islands and a much sought after tourist destination by sun seekers from all over the world, and a haven for the investments of the financial pundits.

Having spent the best part of ten years of my pastoral ministry here on these "Islands of the shallow seas," I was faced with a very significant decision: should I go or should I stay? When I sensed God's call to serve Him in the ministry some forty-five years earlier, I willingly answered "yes." However, I did place some personal provisions on the answer: I didn't want to go to a big city, or to a place with a warm climate. Does God have a sense of humour? From the above you will notice that I have done it all.

Having seen the work and ministry at Calvary Bible Church ... built on a significantly strong and effective ministry of the solid foundations laid by previous pastors ... now growing and maturing into an effective ministry, not only in the Bahamas but also around the world, I was aware of the fact that at this juncture my own preferences must in no way hinder the ongoing work of this bastion of evangelical ministry and vision. We had experienced God's goodness and grace with increased attendance, expansion and improvements of the facilities, significant additions to the staff, and, apart from a few individuals who sought to sow seeds of discord, there was a very good spirit amongst the people. However, now that I was sixty-two years of age and had been living out of Canada for ten years, perhaps it was time to go back and re-establish myself in my adopted land. Another factor came into play. I had a desire to minister in churches that were in pastoral transition or were facing some problems where I could draw upon my extensive experience and help to bring healing. I also had a desire to use my ministry to missionaries in the country where they were serving. So in the light of all of this, I eventually tendered my resignation from Calvary Bible Church.

Over the years, I have never found this easy to do. On June 9, 1990, actually ten years after I had accepted the call to Calvary, Nassau, we had our official farewell banquet. We would actually continue ministering to the church directly and indirectly until August 22, 1990.

The evening of the farewell was very special and very emotional. Around four hundred people attended the banquet. We received a gift from the congregation of over $5,000.00. We were presented with a beautiful quilt from the ladies of the church that was made by the ladies of Spanish Wells, who are well known for their quilt making. In each square of the quilt there were embroidered the names of the people who had contributed to it. We also received an afghan rug and a special plate. Of course, our lovely Bahamian granddaughter stole the show when she presented us with a beautiful bouquet of flowers. Many tributes were shared with us that evening. Two in particular should be mentioned.

Dr. David Allen highlighted my extensive pastoral ministry where I truly cared for the flock—visiting in times of sickness, sorrow, and the struggles of life. He cited one incident in which a member of our congregation had been involved in a very serious car accident and was rushed to emergency at the hospital. On hearing of this, I immediately made my way to the emergency department, only to discover that she was unconscious. While in the room, I heard the doctors discussing what medication they would give her. I intervened and informed them that this lady was on lithium and shouldn't have the medication they were prescribing. I knew this because I had been visiting her prior to the accident because of her ongoing sickness. Dr. Allen was overwhelmed by the fact that I had acquainted myself with her problems as I exercised my pastoral ministry. May I say to the younger men in the pastoral ministry that you need to know your people so that you may be effective in your ministry.

Mr. Brian Moree, well known lawyer and member of our congregation who was very active in several areas of ministry and service in the church, spoke extensively of my almost ten years of ministry at Calvary Bible Church, along with the supporting role of my wife. Here I will quote some selected excerpts from a rather lengthy expression acknowledging the impact of my ministry in the church and community.

Tonight is one of those bittersweet occasions when on the one hand one feels joy and celebration, and on the other hand sorrow and nostalgia … We rejoice that together we have laughed and cried; that we have agreed and disagreed; that we have succeeded and failed; that we have prayed and supported each other. We remember the happy times of social fraternity, the challenging times of resolving difficult issues and tackling tough projects. We recollect that we have even faced death together and comforted one another. We remember the sheer hard work and the many hours of toil and labour that our pastor and his wife have invested in this congregation and the ministries of this church. Many of us tearfully recall the reassuring arm of support when the pastor and his wife visited us when a loved one passed away or when we were ill or confronting another crisis. The fact that they were there just seemed to help; a kind word; a sincere embrace …Give to our honoured guests a tribute which is befitting of their loyal and sacrificial service to Calvary Bible Church and to those of us who comprise that body …When they came to Calvary, our church had been without a permanent pastor for almost two years, and there was an urgent need for strong Biblical leadership. Pastor Russell quickly filled this need and demonstrated both spiritual insight and physical stamina in discharging his responsibilities. In those days there was only Pastor Russell and a small support staff. I know from the records that in those early days he would attend over three hundred and fifty meetings in a twelve month period. Together with his wife they would make over three hundred visits a year to the sick, bereaved, and shut in people of our community, and preach or teach over two hundred and fifty times in a year. In addition to all of this, Pastor Russell carried the administrative burden of the church, performed weddings, baptisms, and funerals. At the same time, he was heavily involved in the radio broadcast and also attended to other pastoral duties. He would work sixteen hours a day and still have time for the individual needs of the people in our church. All of that and he had to plan for the future and seek God's will for the future of the church.

We find in 1 Timothy 3 the biblical qualities of a bishop ... From my point of view, I think that we find all those qualities in Pastor Russell. He is first and foremost a man of God who was ordained over forty years ago. He has been preaching for over forty-four years and is learned in the Bible and theology. God has blessed him with the talent to preach and communicate His Word, which he has faithfully done all over the world ... His well considered and resolute and uncompromising position on important spiritual issues has been instructive as many of us aspire to learn more about His Word... ...He is not the distant aloof pastor who simply preaches on Sunday—his involvement is a personal one ... I clearly remember his involvement with my family when my father was dying of cancer in 1981 ... I recall my father observing on several occasions how easy it was to talk and share with Pastor Russell and how he quickly felt that they had known each other for a long time ... I always got the impression that my father enjoyed a particular peace after the visits from Pastor Russell. An illustration of Pastor Russell's compassion for others is when he visited Jamaica in the aftermath of the devastating hurricane (Hurricane Gilbert) that left many Jamaicans homeless. He did not send the gifts and donations from our church, but personally went himself. That typifies Pastor Russell's way of dealing with people and problems— he has the personal approach, the caring approach, the loving approach. Pastor Russell is an extraordinary administrator. His attention to detail and order is readily apparent to those who have worked with him. His work ethic is unquestionable and disciplined. His vision is progressive, but always relevant and predicated on a devout faith in the unlimited power and authority of God ... I regard it as a privilege to have had the opportunity to work with Pastor Russell on numerous projects ...I have developed a lasting respect for Pastor Russell through my dealings with him which transcends particular differences with regard to a specific issue ... He is someone who is loyal and reliable, wise and understanding. Pastor Russell's ministry at our church can be divided into two phases: 1980 to January, 1986, when he and his first wife laboured together. That first phase was productive and faithful. There was much growth in the various ministries. The faith promise offering increased every year ... and the church expanded our support for missionaries and developed a balanced policy towards supporting local and foreign missions. The Summer Daily Vacation Bible School started under the inspiration of Pastor Russell and his wife. The church enjoyed a stable and healthy financial position and much was achieved for the Kingdom of God. Pastor Russell shared his vision for a counseling centre to extend the outreach of the church to a needy community. Under his inspiration, the church acquired two properties to the north and west of the church to allow expansion in the future. A more timid man might have been intimidated by the size of that project, but Pastor Russell through faith saw immense opportunities arising from the acquisition of the land. This phase ended in January 1986 with the tragic death of Sister Russell. The second phase was from February, 1986 to 1990. From November, 1986, Pastor Russell has been blessed with his second wife, who has been a bastion of support to him and to the church. She quickly became a spiritual leader and counsellor in her own right. I believe I will most remember her for her unconditional, magnanimous kindness, and her peaceful and stable disposition. She has been most gracious of her acceptance of her role in our church. President John F. Kennedy said this: "The credit belongs to the man who is actually in the arena …who knows the great enthusiasms, the great devotions and spends himself in a worthy cause, who at best, if he wins, knows the thrill of achievement, and if he fails, at least fails daring greatly so that his place shall never be with those cold and timid souls who know neither victory nor defeat."

The Concluding Weeks

After the official farewell gathering, I still worked in the church until the month of August. I still did the preaching, the visitation, and conducted some funerals. The last baptism I had was conducted on Monday, June 24, when I baptized Albert Rogers in Lindsey Pinder's swimming pool with a number of friends and family present. It was a wonderful evening of testimony and praise.

Our move from Nassau back to Canada was not without some interesting incidents. One of the well-known shipping companies in Nassau took care of packing our personal things into a container and shipping them to Miami by boat. I arranged to rent a U-Haul van, which I would drive to St. Petersburg to off load some things there, and then take the balance on to Canada. One of the great Scottish bards put it very succinctly when he penned those memorable words: "The best laid schemes o' mice and men gang aft agley" (Robert Burns).

As planned, we took the plane to Miami, picked up the U-Haul, and drove to the dock where our things would be off loaded from the boat and then loaded into the van for our trip north. However, when we opened the container that was marked as containing our goods, we found it was empty. Our things were still in the warehouse in Nassau. We were informed that it would be four days before the ship would be back from Nassau. What then?

The boss was very magnanimous. He was flying out to Nassau and said we could have the use of his car for four days, and the company paid for a suite at the Embassy Suites Hotel. Inconvenient, yet we believe it was ordered by the Lord. We were exhausted from all the last minute activities in Nassau, so this way we could have a rest. It gave me the opportunity to take my wife to some places in the Miami area she had never seen before. Let me note something else that was very significant. We discovered later that we could not have driven north on the day that we were supposed to travel, because the highway we would have travelled was closed after a box of explosives was found under an overpass. The police and the bomb squad had to investigate and remove the hazard.

Four days later we were on our way. We drove to our place in St. Petersburg and offloaded some of our stuff there, and the next day we continued on north to Canada. We had listed everything that we had carried with us to make sure that we accommodated the custom officials upon arrival at the Canadian border. Our trip north was without incident. When we arrived at the customs booth, I handed over the documents. The officer asked a few relevant questions, and each page of our documents was stamped. In handing them back to us he said, "Welcome Home," and sent us on our way.

50

Relaxing, Renewing, and Returning

After a few days of relaxation, visiting with family, and planning for the future, we returned to Nassau to gather our group who were travelling with us to Europe with the main purpose of taking in the Passion Play at Oberammergau. We travelled to Miami, and then got the plane to Toronto. We flew from Toronto to Nuremberg, arriving there on July 13, 1990.

Nuremberg is known for its fame and infamy. Nearby is the site of a beautiful castle. It was in this city that Albert Druer carved those now- world- renowned "Praying Hands." Nearby is the site of the famous rally organized by Adolf Hitler, where over two million people gathered to demonstrate their support for "Der Furher." It was also here that the Nazi War Criminal Trials were conducted in 1946.

We then travelled to Prague, Vienna, and on to Hungary and its capital, Budapest. This was a special time in Budapest. My daughter and son-in-law were with us, so our son-in-law wanted to visit the place where he had lived with his grandparents before he came to Canada. This was very special for him. It was sad to see the damage that had been done when the Hungarians finally got their freedom from Russia and communism. Damage from the bullets and bombs was evident all around.

From there we travelled to Yugoslavia and the famous Plitvice Lakes and waterfalls. In 1949 this spectacular area was designated as a National Park, and is now under the protection of UNESCO. One is awestruck by the spectacular natural beauty. On Sunday we travelled through Slovakia to Lake Bled. This is a glacial lake and was a favourite retreat place for former Marshall Tito. In the middle of the lake is a very unique island. At the high point of the island, some one hundred and thirty-nine metres above Lake Bled, is a beautiful ornate church. This church was once under the leadership of the Bishops of Brixen, at the time of the Holy Roman Emperor. Henry II turned it over to the Bishops of Brixen in 1004. They were the rulers of a separate state. We took a boat out to this island and climbed up to the church. In talking with the custodian of the church, we asked if we could conduct a service for our group there. He very readily concurred. We had some significantly talented singers in our group, and with the wonderful acoustics of the church, we created wonderful harmony, singing some well known hymns. Very soon we had a significant number of other tourists join us and participate in the time of worship. I shared a devotional and prayer. It was one of the significant highlights of our tour.

From there we drove to Germany and headed towards Oberammergau. On the way we stopped at "Mad King Ludwig's Castle," which was rather unique and spectacular. We arrived in Oberammergau in time for checking in at our hotel and dinner. We needed to rest up because the following day was our goal—The Passion Play.

The Passion Play
The Passion Play is presented every ten years by the villagers of Oberammergau. This play has been presented regularly since 1634 as a result of a commitment following the devastating Black Death. Each year that it is performed, some 500,000 people attend, and some 2,000 of the villagers participate in the presentation that covers the prophecies concerning Christ and the happenings of the Passion Week. The whole story of Christ's redemptive work really comes alive. It has been my joy to be there on four different occasions. We then made our way back to Frankfurt where we saw our group off to America and Canada and the Bahamas. My wife and I then flew from Frankfurt to Oslo, Norway, for what would be an incredible trip to see where I had ministered in earlier years.

Returning to Roots
I took my wife on a tour of Norway, Lapland, Sweden, and Finland so that she would see where I had worked with Global Outreach Mission (formerly known as The European Evangelistic Crusade) for the first six years of my fulltime ministry, and personally experience the places and people she heard me speak of.

Our first stop was Drammen in the south of Norway, and I had the joy of seeing many of my friends there, and my wife heard me preach for the first time in Norwegian, my second language. From there we set out on our journey north. What a change from the first time I drove north in 1950. At that time it was gravel highway all the way, taking us four days to get to our destination. Now in 1990, it was a beautifully paved, broad, sometimes multilane highway.

Along the way we drank in the beautiful scenery of fjords and mountains, rivers and lakes. We stopped to greet friends and visited places. We stopped in Oppdal and travelled over Dovrefjell. We stopped in Trondheim and visited the beautiful Cathedral, Nidarosdommen, the site commemorating St. Olav, Patron Saint of Norway. Of course we stopped at the site marking the Arctic Circle, visiting the monument to the thousands who died there building the highway through forced labour during the German occupation of Norway. What a price to pay.

From there we visited Narvik, and then went on to Espenes. Espenes was where we lived most of the time we were in the North. It was here that we started our married life together and matured in our relationship to one another. Here we ministered to children and adults and had the first taste of revival in my ministry. Some of our special friends had since gone to be with the Lord, while others were still serving Him faithfully. What a joy it was to renew fellowship with so many of our friends. From there we travelled on to Tromso, where our eldest son was born. It was here also that I had served in the Baptist church as the interim pastor while the pastor was recuperating from a very serious accident. This experience was to serve me well, as I realized sometime later that God's call on my life was really to a pastoral ministry. This proved to be a good training ground, equipping me for many years of fruitful pastoral ministry.

From Tromso we headed for Nordreisa, where our eldest daughter was born in the mission hospital. While there we visited Birger Ruud, manager of the hospital. There we also met up with some of my Sami friends (Laplanders) from Kautokeino, one of whom had been my interpreter (from Norwegian to Lappish) all the time I travelled and preached amongst them. My dear friend, Berrit, invited us to stay for lunch. It was very tempting, since we saw the very large salmon cooking in a large pot on the fire in the centre of the tent. However, we had to decline since we had some others to see and places to go.

My wife was so excited to see the reindeer and have other experiences and encounters. From there we drove on to Kautokeino, then on the Rovanieme in Finland. Rovanieme is the heart of Lapland in the North. This is now famous for its Ice Hotel and winter tourist attractions. It was very interesting to see how this whole area had developed since I was there in the 1950s, when we saw the ravages of occupation and the Second World War.

We headed south toward the Finnish-Swedish border. The river there is the international border. On the Finnish side the town is Karresuanto, and on the Swedish side the town is Karresuando. We found a small hotel on the Swedish side where we decided to stay the night. Dinner that evening was delicious, as the salmon had just been caught that afternoon. The next day was very special for my wife. Although we had seen reindeer along the way, she really wanted to see a big herd. Well, it happened! Suddenly a huge herd of reindeer came out of the low shrub and crossed the road in front of us, along with the young deer that had been born in the spring. How exciting!

While in the area we visited the area where Lars Levi Laestadius started his work, which became known as the Laestadianer Movement. This was a form of religious revival that spread through Northern Scandinavia and has some centres in North America. I write more extensively about this in the story of my work in Lapland. This place in Sweden is marked by a very simple wooden building that records the history and influence of this movement. From there we drove south to Stromsund where we stayed overnight before crossing over into Elverun in Norway the next day. On our way there we stopped to play Good Samaritan to a man who had been knocked off his bicycle, so my wife was able to apply her nursing skills, using some band aids and antiseptic ointment to cover his abrasions. He went on his way rejoicing.

We arrived back in southern Norway on the weekend that marked exactly forty years since I first went to Norway. We had a special dinner to mark the occasion. The following day being Sunday, and in deference to my wife who cannot speak Norwegian, we went to the English speaking Baptist church to worship. Following this, we flew back to Frankfurt where we got our return flight to Canada.

What an incredible five weeks travelling in eight different countries by plane, by tour bus, and by car. We covered several thousand miles with no accidents and no unpleasant experiences. Thank you, Lord, for watching over us. After a few days in Canada we had another trip down to Nassau. While there we had a reunion of our European tour group with whom we reminisced, shared photos, and had an evening of wonderful fellowship. While there I had a funeral service and also performed the wedding service of a young couple from Calvary Bible Church. We then flew back north to Canada and had a funeral service in Scarborough. So much for retirement from the regular pastoral ministry!

(51)

New Ministries, New Experiences

We realized that we needed to settle back into Canada and get some order into our life up north. The first thing we needed to do was buy a car. Through a friend of ours who was a car salesman, we were able to buy a 1988 Buick LaSabre for $11,000.00. However, we ran into a real snag. Since I had lived and worked out of the country for ten years, I had a problem getting car insurance. Upon investigating several insurance companies I found their quotes for our car insurance ran between $2,500 and $3,000. This was way more than we could afford. Fortunately, we both remembered the name of a Christian insurance agent we had used before. We called him and he was able to quote us insurance for our car for $900.00. Wow! What a difference. So now we had transportation, which we needed to get started on our new ministry with Global Outreach Ministry.

In September we officially got together displays, film, and brochures from Global Outreach Mission. We would be able to use these items in promoting the work of the Mission in Southern Ontario and Eastern Canada. In mid September we headed east to New Brunswick via the U.S.A. This would be our first official tour representing the Mission.

Our first stop was Campobello Island. We spent three weeks in the Atlantic provinces and also spoke at New Brunswick Bible Institute. In the month of October, we continued with missionary meetings around Southern Ontario. In November of 1990, we headed to our place in Florida where we were able to enjoy warmer weather, the fellowship of Northside Baptist Church, as well as talk about the work of Global Outreach Mission. We were able to fly over to Nassau to spend Christmas with family and enjoy fellowship at Calvary Bible Church.

During January, February, and March we had a very busy time ministering in Northside Baptist Church and several churches in the area of St. Petersburg, Tampa, Clearwater, and Kissimmee. We also had a wonderful week of conference at First Baptist Church and School in North Miami. Of course we enjoyed lots of visitors from Canada and Bahamas. It seems a little strange that very few people wanted to visit us when we lived in Lapland! We always enjoyed the fellowship and ministry at the Moody Keswick Conference.

While in Florida, we got word that my sister-in-law in Toronto had lapsed into a coma. We made immediate plans to drive north. I will not soon forget that trip. In northern Florida we encountered a terrible storm of driving rain. In fact, at one point we had to stop and find shelter under an overpass since we couldn't see the road ahead. When we got to the northern States, we encountered an incredible snowstorm all the way into Canada. On March 7, 1991, my sister–in–law went to be with the Lord after years of fighting cancer.

While in Canada, we were also able to finalize the purchase of our house in Ancaster, Ontario. We made our way back down to Florida to stay for another month. We then headed north in time for our son's wedding. In June we were off to Scotland to take in weddings and re-unions. I had the joy of preaching in my home church where I had been ordained on June 25, 1950. It was also a very special event to visit a history night at Larbert Village School, which I had attended as a boy.

A Fresh Call

Back in Canada, I was busy promoting the work of Global Outreach Mission in churches throughout southern Ontario. However, I became increasingly aware of the fact that the primary call of God on my life was that of preaching and pastoral ministry. This was made very clear to me in the late fall of 1991. One Sunday evening I had a mission responsibility in a very active church in the south east corner of Ontario, Canada. That evening I showed a film, then presented a challenge to serve the Lord wherever He would lead. The response was incredible. Several young couples came forward in response to that invitation. God was doing a real work in their life.

Driving back to Brantford that evening was a nightmare. It was heavy rain and thick fog. We followed the tail lights of a tractor trailer, as it was the only way we could navigate. On the way home my wife and I shared a very significant conversation that led to a life-changing ministry. We talked about the wonderful response in the service that evening. Then I made a significant confession. I said to my wife, "I am really not happy doing what I am doing; I'm a pastor at heart. Just think of that group of people who offered themselves for service. I should be pastoring them and mentoring them. My heart tells me that's what I should be doing."

My wife's response was very succinct: "Well, if that's how you feel, we need to pray about it."

We arrived back in Brantford very late and very tired. The next morning we were sitting at the kitchen table after breakfast. We had our devotions, and I had just finished praying that if God wanted me back in the pastoral ministry, He would make this very clear to me. Just as I said "amen," the telephone rang. When I answered, a bright, always cheery, always positive voice greeted me. Following the exchange of a few words of greeting this is what he said: "I'm wondering if you would consider becoming pastor of Rosedale Baptist Church in Toronto, which would also mean being the chaplain of Fellowship Towers Seniors' Residence."

WOW! The decision to contact me had been made before that conversation in the car and before that prayer at the breakfast table. Truly, "before they call I will answer." Who said God doesn't have a call for a man in his mid sixties? Believing this was of the Lord, I did what I've always done when presented with a call—I accepted without knowing what the salary or the terms would be. Upon reflection, in sixty-four years of ministry, God has always been faithful. I would commence my ministry at Rosedale Baptist Church and Fellowship Towers on October 27, 1991. To God be the glory. During this time also we took possession of our new home in Ancaster, Ontario.

This was exciting new job for me, because I'd had the joy of serving on the committee that planned Fellowship Towers under the leadership of Dr. Timothy Starr. Now I was back to pastoral ministry in a wonderful setting. My ministry there included conducting worship services on Sunday mornings. From time to time we would have special services on Sunday evenings. We had Bible study and prayer meeting on Monday evenings and chapel service on Thursday mornings. I visited in the hospitals, conducted funerals, counselled with families, and attended special birthday parties. The only thing we didn't do was have baby dedications. There were no Abrahams or Sarah's amongst our residents. We had four and a half wonderful years of ministry there.

One morning after chapel service, a single lady spoke to me. She made an amazing statement: "Pastor, I had my ninetieth birthday this week. I know that I don't have too many more years left in this world, but I don't know where I'm going." After lunch my wife called her and we made arrangements to visit her that afternoon. We spent two hours sharing the Word of God and praying with her. She came through to a personal and vital commitment to the Lord Jesus Christ as her personal Saviour and Lord. She couldn't wait to get in touch with her nephews and nieces and friends. Her whole life radiated the love that she had for her new found Saviour.

She'd had a very interesting life. She was born in Scotland into a Godly family. Her father worked in an iron foundry. He was a very strong Christian. He read the Scriptures and prayed every morning before the family faced a new day. He was a faithful worker in the Tent Hall in Glasgow. This was a work that had been started as a by-product of the work of D.L. Moody. He had prayed regularly for his daughter, and his prayers for her were finally answered when she was ninety years of age. Our ministry of four and a half years at Rosedale Baptist Church and Fellowship Towers finally came to a close. It was a very real investment for eternity. Little did I realize how God had prepared me for this ministry some years earlier. God moves in mysterious ways His wonders to perform.

52

Twenty Years and Counting

My ministry as a missionary, pastor, and chaplain from 1950 to 1990 prepared me for unique ministries that I have had from 1990 to the present time, 2014. These ministries have taken me to interim pastoral service in five different churches in Southern Ontario, and to the establishing of an International Church on the Island of Bonaire in The Netherland Antilles. Putting into practice what I had learned over the previous forty years was a most rewarding and fruitful experience. My having grey hair, or no hair, seemed to create at least an apparent willingness to listen to and respond to what I had to share with those churches, each with their own particular need.

When invited to a church to serve as an interim pastor, I set certain boundaries. These ministries ranged from two to three years duration. When called to such a situation, I would assume the role of pastor while at the same time making it clear that when they felt ready to call a full time pastor, my ministry would be over. As interim pastor, I'd do what every pastor should do. I would preach and teach at the stated services of the church. Having assessed the status of the church, identifying the areas that needed to be addressed, I would seek to preach appropriate messages and teach appropriate themes to nurture, strengthen, encourage, and prepare the church for the future. I would acquaint myself with the various departments of the church and visit the members, giving attention to the sick and shut-ins. I would spend time with the deacons/elders, praying and planning the ministries as we progressed.

While doing all of this, I wouldn't neglect the outreach in evangelism and the nurturing of the new believers. Not all of the churches had problems;

however, there were usually issues that I could address freely since I wouldn't be safeguarding my future and I'd be able to act without the issue of personal gain. I also had the advantage of my wife being deeply involved with me in this ministry, and she could address issues from her perspective.

One church I was called to had a highly emotional and grieving situation. Their pastor, a relatively young man, had died very suddenly and unexpectedly while on a mission assignment in another country. My immediate role as interim pastor was to bring comfort and healing to his family and to the church. Then I had to prepare them for the future in calling a new fulltime pastor.

Another church had suffered a terrible split and a significant number left with the pastor. Here one had to bring healing and build bridges. Thankfully the main leadership remained, and it was a joy to spend time with these Godly, praying men who would spend one hour in prayer before even attempting to do any business. We did see the church regroup, grow, and catch a fresh vision. Souls were saved. Relationships were restored. God brought them together with a very able young pastor whom they called, and at the time of writing he has been there almost fifteen years and the church is still growing. One of the things we encouraged churches to do was to take care of any renovations or repairs at a time when they were not paying a senior pastor's salary and expenses. In two of the churches, my wife even got them to put in central air conditioning. Hallelujah!

One of the churches called me as interim pastor for a six month period. I ended up being there for about three years. There were still long term hurts that kept raising their ugly head. Two different potential pastors were approached, but both eventually said no. This really hurt the church quite significantly. At the prayer meeting one evening, there was earnest prayer that the church might be led to the right person. One of the senior men in the church expressed himself in the following prayer: "Dear Lord, we would like you to send along the right pastor for us, but we are not in a hurry, since we like the interim pastor we have now." However, I was able to continue my interim ministry there until such time as they called a very fine young man who was able to lovingly shepherd the flock.

Very soon I was invited to another church as interim following an issue they had with their pastor and his theology. This was a very difficult situation— dealing with "us" and "them." Apart from one or two people, there was very little significant prayer within the church. There were two strong, differing factions of theology within the church. One group had a strong desire to reach out to a rapidly growing community. The other faction was happy to protect their "holy huddle." After two years there, they were still content to maintain the status quo—as one well known preach was heard to comment: "That's Latin for 'the mess we are now in'".

The last interim ministry I had lasted for a little over two years. There had been some major problems in the personal life and ministry of the pastor. The congregation was fractured and polarized. The membership was made up of several different ethnic backgrounds. Having lived and work amongst most of these groups in my full time pastoral ministry in different countries, I was very cognizant of the issues at hand. We were blessed with a good group of men in the leadership of the church. As a result, we were able to prayerfully address and work through the issues. It was a joy to see some come to a personal relationship with Jesus Christ and some follow the Lord in baptism. There were also funerals and weddings. Eventually the congregation was able to call a young man and his wife to the ministry of the church. Under his ministry, the church has grown significantly both numerically and spiritually. To God be the glory, great things He has done.

I have been very much aware of the fact that God has allowed me to have ministries and experiences that have uniquely equipped me to cope with situations, circumstances, and cultures and to adjust so easily and readily in language and cultures and customs. My interim ministries have been most rewarding over the last twenty years. I made a commitment to the Lord when I resigned from Calvary in Nassau that I would be available for whatever He would provide. I would love to do a ministry to churches in need, serve on any mission field that He would open for me, and be available for whatever the Lord would provide. The Lord took me at my word. The Lord has blessed me with reasonably good health, and divested of administrative responsibilities and committee duties, I was still able to do the work of the ministry as a pastor. This I have been able to do over the past twenty years plus. I can testify with the Psalmist in Psalm 37:25, where he says it so beautifully: *"I have been young, and now am old; yet I have not seen the righteous forsaken nor his descendents begging bread."* It has been my joy to invest my life in service—I lay up my treasures in Heaven. The rewards are out of this world.

In the middle of all my interim ministries, I received a very interesting invitation. There was a need in a missionary situation. Would I consider going there to minister in a critical and crucial need? I had already made a commitment to go wherever the Lord would lead. My wife and I prayed about it, and we asked the church where we were serving at the time if they would release us for a period of time. They readily agreed, and so we went. I felt a little bit like Abraham—we didn't know where we were going.

Plans were made and we set out for the Island of Bonaire. We took a flight from Toronto to Miami, then a flight from Miami to Bonaire, stopping briefly on the island of Curisau and finally landing in Kraalendyk on the island of Bonaire. There we were welcomed by a group of the staff from the TWR radio station located on the Island.

"Bon Binni!" A Warm Welcome Awaits You Here

What did this warm welcome really mean? Little did I realize all that would be expected and accomplished in the time we would spend on the Island of Bonaire! Initially we had anticipated a stay of about four weeks; however, we did have a break after the four weeks, but we left with the promise that we would return at a later date. It turned out that our total time on the Island would be four and a half months. Before sharing what was accomplished in that time, let me introduce you to this incredible, world renowned island jewel in the Caribbean called Bonaire.

Bonaire is one of a group of islands often spoken of as the "ABC "Islands, meaning the islands of Aruba, Bonaire, and Curacao. They are part of what is referred to as the "Netherland Antilles." Bonaire is one hundred and eleven square miles in area, and about twenty-four miles long. It has a population of around 17,000 people. A short distance off the west coast of Bonaire is a small unpopulated island called Klein Bonaire. It's just two square miles in size. Bonaire has an average rainfall annually of twenty-two inches, and average temperatures between eighty and ninety degrees, sometimes peaking to one hundred degrees. However, the gentle trade winds from the east help to make it bearable.

The administrative centre and Kraalendyk, the capital, are located in the centre of the island. There are four main languages spoken: Dutch, the official language, English, Spanish, and the local language called Papiamentu. A missionary who worked on the island for many years produced the first dictionary for the Papiamentu language. There is a good school system, and for further education most of the young people go to Holland.

In the early days, the island was largely populated by Arawak Indians, the same tribal group as those that were found in Newfoundland and Bahamas. They were a very peaceful people. However, in the days of the Spanish influence in this part of the Caribbean, the Spanish took them as slaves to the other islands and also to Spain.

During the war years, the American military built an airport in the centre of the island. Later this was turned over to the local authorities, and it was expanded and is now named "Flamingo Airport." There is also a relatively good road system throughout the island.

Donkeys roam freely throughout the island. In former days, they were brought here as work animals, but were abandoned with the introduction of more modern machinery and transportation. Goats also roam everywhere. In days gone by they were raised here to provide hides for the making of the very expensive "Kid Gloves" that were very much in demand by the European market in days gone by.

In the northern section of the island is the Washington Slag Baai National Park. Here was brought about a strong influence to protect nature. In this they took the lead in the world. Bonaire boasts of having the best diving location in the world, and it has very strict laws for the protection of those amazing coral reefs. There is also a spectacular variety of fish and other sea life. Tourists and divers come from all over the world, thereby making a significant contribution to the local economy. There is also an interesting population of wildlife throughout the island. There are large iguanas and various types of lizards, particularly in the north. Birds of every size and colour are found throughout the entire island. They include lora, parrots, and parakeets. The northern part of the island is largely desert with a large variety of cacti. There is also the acacia plant and aloe vera plants left over from the era when they were grown commercially.

In the southern part of the island it almost seems like another world altogether. There are remnants of rows of low huts, which were the living quarters for slaves from bygone days. When flying over the islands, one gets the impression of flying over small hills covered with snow. In fact, they are mounds of sea salt. In this area there are large lagoons full of salt water. With the high temperatures and low rainfall, the water evaporates. The salt moves through a series of lagoons until it forms large mounds. From here the salt is moved on conveyer belts and loaded on to waiting ships. From there it is taken to processing plants around the world, where it's packaged for sale.

In the waters and low lying areas, one is absolutely captivated by the thousands of flamingos to be found there. It's reported that there are some 15,000 of them. They feed and breed here because of the endless supply of shrimp in these waters. Of course, this diet of shrimp is what gives the flamingo the vibrant colour of pink. They build their nests of mud in the shape of an upside down cone. There they lay a single egg and sit on it until it's hatched. One interesting thing about the flamingo is their weekend activity. On Fridays we saw them take off in large flocks. We discovered that they headed to the north coast of South America, about forty miles away. We jokingly said that they had gone there for a weekend shopping trip.

Bonaire lies outside of the hurricane belt. It boasts several large marinas. It's here that many of the small craft find shelter from the hurricanes. A number of years ago, a large pier was built that could accommodate large cruise ships. This naturally brought more tourist traffic to the island. Quite often American Coast Guard ships would dock here and the crew were able to have a few days shore leave.

We had the joy and privilege of experiencing this unique paradise as we travelled the length and breadth of the island during our stay. Also, we were the recipients of the hospitality provided by officials of the government and the local inhabitants. Above all, we enjoyed the warm welcome extended to us by the missionary staff of Trans World Radio. We were called there to be their pastor, counsellor, and co-workers in the proclamation of the Gospel and in the advancement of the Kingdom of God.

I found it intriguing and unique that here I would see fulfilled my commitment to God upon my stepping down from my ministry in local churches. I had said to the Lord that I would be available for whatever He called me to do in preaching and teaching the Word of God, ministering to churches in transition, or in encouraging missionaries in their ministry. The Lord has taken me at my word.

When I ministered in Europe under the European Evangelistic Crusade (now known as Global Outreach Mission), I had met Dr. Paul Freed on two different occasions at our missions conference in Switzerland in the early 1950s. Dr. Freed had established a radio station in Morocco for the purpose of broadcasting the Gospel into Spain. At that time there was a strong desire that the two missions would co-operate on this project. Little did I realize then that one day I would be ministering to the staff of Trans World Radio, which operates the most powerful Christian radio station in the world. This station has a medium wave transmitter and several short wave transmitters. The antenna for this station consists of four 231.6 metre tall masts. TWR is now broadcasting the Gospel in two hundred and thirty languages and dialects, and is still faithful in their over sixty-five years.

My ministry on Bonaire was originally planned for four weeks, but ended up being for four and a half months. While I ministered to the staff and to the wider community on Sundays, my wife worked as an assistant to one of the missionaries. She helped process mail that came from the listeners in response to some of the broadcasts.

My wife, who is a registered nurse and taught nursing for twenty-one years, was so excited to discover that one of her former students was on the staff at the station. Her husband was there also. His role was to maintain those tall masts. Because they were located where the island was surrounded by the high salt density of the ocean, their metal antenna ran into problems. He had to climb the masts and scrape off the salt deposit to make sure the signal was not compromised. Periodically he would paint the masts and replace the parts that were beyond repair. It is wonderful to see how God has His servants in strategic places.

When God Calls He Equips

So often one has in mind that the missionary is unique in any given mission station, and rightly so. They are strong in their spiritual commitment, deep in their devotion, and uncompromising in their dedication. This is true in a very real sense. However, having acknowledged all of this, it is no less true that they are strong in their personality and very convinced in their vision and goals. By the same token, all of this can result in conflicts and clashes when brought together in an environment that isolates them from the wider population. This can strain their relationships and compromise their primary commitment to service for their Lord and Saviour Jesus Christ. The result may be that they fall short of glorifying their Master and are diverted from their goal of reaching the lost with the Gospel and building His Church.

Satan is a master, like the wolf, at seeking out the vulnerable and pouncing on his prey. Having been a missionary myself, having had the great joy of seeing individuals, couples, and families responding to God's call to service, and having pastored churches for sixty plus years, God has enabled me to respond to a wide range of issues. I was soon to discover that this was no less true of my call to minister to the missionary families of Bonaire, along with ministering to the local resident community along with the large tourist population. One Sunday in particular I counted at least sixteen different nationalities represented in the morning congregation. Not only were we reaching out to the world, but the world was coming to us. I soon learned that my call to minister on the island of Bonaire would be multi-facetted and would tap into my years of international, cross cultural, multi-lingual, and varied climate experience. In God's initial call to full time service, I had offered myself willingly and totally, but with the two reservations mentioned previously. Well, God certainly has a sense of humour. He took me to Toronto, Canada's largest city! Although I started my ministry three hundred miles above the Arctic Circle in Lapland, He finally brought me to the Island of Bonaire with its tropical climate

My Ministry on Bonaire

While on Bonaire, I was pastor, preacher, teacher, counsellor, advisor, bridge builder, church planter, and grandfather figure to the children of the missionaries. The combination of age and experience was very valuable. My first trip there in 1998 gave me an opportunity to evaluate the issues and opportunities that required attention. It also gave me an opportunity to become acquainted with the culture, the country, and the congregation. I also was able to understand the relationship of one to the other. Ministering to the staff at their weekly meeting was most encouraging, and it also gave me the opportunity to check the temperature and assess the issues. The general ministries on Sunday and Bible studies during the week were most rewarding, resulting in individuals making commitments to the Lord Jesus Christ as well as growth in the life of the Christians. Some off times we acted like tourists and toured the island and relaxed at the beach.

Church Planting

In addition to the regular activities, we began to discuss the wisdom of establishing an International Church that would provide an effective ministry to the entire community. Part of the concern was that here at the station was a group of very talented, well equipped missionaries ministering to a large segment of the world "out there," but not having a significant ministry to the "world at their door." So we initiated plans for outreach to the local and tourist population. We had early morning prayer times with the staff leadership, followed by laying plans for the establishing of a local church. This was the ground work upon which we would build when we returned to the island in early 1999. This was the time to bring to reality plans and preparations that were accomplished in our previous visit. Thus we began to build upon the ground work already established and bring to reality the plan to have what became known as "The International Bible Church of Bonaire."

In January of 1999, we were able to announce that we had sixty-one charter members and were in the process of selecting elders and officers. Part of the whole process required that we register with the local Dutch authorities. One of the key government officers was one of our charter members, and he was appointed our treasurer. It was a very special day when we installed five of our men as elders of the church. This ministry continues reaching out and touching many people who come from many countries and cultures around the world.

La Grande Finale

For me, this story of my life has been a marathon experience of emotions. At eighty-eight years and counting, this life lived in the service of my Lord can best be capsulized in the words of the hymn "To God be the Glory, Great Things He has Done." To think that God would be so gracious in calling, sending, and using me in the way He has done is beyond all human comprehension. If in the reading of this story you have been blessed, challenged, encouraged, or even called to the service of my Master, or perhaps have come to know Christ as your Saviour and Lord, it will have been worth it all.

I am far from perfect, but I have sought to be a humble servant of my Lord and Saviour Jesus Christ. I am living proof that God uses weak, flawed, and insignificant people in His service. Oh to grace how great a debtor daily I'm constrained to be!

I am thankful for my dear widowed mother who was willing to sacrifice to make it possible for me to attend college that I might be equipped for the ministry. I thank God for those in the Larbert Baptist Church who encouraged me along the way. My thanks goes to Mr. James D. Taylor, deacon, lay preacher, and local county councilor, who knew that my father was a military veteran, and was able to secure financial help for me during my years in college. I am thankful for the pastors and leaders who were a great encouragement to me along my spiritual journey. It was in that church that I came to personal faith in Jesus Christ and later followed Him in baptism. Thanks also go to Agnes Nicol and Katie Thompson for their sacrificial service in leading our youth group and encouraging us in our Christian growth. It was in this church, on June 25, 1950, that I was ordained to the Christian ministry and commissioned as a missionary to Lapland, Norway.

I thank God for Adaline Betty, my wife of thirty-six years. I am thankful for the family we had together and for her significant contribution to our ministry as missionaries in Lapland and our pastoral ministries in New Brunswick, Newfoundland, Toronto, and Bahamas.

My thanks also to my wife, Sarah (Morag), of twenty-nine years. She has provided support in my pastoral ministry, missionary outreach, and interim ministries for twenty years in Ontario and beyond.

I thank the Lord for allowing me to work through Global Outreach Mission (formerly known as European Evangelistic Crusade) and for allowing me to partner with colleagues in Norway in pastoral ministry there. I'm thankful also for my pastoral ministry in Grand Bay/Browns Flat, Sussex, New Brunswick, St John's and Gander, Newfoundland, Long Branch, Ontario, Nassau and Treasure Cay, Bahamas, Fellowship Towers, Toronto, Calvary and Pineland in Burlington, St.Catharines and Binbrook, Bonaire in the Netherland Antilles, and Unionville, Ontario. What a joy to serve in those intra-cultural and intra-lingual ministries.

Along the way I cannot say I was perfect. There were temptations, conflicts, and sometimes human errors, but with God's unfailing grace, may it be said, "*I have fought the good fight, I have finished the race, I have kept the faith*" (2 Timothy 4:7).

Yours in His Glorious Service,
Rev. A. Morris Russell.

Thank You

I have always been most grateful for being born into a humble, yet loving, family. I was the youngest of seven children. I only had my father in my life for eleven years. He was only fifty-six when he died from the consequences of having been gassed in the First World War. However, in the short time I knew him, he taught me much of the values of life that have stayed with me all these years .My mother was widowed when only fifty-three years of age. The older four of my siblings were all working and making their own way in life, but we three younger ones were still in school. My mother had only a very small pension, but she was still able to provide us with the essentials of life. She taught us the values of life and the importance of commitment and hard work. We each had our regular chores, and we were able also to do some work and earn some extra money. She insisted that we value an education, which she herself was denied.

Upon the death of my father, the local Baptist Pastor, Rev. W.C. Inglis, B.D. (graduate of the original McMaster College in Toronto), ministered to our family. As a result, we started to attend the Baptist Church. This marked the beginning of my spiritual journey.

Thank God for two of His unclaimed treasures, who never married, but devoted their life to leading the youth group in the church. They discipled us and encouraged us to use our talents in the Lord's service.

I am deeply grateful to one of the Deacons in my home church. Mr. J.D. Taylor was a great encourager to all of us. He was a lay preacher, school teacher, and local county councillor. He took a great interest in me as I was preparing the Christian ministry. Through his influence and realization that my father was an ex-soldier, he was convinced that I would be eligible for financial support toward my college expenses. Through his influence, the county council granted me sufficient finances to cover all of my college expenses.

I am thankful for all of the churches where I have ministered ... for their support and influence in my life and ministry, and the contribution they made to my development and maturity in my Christian service.

I am deeply grateful to the Lord for my first wife, Adaline Betty Jamieson, who served with me for thirty-six years. I'm thankful also for my wife, Sarah (Morag) D.A. Forrester, who served with me for twenty-nine years. Both have made significant contributions as they supported me in my ministry.

To God be all the glory and praise for whatever has been accomplished over these sixty-five years of ministry and service.

A. Morris Russell